Assassins of Memory

EUROPEAN PERSPECTIVES

European Perspectives

A Series in Social Philosophy and Cultural Criticism

Lawrence D. Kritzman and Richard Wolin, Editors

European Perspectives seeks to make available works of interdisciplinary interest by leading European thinkers. By presenting classic texts and outstanding contemporary works, the series hopes to shape the major intellectual controversies of our day and thereby to facilitate the tasks of historical understanding.

Julia Kristeva	*Strangers to Ourselves*
Gilles Deleuze	*Empiricism and Subjectivity*
Theodor W. Adorno	*Notes to Literature,* vol. 1
Richard Wolin, ed.	*The Heidegger Controversy*
Antonio Gramsci	*Prison Notebooks,* vol. 1
Theodor W. Adorno	*Notes to Literature,* vol. 2
Jacques LeGoff	*History and Memory*
Alain Finkielkraut	*Remembering in Vain*

Assassins *of Memory*

Essays on the Denial of the Holocaust

Pierre Vidal-Naquet

Translated and with a foreword by
Jeffrey Mehlman

COLUMBIA UNIVERSITY PRESS
New York

Columbia University Press wishes to express its appreciation
for assistance given by the government of France through Le
Ministère de la Culture in the preparation of the translation.

Columbia University Press
New York Oxford
Copyright (c) 1992 Columbia University Press
All rights reserved

*Les Assassins de la mémoire: "Un Eichmann de papier et
autres essais sur le révisionnisme."* (c) Editions La Découverte, 1987.

Library of Congress Cataloging-in-Publication Data

Vidal-Naquet, Pierre, 1930–
[Assassins de la mémoire. English]
Assassins of memory : essays on the denial of the Holocaust /
  Pierre Vidal-Maquet ; translated and with a foreword by
  Jeffrey Mehlman.
p.   cm. — (European perspectives)
Includes index.
ISBN 0–231–07458–1
1. Holocaust, Jewish (1939–1945)—Errors, inventions, etc.
2. Holocaust, Jewish (1939–1945)—Historiography.
I. Title. II. Series.
D804.3.V5313   1992   940.53'18'072—dc20   92-
  26654
CIP

Contents

FOREWORD by Jeffrey Mehlman   *ix*

PREFACE   *xxiii*

1. A PAPER EICHMANN (1980)   *1*

   Anatomy of a Lie

   1. On Cannibalism, Its Existence, and How It Has Been Explained

   2. On La Vieille Taupe and Cannibals

   3. On History and Its Revision

   4. On the Revisionist Method

   5. Moscow, Nuremberg, Jerusalem

   6. The Fantastic Calculations of Paul Rassinier

   7. The Jewish War

   8. On the Art of Not Reading Texts

   9. On Plato, Lies, and Ideology

   10. Living With Faurisson?

   Appendix: Zyklon B (by Pitch Bloch)

2. ON FAURISSON AND CHOMSKY (1981)   *65*

Contents

3. ON THE SIDE OF THE PERSECUTED (1981)   75

4. THESES ON REVISIONISM (1985)   79

    1. From One Revisionism to Another

    2. On Myths of War and the Advance of Truth

    3. That There are Several Abodes . . .

    4. On an Explosive Mixture

    5. On the Nations and Israel

    6. History after Auschwitz

5. ASSASSINS OF MEMORY (1987)   99

    1. The Destruction of the Helots of Sparta

    2. History and Stories

    3. Discourse-Memory-Truth

    4. The Sect

    5. History and the Nation

    6. Auschwitz and the Third World

    7. The Confusion of Feelings

    8. In the Guise of a Conclusion

NOTES   143

INDEX   193

In memory of my mother,
Marguerite Valabrègue

Marseilles, May 20, 1907–
Auschwitz, June 2 (?), 1944

Forever young

Foreword

Jeffrey Mehlman

The term *intellectual*—with its resonances of political commitment and progressivism, its refusal to be confined by the bounds of any guild-defined discipline or genre—is one of the linguistic legacies of the Dreyfus Affair, and it seems (at least) doubly fitting to recall that fact in approaching the work of Pierre Vidal-Naquet. For he is not only one of the masterly renewers of French classical scholarship, an innovator in the heuristic inclusion of the insights of structuralism in our understanding of ancient Greece, but also the author of a number of books revealing—and denouncing—the systematic use of police and army torture during the Algerian war.[1] Vidal-Naquet, that is, in his willingness to take on the political—and military—establishment, is an intellectual in the grand (and perhaps waning) tradition that can be dated to Zola's "Manifeste des Intellectuels" of January 14, 1898.[2]

If the reference to the Dreyfus Affair seems *doubly* appropriate in the case of Vidal-Naquet, however (and here we approach the subject of *Assassins of Memory*), it is because as heir to a Dreyfusard family of assimilated Jews, he has always remained something of a child of the Affair. Prefacing Michael Marrus's history of Jewish assimilation in the last years of the nineteenth century, he confesses to reading it as something of a family history.[3] Indeed, he observes that "it was with the example of the Dreyfus Affair in mind, that, years later, as an adult, but not without illusions," he embarked on the polemical activity that marked his engagement in the "Algerian affair."[4]

The Dreyfus Affair, which was marked by anti-Semitic riots in war into which France was plunged in the course of the struggle to reopen the case of Alfred Dreyfus, an army captain (and assimilated Jew) unjustly sentenced to life imprisonment on Devil's Island for high treason. It has been interpreted by Hannah Arendt, among others, as a dress rehearsal for the catastrophe that was to befall European Jewry under Hitler.[5] Indeed, without an awareness of the Affair it is impossible to appreciate the historian's grim quip that if, in 1925, one were to have predicted the massacre of six million European Jews within twenty years, the only intelligible response, beyond the shock of initial disbelief, might well have been: *Ah! ces Français.* . . . Vidal-Naquet himself is too much the historian to be willing to read back the events of the 1940s into those a half-century earlier.[6] And yet one is hard put to read the moving excerpt which he has quoted from his father's diary for the date September 15, 1942, without hearing the bitter lesson Alfred Dreyfus—had he been a bit more lucid—might have derived from his own ordeal: "I experience as a Frenchman the insult visited on me as a Jew; and it is frightfully painful for me to acknowledge it (but I have promised myself total frankness): this blight on France's reputation has snuffed out the love I bore my country. I believe quite firmly today, since a distinction has been made between 'us' and France, that France was 'us' and I shall turn away from her, however awful the rift within me, if, as the sneers of the masters of the hour contend, France finds its embodiment in 'them' and not in 'us.'"[7] It is perhaps the imperfect tense—the present belief that France *was* us—which is most wrenching. Vidal-Naquet's parents were deported during the Occupation.

We approach the subject of *Assassins of Memory*, for it too hinges on what Vidal-Naquet rightly identifies as another linguistic legacy of the Affair, the word *révisionnisme*. At the end of the nineteenth century, the term referred to the movement pressing for a judicial review or reopening of the Dreyfus case. Its adepts were popularly known—and frequently excoriated—as *révisionnistes*. If Vidal-Naquet has subtitled his book in French "Essays on Revisionism," it is because that term has resurfaced in French life, and is identifiable as the movement to revise historical understanding of a specific crucial episode: the Nazi destruction of the Jews of Europe. A few chronological notes will help situate this latter-day "revisionism."

In the fall of 1978 the French weekly *L'Express* ran, without editorial comment, an openly anti-Semitic interview with Louis Darquier de Pellepoix, one of the villains of Vichy France and, from 1942 to 1944, its Commissioner for Jewish Affairs.[8] Darquier's principal point was summarized in the magazine's headline: "Only Lice Were Gassed in Auschwitz." Speaking from the comfort of exile in Madrid, Darquier implied that the Nazi "genocide" was in fact a—typical—Jewish hoax. France had not seen anti-Semitism of so crude a stamp since the war, and the result, as Jean-François Revel has suggested, was something of a "national psychodrama."[9] French anti-Semitism, the role of French collaborators, but also the "Jewish question" in general became topics on the public agenda.

It was on December 29, 1978 that *Le Monde*, with some embarrassment, yielded to the legal pressures of an iconoclastic professor of French literature, Robert Faurisson, who had been attacked in the paper several years earlier, and published his article entitled "The Problem of the Gas Chambers or the Rumor of Auschwitz."[10] The title itself bespoke a substantial advance in the sophistication of those prepared to deny the genocide. The phrase "the problem of the gas chambers" was in fact a borrowing from the respected thesis of Olga Wormser-Migot, *Le système concentrationnaire nazi*; the implication was that the "problematic" status of the gas chambers was not an invention of Faurisson's own, and that he was merely raising a perceived problem to a new level of awareness.[11] "The rumor of Auschwitz" deliberately echoed another phrase, "the rumor of Orléans"; this was a much commented on case in the 1960s involving an alleged white slave trade, run by Jews, in the provincial city of Orléans. The Orléans trade in prostitution turned out to be a fantasy fueled by vile prejudice—but so, suggested Faurisson, was the much repeated "legend" of the gas chambers.

Faurisson's argument lay in positing that the technological requirements for mass gassings were totally incompatible with the installations described by numerous witnesses, and would have resulted in a "catastrophe" for those administering the gas chambers themselves. Moreover, since numerous eyewitness reports had already been discredited, on what basis could one accept *any* such testimony? The hell of Auschwitz, for Faurisson, was that of a protracted typhus epidemic: whatever gassing (of lice)—or cremation (of infected corpses)—may have been going on at Auschwitz was part of an effort to control that epidemic.

Finally, what was most distressing about Faurisson was the tone of his conclusion: "Nazism is dead, quite dead, and its Führer along with it. What remains today is the truth. Let us dare to proclaim it. The nonexistence of the 'gas chambers' is good news for beleaguered humanity. Good news that it would be wrong to keep hidden any longer." For where Darquier appeared to be delivering his message out of festering rancor and anti-Semitic fury, Faurisson pretended to be an evangelist, a bearer of good tidings. He would subsequently write to *Le Monde*: "If through some misfortune the Germans had won the war, I suppose their concentration camps would have been presented to us as reeducation camps. Contesting that presentation of the facts, I would no doubt have been accused of being objectively in the service of 'Judeo-Marxism.' I am neither objectively nor subjectively a Judeo-Marxist or a neo-Nazi. I have admiration for those Frenchmen who fought bravely against Nazism. They defended the right cause. Today, if I affirm that the 'gas chambers' did not exist, it is because the difficult duty of being truthful obliges me to say so."[12] The tone was at once scholarly and seductive, and yet the political implication of Faurisson's case was plain: the villains of the historical episode which only recently in France, following broadcast of the American television film, had come to be referred to as the Holocaust, were not the Nazis but the Jews. In a radio interview of December 17, 1980, the professor from Lyon, residing—as if by provocation—in the city of Vichy, had summarized the upshot of his conclusions: "The alleged Hitlerian gas chambers and the so-called genocide of the Jews form a single historical lie whose principal beneficiaries are the State of Israel and international Zionism and whose principal victims are the German people, but not its leaders, and the Palestinian people in its entirety."[13] It was that statement which eventually led to Faurisson's conviction by the first chamber of the Paris Court of Appeal on April 25, 1983, not for the falsification of history, but for the maliciousness with which he had reduced his research (which was said to be serious) to offensive slogans.[14] It was indeed, to use the language of the second Dreyfus trial, as though he had been found guilty "with extenuating circumstances."

Thus did the revisionist thesis about the Judeocide make its way into French public awareness—through the grand gateway of France's newspaper of record. A rebuttal of the initial article, entitled "An Abundance of Evidence," by Georges Wellers of the Centre de Documentation Juive Contemporaine, appeared along with it. But that format contributed to the appearance that there were two sides—"revisionist" and "exterminationist"—of an argument, either of which reasonable men might entertain. And since Wellers had a clear institutional investment in his side of the argument, the scales—to the uninformed—might appear to tilt in favor of the apparently neutral Faurisson. In any event the equivalent space granted to both positions was a major coup for the "revisionists." The appearance of "reasonable doubt," in this case as in others, was a decisive achievement. By 1983 *Le Monde* would be running an article headlined "Academics Confront Each Other over the Faurisson Case."[15] It was at about that time, moreover, that France's pioneer gay liberationist, Guy Hocquenghem, could preface a book on the Nazi persecution of homosexuals by writing: "This book is our anti-Diary of Anne Frank. At a time when French intellectuals debate the question of whether or not there had been an extermination through gassing, it vividly reveals a far more important mystification [*truquage*] in the hagiography of anti-Nazism."[16] The mystification would be the claim that the Jews suffered a worse fate than the gays under Nazism. But in the process of saying as much, Hocquenghem endorsed in passing the notion that the gas chambers themselves were a hoax. In a single stroke, with an assist from Faurisson, gay liberation, in the voice of one of its principal French spokesmen, had managed to turn—however fleetingly—anti-Semitic. The "question" of the gas chambers had infiltrated still another register of discourse. If it was surely an exaggeration to pretend with the revisionists that the gas chamber "question" had become a "touchstone" of French culture, it was nonetheless a telling sign of the times that a philosopher as attuned to the winds of change as Jean-François Lyotard could fix on the revisionist debate as the prime example of the language game he began thematizing as *Le Différend*.[17]

It was in the face of what many thought could only be a dishonorable debate that the French historical establishment closed ranks in a collective declaration, written by Vidal-Naquet and the historian of anti-Semitism Léon Poliakov and published in *Le Monde* on February 21, 1979. Its conclusion read: "The question of how *technically* such a mass murder was possible should not be raised. It was technically possible because it occurred. This is the necessary starting point for all historical investigation of the subject. It has fallen to us to recall that point with due simplicity: there is not nor can there be a debate over the existence of the gas chambers."

Two other aspects of Faurisson's activities should be mentioned in this context. The first concerns the disastrous turn taken by Faurisson's personal fortunes in the wake of the notoriety he achieved. It soon became impossible for university authorities in Lyon to ensure his physical well-being and he was forced to leave his academic post. He was involved in numerous lawsuits and claimed to have suffered in his health as a result. Access to the Centre de Documentation Juive Contemporaine, which had sustained his research, was denied him. The second concerns the surprising political support he received from an unexpected quarter: the extreme-left group known as La Vieille Taupe [Old Mole], which recognized in Faurisson's position an ideological bombshell, and in the much touted volume of documentation he was prepared to adduce, no doubt, a touchstone of authentic materialism. We shall return to the rationale of Faurisson's supporters on the far left shortly. For the moment suffice it to say that one of the major turns in what became known as the "Faurisson affair" occurred when his book—*Mémoire en défense: contre ceux qui m'accusent de falsifier l'histoire; la question des chambres à gaz*—was published by La Vieille Taupe (reconstituted as a publishing house specializing in "revisionist" literature) with a preface by none other than Noam Chomsky.

Chomsky was in all probability drawn into the affair by way of his own critique of the use the Western media had been making of Pol Pot's massacre in Cambodia.[18] Régis Debray, in discussion with Chomsky, had put it as follows: "The West's best propaganda resource is Pol Pot's regime. We needed that scarecrow."[19] For Hitler too, after all, serves as something of a "scarecrow" for liberal democracies, and the conflation of the two cases, as Alain Finkielkraut has suggested, seemed particularly apposite. It was not for nothing that the back cover of Faurisson's book featured a photograph of American Congressmen gawking reverently at what historians have now determined could *not* have been a gas chamber at Dachau.[20] But Chomsky's preface—which is discussed at some length by Vidal-Naquet—did not mention Cambodia. Nor did it support Faurisson's position on the gas chambers. Indeed, Chomsky claimed to have scant familiarity with Faurisson's work. The preface was offered instead under the title "Some Elementary Comments on the Rights of Freedom of Expression."[21] It was in large part a disquisition on the apparent French inability to assimilate a basic civil right, which in the United States had long been regarded as a fundamental achievement of the eighteenth century. The French intelligentsia seemed to subscribe to "a vicious campaign of harassment, intimidation, [and] slander" against the Lyon professor in an "attempt to silence him." But "for those who have learned something from the eighteenth century (say, Voltaire), it is a truism, hardly deserving of discussion, that the defense of the right of free expression is not restricted to ideas one approves of, and that it is precisely in the case of ideas found most offensive that this right should be most vigorously defended."[22]

Vidal-Naquet's response to Chomsky concerns an apparent whitewash of Faurisson's activities (as a "relatively apolitical liberal") incidental to the linguist's defense of the right to free speech. But those arguments—against Chomsky, and more fundamentally against Faurisson and the revisionists—are best followed in the detail of Vidal-Naquet's text. What will perhaps be most interesting to an American readership is a tone—between rage and pessimism—characterizing this work. It is best emblematized by the surprising section in the "guise of a conclusion" to the volume's titular (and final) essay. For it gives to this record of Vidal-Naquet's decade of sparring with the revisionists something of the disenchanted quality of a journal. That concluding section consists for the most part of a translation of a celebrated and cynical tango by the Argentine poet E. S. Discépolo. Entitled "Cambalache," it evokes a kind of leveling of all values in the moral and intellectual junkshop (*cambalache*) the twentieth century has become. In the Argentine's words:

> Todo es igual!
> Nada es mejor!
> Lo mismo un burro
> que un gran professor!

(All is the same / Nothing any better. / A donkey the same / As a great professor!) A bizarrely pessimistic conclusion indeed for the "gran professor," fighting the good fight, in whom many may be inclined to see Vidal-Naquet himself.

I confess that it was that aberrant ending to his book that I found most intriguing. Here then are three speculations on the enigma of what Vidal-Naquet himself hesitates to call a conclusion. First, one should consider that by intellectual temperament Vidal-Naquet is anything but a defender of orthodoxies, and can only have been irritated by the discursive position into which the Faurisson affair seemed to have forced him. One of his more interesting essays in *Les Juifs, la mémoire et le présent,* for instance, resorts to a structural analysis of the historian Josephus in order to discredit the efforts of Yigael Yadin to shore up through archaeology what can only be termed the Zionist myth of another Jewish catastrophe, the mass suicide at Masada.[23] And yet here he was, the skeptical historian all but forced by a bogus debunker into the camp of the dogmatists. *Cambalache*!

A second basis for Vidal-Naquet's dispirited conclusion may pertain to a work (in manuscript form) invoked on several occasions in the notes of *Assassins of Memory.* The book contains several warm references of indebtedness to Arno Mayer and what was to be his future publication, *Why Did the Heavens Not Darken?: The "Final Solution" in History.*[24] Now Mayer's controversial work, which appeared with a blurb by Vidal-Naquet, advanced the thesis that the "Judeocide" was in large part the—gradual—result of Nazi frustration at the failure of Germany's Eastern campaign. He in no way denied the Nazi extermination of the Jews. And yet the "revisionists" A. Butz and P. Rassinier—referred to as "skeptics"—had made their way into Mayer's bibliography.[25] Mayer's take on them was in certain respects uncompromising: "The skeptics, who are outright negationists, mock the Jewish victims with their one-sided sympathetic understanding for the executioners. They are ill-disguised anti-Semites and merchants of prejudice, and this morally reprehensible posture disqualifies them from membership in the republic of free letters and scholarship."[26] The passage reads as though it had been dictated by Vidal-Naquet. Butz, who teaches computer science at Northwestern University, wrote a review denouncing Mayer's history as "shoddy."[27] In *his* review, Faurisson, however, for whom this entire matter has taken on a distasteful air of academic gamesmanship, could not help fixing with utter delight on two passages in Mayer's book. The first began: "Sources for the study of the gas chambers are at once rare and unreliable," and ended: "There is no denying the many contradictions, ambiguities, and errors in the existing sources."[28] This was a far cry from the title of the article in *Le Monde*, "An Abundance of Evidence" by Georges Wellers, with which the anti-revisionist camp initially responded to Faurisson's piece in the same newspaper. Coming from an author whom Faurisson could not help touting as "Pierre Vidal-Naquet's friend," Mayer's statement could only have the appearance of a carefully hedged concession.[29] The second passage reads as follows: "At both camps [Auschwitz and Majdanek], the line between egregious exploitation and outright exterminism kept wearing thin. Indeed, ultimately the execrable living, sanitary, and working conditions in the concentration camps and ghettos took a greater toll of life than the willful executions and gassings in the extermination centers."[30] Here too the willingness to affirm that disease and exhaustion (which presumably characterize all wars) exacted a greater toll among Jews than outright murder could be read as a concession—however carefully qualified—to the "revisionist" position. My interest here is not in affirming (or challenging) the accuracy of Mayer's argument, but in gauging the toll that the Princeton historian's book, when it finally did appear, can only have taken on the Frenchman's spirits. *Cambalache*, then, again.[31]

But perhaps the major justification for Vidal-Naquet's oddly dispirited pseudo-conclusion lay in an awareness of what a bizarrely exact parody of Dreyfusard "revisionism" twentieth-century French "revisionism" had become. Faurisson's stance was that of a member of a small group challenging a theologically based error. Providentially, the television miniseries *Holocaust* came to consecrate the fate of the Jews under Hitler in theological terms. (Before its broadcast, the term generally used in France was *genocide*.) And from the revisionist point of view the gas chambers functioned as the holy of holies of that religious construct. (Are there grounds, then, for excluding the Holocaust from the *religious* curriculum of American Hebrew schools?) Faurisson's language, moreover, is that of the positivist; he is endlessly calling for the opening of archives and the engagement of debate. He can be perversely resourceful in disqualifying the documentary evidence marshaled by his adversaries on internal grounds. (The doubts he has cast on the authenticity of parts of *The Diary of Anne Frank* appear, initially, to have convinced Vidal-Naquet himself.) He greets the copiousness of the evidence marshaled against him as a fraudulent joke. For better or worse, this was the initial ambience of those fighting—during the heroic phase—for a judicial review of the Dreyfus case. Moreover, Faurisson's efforts to exonerate the Nazis have increasingly taken the form of a judicial effort to defend himself. The title *Mémoire en défense* is eloquent in this regard. Whereas Vidal-Naquet is left dispirited at the end of his volume as to the future prospects of truth, Zola's great slogan has fallen—diabolically—into the adversary camp. "Historical truth is on the march," writes Faurisson, and "one is hard put to see who might stop it."[32]

With Faurisson having staked out a "revisionist" position so uncannily parodic of Dreyfusard "revisionism," Vidal-Naquet, perhaps France's quintessential heir to the Affair's noblest legacy, finds himself at times in the depressing discursive stance of those, at the end of the century, who were busy closing ranks against the slandered captain. The refusal of open debate—lest it grant a shadow of legitimacy to the other side; lest, that is, the Judeocide fall into that media void in which pro and con end up being mere echoes of each other—is understandable.[33] Yet it opens Vidal-Naquet up to the charge of having written a book about (and against) arguments which he claims to regard as beneath serious consideration. Whence a tendency to drown the other side in stridency and insult (the idea that a debate would be "obscene," knowledge that Faurisson is an anti-Semite, etc.), a venting of outrage at being expected to *prove* what is already *known*. Moreover, the statement—in the historians' manifesto in *Le*

Monde—that the question of how the mass murder was technically possible need not be raised since it did indeed occur seems
both like a closing of establishment ranks and an a priori refusal
of discussion. Finally, whatever the initial grounds for Chomsky's association with Faurisson, and however outrageous the
linguist's incidental whitewash of Faurisson's efforts may have
seemed to Vidal-Naquet, he can not have been happy at having
to denounce an article whose central thesis did indeed lie in affirming a difficult lesson—of tolerance—one might have hoped
was a permanent legacy of the eighteenth century. Press *one* tendency in *Assassins of Memory* to the extreme and one arrives at
the recently introduced French legislation to criminalize the falsification of the history of the Second World War, a law that
Vidal-Naquet has, to his credit, opposed.[34] "To criminalize the
tendentious interpretation of history is grotesque," as Tzvetan
Todorov has written, "and can only produce effects contrary to
those anticipated."[35] Contrary indeed: in the reverse replay of the
Dreyfus Affair into which Vidal-Naquet and Faurisson occasionally seem locked, one is inclined to attribute diabolically emblematic value to the publication—prefaced by Faurisson's far-
left supporter from La Vieille Taupe, Pierre Guillaume—of two
problematic texts on anti-Semitism by the future hero of the
Dreyfus Affair, Bernard Lazare.[36]

It is the support Faurisson has received from Guillaume—formerly of the radical group Socialisme ou Barbarie—and his colleagues at La Vieille Taupe that is no doubt the real enigma of
the Faurisson affair. It will as well furnish us with a way out of
the mirror-world in which we have been straying. Faurisson himself, after all, is a literature professor whose principal claim to
fame had been a volume sensationalistically purporting to de-
mystify a hoary illusion—not the existence of the gas chambers,
but the transgressive greatness of the poet Lautréamont: "A hundred years. The mystification will have lasted a hundred years,"
as the first line of *A-t-on lu Lautréamont?* reads.[37] No need then
to conjure up the shade of Dreyfus to account for the situation
of *this* "revisionist." The left-wing support he has received in his

denial of the existence of the gas chambers does, however, resonate with a dimension of the Affair in a manner that has been rather splendidly analyzed by Alain Finkielkraut.[38] For Jules Guesde and a significant fraction of the French Socialist party, the fight to establish the innocence of Dreyfus, a wealthy military officer, was so much a diversion from the class struggle that out of opposition to that juridical distraction it became possible to make the transition to an anti-Dreyfusard stance *tout court*: Karl Liebknecht, one of the tutelary eminences of the Socialist International, would thus find his articles on the Affair translated from *Die Fackel* into the French of *Action Française*. During the interwar period the purist refusal to be diverted from the class struggle took the form of a resolute rejection of the slogans of antifascism: even as Dreyfus was *ultimately* guilty for reasons of social class, for identical reasons no bourgeois regime, no matter how allegedly odious its (fascist) adversaries, could ever be found innocent. As one formulation had it: not only anti-Semitism, but also antifascism was the socialism of fools.[39] But at the end of World War II, the principal obstacle to such a rationale was the sheer horror provoked by the revelation of the Nazi gas chambers. Whereupon the grounds were laid, among left-wing purists, for making a transition from the ultimate irrelevance of the gas chambers (in terms of the class struggle) to their alleged nonexistence. Even as pique at the diversionary struggle over Dreyfus's innocence had led some socialists, nobly opposed by Jaurès, directly into the anti-Dreyfusard camp.

The link with the Dreyfus Affair, in brief, is less between one "revisionism" and another than between the left-wing aversion to the struggle against anti-Semitism at the time of the Affair, on the one hand, and the lingering left-wing distrust of the politics of antifascism on the other. Add to that nexus the Gallo-structuralist wish to read out of existence whatever is deemed to be lacking in structural pertinence, and Vidal-Naquet's subject—the Faurisson affair—begins assuming its contour as one of the strategic nodes of French cultural life in the 1980s.

Preface

This short book was born of an observation: for about two years now, the "revisionist" effort—by which I mean the attempt to deny the Nazi gas chambers and the extermination of the mentally ill, the Jews, and the Gypsies, as well as members of races deemed racially inferior, and specifically the Slavs—has taken on alarming proportions. A quite small but remarkably energetic sect has devoted all its efforts and a variety of means—political tracts, fables, comic books, allegedly scholarly articles, a specialized journal—to destroying not the truth (which is indestructible) but a general awareness of the truth. In point of fact, it is interested in neither the mentally ill nor the Gypsies, and even less in Soviet prisoners of war, but solely in the Jews. Why this choice? The studies that follow will attempt to supply an answer.

The five texts gathered in this volume were written between June 1980 and June 1987. The first four have already been published, and some several times over.[1] The fifth, "Assassins of Memory," which gives its title to this volume, has not appeared before.[2] Why this title—for that chapter and this book? A historian myself, I am as aware as anyone else that memory is not history: not that the latter follows the former through some unidentifiable mechanism, but because history's mode of selection functions differently from that of memory and forgetting. Between memory and history, there can be tension and even opposition.[3] But a history of the Nazi crime which did not integrate memory—or rather, diverse memories—and which failed to account for the transformation of memories would be a poor history indeed. The assassins of memory chose their target well: they are intent on striking a community in the thousand painful

fibers that continue to link it to its own past. They have launched
against it a global accusation of mendacity and fraud. I am part
of that community—which in no way implies that I find myself
in solidarity with all that its representatives, or those claiming to
be such, proclaim or do. But it is not my intention to reply to
that global accusation on grounds of sentiment. What is at stake
here is not feeling but truth. That word, which had a certain
gravity, nowadays appears to have entered into decline. Such is
one of the impostures of our century, a domain in which it is
rather rich. I spoke of answering an accusation. It should be
understood once and for all that I am not answering the accusers, and that in no way am I entering into a dialogue with them.[4]
A dialogue between two parties, even if they are adversaries, pre-
supposes a common ground, a common respect—in this case for
truth. But with the "revisionists," such ground does not exist.
Could one conceive of an astrophysicist entering into dialogue
with a "researcher" claiming that the moon is made of Roquefort cheese? Such is the level at which the parties would have to
be situated. And, of course, no more than there is an absolute
truth is there an absolute lie, even though the "revisionists" have
made valiant efforts to attain that ideal. By which I mean that
were it to be determined that the passengers of a rocket or a
spaceship had left a few grams of Roquefort on the moon, there
would be no point in denying their presence. Until now, the contribution of the "revisionists" to our knowledge may be compared to the correction, in a long text, of a few typographical
errors. That does not justify a dialogue, since they have above all
amplified beyond measure the register of falsehood.

I have thus imposed on myself the following rule: one can and
should enter into discussion *concerning* the "revisionists"; one
can analyze their texts as one might the anatomy of a lie; one can
and should analyze their specific place in the configuration of
ideologies, raise the question of why and in what manner they
surfaced. But one should not enter into debate *with* the "revisionists." It is of no concern to me whether the "revisionists" are

neo-Nazi or extreme left wing in their politics: whether they are characterized psychologically as perfidious, perverse, paranoid, or quite simply idiotic. I have nothing to reply to them and will not do so. Such is the price to be paid for intellectual coherence.[5]

ONE

A Paper Eichmann

(1980)

The Anatomy of a Lie

I hesitated a long while before responding to the friendly request of Paul Thibaud, the director of the journal *Esprit* (and who was also, from 1960 to 1962, the editor of *Vérité-Liberté*, a documentary publication on the Algerian war), and writing these pages on the so-called revisionist movement, concerning a work whose publishers tell us without the shadow of a smile: "Faurisson's arguments are serious. They should be answered." The reasons for not answering are many, but differ in value. As a historian of antiquity, what was I to do in a period "not my own"? As a Jew, was I not too directly party to the issue, incapable of being completely objective? Would it not be preferable to relinquish the business of responding to historians less immediately concerned? And finally, was not answering in itself tantamount to giving credit to the idea that there was indeed a debate, and thus giving publicity to a man all too eager for it?

The first argument does not impress me very much. Having always fought against the overspecialization of historical guilds, having always done battle for a history untrammeled by artificial divisions, I had a chance—and not for the first time—to practice the position I had advocated. Moreover, the subject is not so difficult as to preclude one's apprising oneself of it in short order. I reject, to be sure, the notion that a Jewish historian should abstain from treating certain subjects. But it is, alas, the case that, on the whole, the historians' guild in France has shown little interest in such questions. And they do indeed have a repugnant aspect that must be confronted. It is enough to consider the state of our major libraries. Neither at the Sorbonne nor at the Bibliothèque Nationale can one find fundamental documentation concerning Auschwitz, which has to be consulted, for the most part, at the Centre de Documentation Juive Contemporaine, which itself is far from possessing all that it should. A large number of historians signed the declaration published in *Le Monde* on February 21, 1979,[1] but very few set themselves to work, one of the few exceptions being François Delpech.

The final objection is in fact the most serious one. It is true that it is absolutely impossible to debate with Faurisson. Such a debate, which he persists in calling for, is excluded because his way of arguing—what I have called his use of the nonontological proof—makes discussion futile. It is also true that attempting to debate would amount to accepting the unacceptable premise of two "historical schools"—one "revisionist" and the other "exterminationist." There would be, as a tract signed in October 1980 by various "extreme left" groups dared to maintain, the "advocates of the existence of lethal 'gas chambers'" and the others, just as there are advocates of a higher or lower chronology for the tyrants of Corinth, or as there are at Princeton and Berkeley two schools of thought at loggerheads over what, at bottom, the Attic calendar was. When one knows how the "revisionists" work, the idea has something obscene about it.

But does one know? And can we proceed in France, in our centralized society, as one does in the United States where the most skillful revisionist, Arthur Butz, peacefully teaches computer science at a small university in Evanston, Illinois, admired by a minuscule sect and completely unknown to those, from New York to San Francisco, who practice the historian's craft?

For better and for worse, the French situation is not the same. From the day that Robert Faurisson, a duly certified academic, teaching in a major university, was able to express his views in *Le Monde*, even though he was refuted immediately thereafter, the question ceased being marginal and attained a certain centrality. And those without any direct knowledge of the events in question, specifically young people, were right to ask whether there had not been an effort to conceal something from them. Whence the decision of *Les Temps modernes* and *Esprit* to respond.[2]

But how to respond since discussion is impossible? By proceeding as one might with a sophist, that is, with a man who *seems* like a speaker of truths, and whose arguments must be dismantled piece by piece in order to demonstrate their fallaciousness. And by also attempting to elevate the debate, by showing that the revisionist fraud is not the only one to adorn contemporary culture, and that not merely the *how* but also the *why* of its lie needs to be understood.

1. On Cannibalism, Its Existence, and How It Has Been Explained

Marcel Gauchet devoted his first column in the journal *Le Débat* (May 1980) to what he has called "inexistentialism." It is in fact a characteristic of contemporary "culture" to declare of a sudden "inexistent" social, political, intellectual, cultural, and biological realities which were assumed to be well established. There have thus been relegated to nonexistence sexual relations, woman, domination, oppression, submission, history, the real, the individual, nature, the state, the proletariat, ideology, politics, madness, and trees. Such minor diversions, however sad, may indeed also amuse, but are not necessarily dangerous. The notion that sexuality and sexual relations do not exist hardly inconveniences lovers, and the nonexistence of trees has never taken the bread out of the mouth of a logger or a manufacturer of paper pulp. It is occasionally the case, however, that such a diversion ceases to be innocent. This situation maintains when what is called into question is no longer an abstraction such as "woman," "nature," or "history," but a specific individual expression of humanity, a specific painful moment of its history.

In the long undertaking of supplying a definition of man—in relation to the gods and to animals—the fraction of humanity to which we belong has chosen, at least since Homer and Hesiod in the eighth century before our era, to posit man, as opposed to animals, as he who does not eat his fellow creatures. Thus, in *Works and Days* does Hesiod say: "Such is the law prescribed by Zeus the son of Kronos to men: that fish, beasts, and winged birds devour each other, since there is no justice among them." There are transgressions of the law, which are rather rare in practice, but more frequent in myth. There are above all transgressors, who are cataloged as such: these are certain categories of barbarians, who are thus excluded from the ranks of humanity. A cyclops is not a man.

Not all societies place the barrier at precisely that level. There are some that are neither less nor more "human" than Greek society or modern Western society, and which accept the ingesting of human flesh. There are, I believe, none that regard such a practice as an act commensurate with others: human meat does not fall into the same category as game meat or the meat of agriculturally raised animals. To be sure, such differences are not apparent to outside observers, rushed as they are to treat as nonhuman men who are simply *other*. Here, for instance, is the view of Bernal Diaz del Castillo, who was one of Cortés's companions in Mexico during the beginning of the sixteenth century, in his *True History of New-Spain* (1575):

> I must say that most of the Indians were shamefully ridden with vice: . . . they were almost all given over to sodomy. As far as the eating of human flesh is concerned, it may be said that they make use of it exactly as we do with butcher's meat. In every village, their custom is to construct cubes of huge wooden beams, in the form of cages, in order to enclose men, women, and children in them, to fatten them up and dispatch them to be sacrificed when they are ready and then to delect in their flesh. In addition, they are constantly at war, province

against province, village against village, and the prisoners they succeed in taking are eaten after first being sacrificed. We observed the frequency of the shameful practice of incest between sons and mothers, brothers and
sisters, uncles and nieces. Drunks are numerous, and it
is beyond me to depict the filthiness of which they are
capable.[3]

The author of this narrative combines two different types of
data: factual information, which meshes with other sources on
human sacrifices and cannibalism; and a strictly ideological discourse intended to justify the Christian conquest. It goes without
saying that the generalized incest that has just been evoked does
not exist in any society.

Sorting out reality from fiction and attributing a meaning to
each are the tasks of the anthropologist and the historian,
whether the focus be anthropophagy, marriage rites, or the ini-
tiation of the young.

Anthropophagy, or (to use a word generalized from a Carri-
bean term meaning "bold") cannibalism, has provoked in recent
years two different—and oppositely symmetrical—interpretive
models. The first, which is "materialist" in tendency, has been
proposed by Marvin Harris in a book intended quite simply to
explain simultaneously "the origins of war, capitalism, the state,
and male supremacy." If men eat human flesh, it is, in the last
analysis, because they need protein: a perfect example of a total-
izing explanation that, in fact, explains nothing at all.[4] How is
one to account for the fact, under such conditions, that Aztec
society disposed of ample sources of nourishment? And how account for an additional fact: the inhabitants of Mexico, besieged
and starved by Cortés's men in 1521, sacrificed their prisoners,
and them alone, but without consuming anything other than the
bodily parts ritually permitted, none of which prevented them
from dying of hunger? As Marshall Sahlins has written: "Clearly
the cultural content at issue, this stupendous system of sacrifice
is too rich, logically as well as practically, to be explained by the

natural need for protein by which Harris proposes to account for it. To accept his view, we have to make some sort of bargain with the ethnographic reality, trading away what we know about it in order to understand it. Or, at the least, it takes a heroic act of utilitarian faith to conclude that this sacrificial system was a way the Aztecs had of getting some meat." Posing the problem of human sacrifice and anthropophagy in terms of economic rationality and considerations of profit leads to incredible absurdities: the system was in no way profitable and in fact partook of an economy of wasteful expenditure.

But what then are we to do with cannibals if they sought neither nourishment nor a maximization of profits? It is at this juncture that a second explanation intervenes: cannibals don't exist; in other words, they are a myth.

Let us open up a parenthesis here: like many historians, my predecessors and contemporaries, I am interested in myths, in the history of imagination, believing that the imagination and its products are an aspect of reality, and that their history should be undertaken exactly as one attempts a history of grains or of marriage practices in nineteenth-century France. No doubt; and yet that "reality" is nonetheless plainly less "real" than what normally passes under that rubric. Between the phantasms of the Marquis de Sade and the Terror of the Year II of the Revolution, there is a difference of nature and even, to take things to the limit, a radical opposition: Sade was a rather gentle individual. A certain vulgarization of psychoanalysis has played its role in this confusion between phantasm and reality. But matters are more complex: it is one thing to account for the role of the imaginary within history, one thing, that is, to define, as does Castoriadis, the imaginary institution of society, and quite another to decree, in the style of J. Baudrillard, that social reality is composed only of imaginary relations. For that extreme affirmation entails another, which I will have to take into account: one decreeing a whole series of quite real historical events to be imaginary. As a historian, I feel a measure of responsibility for the delusions I shall presently be discussing.

It is W. Arens who has bestowed on us this dazzling bit of evidence: there never were any cannibals.[5] As is the rule in this kind of discovery, Arens arrived at it through several stages, which he explains to us at great length. Convinced that anthropophagy was a rather common practice, he was surprised by the rather imprecise character of the anthropological literature. He then set out in search of decisive proof, and placed a personal ad in a journal, searching for an eyewitness. The responses were vague, but a young German researcher, Erwin Frank, told him that he had scoured the entire literature on cannibalism among Indians in the Amazon basin from the sixteenth to the twentieth century, and that he was unable to find a single instance of first-hand testimony concerning the act of eating a fellow human being. Little by little, he thus arrived at the bitter and joyous realization that there were no cannibals, and that anthropophagy was an invention of anthropologists on the basis of inconsistent testimony. The function of that invention was to justify the domination of conquered societies by their conquerors.

A few lines will suffice to establish the grotesqueness of such a theory: we will, no doubt, always be lacking the testimony of the victims, the only testimony capable of satisfying Arens's requirements, but there does exist a quite sufficient quantity of testimony and information for no doubt to subsist. Marshall Sahlins and others have reminded us of as much, but the American anthropologist has had the singular merit of analyzing the logic underlying this kind of exercise, which is less in the order of research than of academic gamesmanship. In concluding, he also pointed out the inevitable connection with what will henceforth be the central theme of this essay:

> It all follows a familiar American pattern of social science journalism: Professor X puts out some outrageous theory, such as the Nazis didn't really kill the Jews, human civilization comes from another planet, or there is no such thing as cannibalism. Since facts are plainly against him, X's main argument consists of the expression, in the highest moral tones, of his own disregard for

all available evidence to the contrary. . . . All this pro-
vokes Y and Z to issue a rejoinder, such as this one. X
now becomes "the controversial Professor X" and his
book is respectfully reviewed by non-professionals in
Time, Newsweek, and the *New Yorker.* There follow appearances on radio, TV, and in the colums of the daily
newspapers.[6]

In other words, what we are confronted with in this manner of
affair is neither truth nor science, but quite simply public relations and academic gamesmanship.

We may state things differently: take the case of a poorly
known individual from ancient history, whose existence has
hitherto been accepted without question—such as the Athenian
legislator Cleisthenes, who lived at the end of the sixth century
B.C. One fine day I decide that he did not exist and I prove it:
Herodotus was in no position to know; Aristotle was repeating
sources that were themselves untrustworthy. But my actual objective is different: to impose a split among historians on my own
terms. I will call all historians preceding me "Cleisthenians,"
while I and my followers will together constitute the anti-
Cleisthenians. Everyone will realize that my theory is absurd, but
since I will have respected the rules of the game, my reputation
will not suffer from it. Marshall Sahlins says rather harshly what
should be said about such customs: "So the publishing decisions
of academic presses and ultimately the nature of scholarly research are drawn irresistibly into the orbit of the average common opinions of the consumer public. It's a scandal."

2. On La Vieille Taupe and Cannibals

If there exist, as we have seen, two extreme and opposite
forms of delusion concerning cannibals—Harris's reductionist
delusion and Arens's delusion of denial—we may expect to find
the same two delusions concerning an event that is far more traumatic for our history than all past, present, and future cannibals

combined: the massacre by Hitler's Germany of several million European Jews. It is always satisfying for the mind to observe a logic in action. It will thus be pleasing to see that the enterprise known as La Vieille Taupe (or the Old Mole) published at several years' distance two equally simplistic explanations of the Hitlerian genocide: a materialist reduction and—if it may still be called an explanation—a negation pure and simple.

La Vieille Taupe, it will be recalled, is a bookstore turned publisher of a tendency that might be characterized, for lack of a better term, as anarcho-Marxist. From Marxism it has retained neither its critical philosophy, which prevails in Marx and several of his disciples, nor the statist perversion of Lenin and Stalin, but the obsession with a total explanation of the world, whose strictly "ideological" cast is apparent. To a humanity one day reconciled with itself, which is the hope of the future, are opposed all existent regimes. Whether bourgeois-democratic, Stalino-Brezhnevian, social democratic, Maoist, third world, or fascist, all such regimes represent so many forms of capitalist domination. More specifically, La Vieille Taupe opines that there was no fundamental difference between the two opposing camps in the Second World War, and thus no particular perversity characterizing Hitlerian national socialism. It may be intuited that starting from such premises, La Vieille Taupe will be poorly equipped to appreciate the rather odd place occupied by the Jews in the history of our society since the triumph of the Christian dissidence.

Thus it was that in 1970 La Vieille Taupe published a brochure entitled *Auschwitz ou le Grand Alibi*, the reprint of an anonymous article which had appeared in 1960 in *Programme communiste*, the organ of another Marxist sect (founded by Amadeo Bordiga). The "grand alibi" of the antifascists was the extermination of the Jews by Hitler. That crime alone establishes the distance separating the democrat from the fascist. And yet, according to the Bordigists, this is by no means the case. For the anti-Semitism of the imperialist era must be given the requisite economic and social explanation. "As a consequence of their prior history, the Jews today find themselves for the most part in the middle and petty bourgeoisie. *But that class stands condemned in advance by the irresistible advance of the concentration of capital.*"[7] The reaction of the petty bourgeoisie to that condemnation lay "in sacrificing one of its segments in order to thus save and ensure the existence of the others." The German petty bourgeoisie "thus threw the Jews to the wolves in order to lighten its load and save itself." Large capital, for its part, was "delighted by the boon: it could liquidate a section of the petty bourgeoisie with the agreement of the petty bourgeoisie."[8] As for demonstrating how the "petty bourgeoisie" was more threatened in 1943 than in 1932, the brochure does not choose to take up the question. But at least it attempts to account for the methodical nature of the endeavor: "In normal times, and when only a small number are at stake, capitalism can allow those it ejects from the process of production to die on their own. But this was impossible to do in the middle of a war and for millions of men: that much disorder would have issued in a general paralysis. Capitalism had to organize their death." But with what profit? "Capitalism cannot execute a man it has sentenced if it does not extract some profit from that very punishment." Profit will thus be sought through the exhaustion of workers, and those incapable of working will be massacred directly. But is it profitable? "German capitalism could resign itself to murder pure and simple only with difficulty . . . because *it brought no revenue.*"[9] The authors of the brochure thus expatiate on the famous mission of Joël Brand, who left Hungary with the blessings of Himmler, to exchange the Hungarian Jews slated for the "mill" of Auschwitz for ten thousand trucks.[10] The authors do not for an instant appear to notice that we are then in 1944, not 1942, that Himmler has good reason to realize that the war has been lost, and that the time has come to attempt to make use of the legendary "Jewish influence" on the Western allies. The Jews, despite such attempts, were destroyed "not as *Jews* but as *rejects from the process of production*, useless for production."[11]

Was it the manifestly absurd nature of that explanation that led La Vieille Taupe to an inverse explanation, one denying the genocide? I do not know, but if mutation there was, it was a rather sudden one, for Pierre Guillaume informs us that as of 1970, "La Vieille Taupe shared in essence the theses of Paul Rassinier."[12] I shall return shortly to Paul Rassinier, to the two of his books republished by La Vieille Taupe,[13] and to several others. We shall retain only the fact that from a "materialist" explanation a path has been taken to denial pure and simple (Rassinier, Faurisson)[14] or to a more or less methodical skepticism (Serge Thion). A formula of Serge Thion's effectively reveals how the unfulfilled dream of a "materialist" explanation lies behind current dissatisfactions: "There were, no doubt," he writes, "artisan-like gassings, but the question of industrial methods of extermination has not been treated in a manner responsive to all the questions appropriately raised with regard to the functioning of any other industrial enterprise, in any other context." What is being discussed here? Technology? But large-scale gassing does not pose problems essentially different from "artisan-like" gassing. Or are we dealing with an economically based interpretation of Auschwitz? But if such is the case, Thion would be revealing that he does not understand the Nazi undertaking any more than Marvin Harris understands cannibalism. For exterminating human beings, even with industrial methods, is not, in this century, quite the same thing as canning peas. Even as eating human meat and eating butcher's meat are not the same thing and are not similarly charged with the sacred. What is it that the "materialists" need and what are they dreaming of? Huge registers in which the entries are marked as living and the exits as dead? In point of fact, we are not so far, as we will see, from possessing them, once one makes the requisite effort of elementary decoding. Would they like a statistical chart showing the productivity of the gas chambers?

The quarrel over industrial rationality in fact hides a profound ignorance of what constitutes a totalitarian system. Such a system is not an organism functioning in unified manner under the leadership of its head. In Nazi Germany, for example, the Gestapo, the Ministry of Foreign Affairs, and the Ministry of Occupied Territories formed as many clans that had neither the same interests nor the same policies. The juridical and police (or deportation) apparatuses did not function at the same pace.[15] For a long time, for example, Jews condemned under common law escaped deportation. It was possible for there to be, quite normally, at Auschwitz, both hospitals *and* extermination installations into which healthy people disappeared. Conflicts of interest between those concerned above all with killing and those who wanted above all to exploit workers (and even Jewish ones) are attested to by documents of the period as well as by subsequent testimony. Beyond the oppositions between various clans and strata of society, one finds, however, in those doing the speaking, a common fear in the face of reality, a common masked language.

In point of fact, the mass murder encounters, in its executants themselves, such tenacious resistances that one finds Himmler, for example, resorting on occasion to straightforward (or almost completely straightforward) language: "The following question has been put to us: what is to be done with women and children? I have taken a decision and here too I have come upon an obvious solution. I did not feel I had the right to exterminate [literally, to extirpate: *auszurotten*] the men—say, if you like, to kill them or to have them killed—and to allow the children to grow up and avenge themselves on our children and descendants. It was necessary to take the grave decision to make this people disappear from the Earth [*dieses Volk von der Erde verschwinden zu lassen*]."[16] Himmler is here, if I may say so, at his most frank, even if a description of the actual process would be a thousand times more traumatic. But it also befalls him, even before an "informed" audience, to inject a sudden note of attenuation. Thus before the officers of the SS, on April 24, 1943: "It is with anti-Semitism as with delousing. Removing or distancing [*entfernen*] lice is not a matter of world-view. It is a matter of cleanliness."[17]

In this case it is the metaphor of lice which gives its true sense to "distancing." For does one in fact "distance" a louse? Finally, Himmler on occasion encodes matters and even overencodes them; thus, upon receiving a report in April 1943 from the SS "Inspekteur für Statistik" R. Korherr, he informs him briefly that he hopes that it in no place makes mention of the "special treatment" (*Sonderbehandlung*) of the Jews.[18] And one recalls that "special treatment" was already a coded term meaning extermination.[19] All this is obvious, sadly obvious, but can one expect the "materialist" Serge Thion to have opened up Jean-Pierre Faye's massive volume on *Langages totalitaires*?[20]

3. On History and Its Revision

Barely did the war come to an end when historical work on the world of the concentration camps began: modest work establishing details, as well as syntheses associated with such well-known names as Gerald Reitlinger, Martin Broszat, Raul Hilberg, Léon Poliakov, Olga Wormser-Migot, and a few others. The work was difficult since it entailed both knowledge and experience. Michel de Boüard, a historian and a former deportee, concluded his admirable sketch of Mauthausen as follows: "When the survivors of the deportation will have disappeared, the archivists of the future may dispose of a few more documents, which still remain hidden today, but they will lack the principal source: the living memory of the witnesses." Great books on the deportation have been written by deportees: David Rousset, Eugen Kogon, Germaine Tillion. A book like Paul Rassinier's *Le Mensonge d'Ulysse* should be mentioned at this juncture: excellent as testimony by the author of what he experienced, interesting when criticizing other witnesses of Buchenwald and Dora and revealing those in charge of a political apparatus run principally by communist deportees, it becomes frankly absurd, even heinous, when dealing with what the author had no knowledge of: the extermination camps, and principally Auschwitz. As it has come to be written, that history has meaning, if not *a* meaning. It has its zones of opaqueness and its progressive logic:[22] "euthanasia" (partly by gassing) of the mentally ill from 1939 to 1941 and of communist "commissars" in occupied Soviet Union from 1941 to 1942; the organization, then the rationalization, of the extermination by gas (carbolic oxide first, then Zyklon B) of Jews, Gypsies, and certain groups of Soviet prisoners in specialized centers in Poland, then, for the most part, in Auschwitz; cessation of the policy of exterminating the Jews on orders from Himmler at the end of October 1944, but the use of certain exterminatory techniques in camps in Austria, Germany, and Alsace (small gas chambers at Mauthausen, Ravensbrück, and Struthof).[23]

That history, to be sure, like all historical narratives, is in need of criticism. The critique can and should be conducted at several levels. First of all, a vast subliterature representing a truly obscene appeal to consumption and sadism should be pitilessly denounced.[24] Equally deserving of elimination is whatever partakes of fantasy and propaganda. The task is not always easy, since fantasy and propaganda are largely based on reality. But clear cases do exist, such as one that has eluded the ardor of the revisionists, that of a Protestant theologian, Charles Hauter, who was deported to Buchenwald, never saw any gas chamber, and who went on to rave about them:

> An obsession with machinery literally abounded when it came to extermination. Since it had to occur quite rapidly, a special form of industrialization was required. The gas chambers answered that need in a very different way. Some, rather refined in conception, were supported by pillars of porous material, within which the gas formed and then seeped through the walls. Others were more simple in structure. But all were sumptuous in appearance. It was easy to see that the architects had conceived them with pleasure, devoting great attention to them, gracing them with all the resources of their aesthetic sense. These were the only parts of the camp that had truly been constructed with love.[25]

Concerning propaganda, we may mention the report on Treblinka by the Soviet journalist V. Grossmann, in which everything is distorted and monstrously exaggerated, from the number of victims, which is multiplied by more than three (from about 900,000 to 3,000,000) to the techniques used to inflict death.[26]

It goes without saying that the testimony, all testimony and documents—whatever one may read in Faurisson (*Vérité*, p. 210*n*45), the archives of the Third Reich are accessible to researchers, unlike the archives of France and the Soviet Union—should be criticized (as they already are, and it is true that some are completely fictitious) according to methods that have been used for centuries. That means, of course, that nothing in this matter is untouchable. The figure of six million Jews murdered, which comes from Nuremberg, is neither sacred nor definitive, and many historians have arrived at a figure which is slightly lower.[27] Similarly, Serge Klarsfeld, through the detailed work characterizing his *Mémorial*, has reduced by about 40,000 the figure habitually given for the deportation of the Jews of France (from 120,000 to a little more than 76,000).[28] Who would not approve of such research? Who would object to a proliferation of theses and studies on the subject—which is not the case?[29]

Finally, it is plain that the mass murder has to be resituated within the larger realities of which it is a part: the whole of Hitler's policies, first of all. (And even here, one should compare only what is comparable: the only "counterpart" to the genocide of the Jews is that of the Gypsies and, to a relative extent, that of a fraction of the Polish and Soviet populations.) The whole of the Second World War, next: it is clear that a history can not be written by the victors alone. The massacre of Katyn, the bombing of Dresden, the destruction of Hiroshima and Nagasaki, the "return," in frightful conditions, of the Germans fleeing from eastern Europe, the camps established near Perpignan by the Third Republic and the French state, and the delivery to the Soviets of the Russian prisoners seeking refuge in the West are as much a part of it as Auschwitz and Treblinka. But here too the comparisons must be honest. It is a bold-faced lie to compare the Hitlerian camps to the camps set up, in a perfectly scandalous decision, by the Roosevelt administration to house Americans of Japanese origin (*Vérité*, p. 189). The last context is planetary, that of our contemporary world so fertile in massacres (the Armenians in 1915, the victims of the colonial wars) and in populations exploited to the limits of survival (the third world). Here too an elementary measuring stick is called for: thus, the expulsion of the Palestinians can not be compared with the Nazi deportation, and the massacre of Deir Yassin by the men of the Irgun and the Stern gang (April 9 and 10, 1948) can be compared with Oradour, not Auschwitz. Finally, it remains for historians to withdraw the data from the hands of the ideologues that exploit them. In the case of the genocide of the Jews, it is clear that one Jewish ideology, Zionism, exploits the great massacre in a manner that is on occasion scandalous.[30] But the fact that an ideology has seized on a fact does not do away with its existence, as the entirety of Thion's book seems intent on demonstrating, for reasons more applicable to his personal approach than to that of those he would attack. Since when, to take an extreme example, does the fact that Hitlerian propaganda revealed to the world the Katyn massacre do away with its reality? Why can it not be the case that LICRA (International League against Racism and Anti-Semitism) might both speak the truth about Auschwitz and make use of the services of a racist buffoon like Paul Giniewski (*Vérité*, pp. 152–153)? Conversely, it is incredible that one might accept simply as "an individual who has always spoken his mind openly" a recently rallied supporter of Faurisson named Vincent Monteil, a relentless (and perhaps paranoid) partisan of the most extremist Arab theses concerning Israel and the Jews (*Vérité*, pp.130–131).

The program I have just sketched is in the order of historical research. It is not entirely accomplished, and like any historical research, it can never be completed.

Is such the critical vision brought to us, even in excessive form, by the literature of "revisionism"?[31] Not by any means. The contribution of that literature concerns, for the most part, not the history of the war of 1939–1945, but the study of contemporary mentalities, above all since the 1960s. One of the very rare bits of information to be derived from Thion's book, for example, besides his bibliographies, is Faurisson's demonstration that Anne Frank's *Diary*, as it was first published, is, if not a "literary hoax," at the least a document that has been tampered with (*Vérité*, pp. 213–298). Thion, who is for once lucid, notes as much: "This does not diminish in any way the tragic fate she [Anne Frank] knew." On the scale of Hitler's genocide, that modification is equivalent in importance to a comma."[32]

In point of fact, the idea that one would have to oppose a "revisionist" school to an "exterminationist" school is an absurd idea that is naturally a creation of the alleged "revisionists," an idea taken up for his own ends by Thion. There exist historical schools that confront others when new problematics, new types of documents, or new "topographies" (in Paul Veyne's sense) surface. Everyone can bring examples to mind. But would one say that there is one school maintaining that the Bastille was taken on July 14, 1789, and another one claiming it was taken on the 15th. We are at this point on the terrain of positive history, *wie es eigentlich gewesen*, as things actually transpired, according to Ranke's nineteenth-century formula, a formula in which truth is opposed to falsehood, independently of any interpretation.

There are, to be sure, historical schools claiming to be "revisionist." Taking the opposite tack from what is taught is a slightly perverse habit, however salutary the reflex from which it springs. One might explain, for instance, that Stalin possessed no more than a shadow of power at the end of the 1930s,[33] or that the U.S. government, and it alone, was the origin of the Cold War (works by Joyce and Gabriel Kolko),[34] which is all the more easy to demonstrate in that the American archives are accessible, and the Soviet archives are not. These are eminently contestable works, but which all the same partake of the historian's ethic and practice. There is nothing comparable in the case of the revisionists of the Hitlerian genocide, in which it is simply a matter of replacing the unbearable truth with a reassuring lie.

4. On the Revisionist Method

To all appearances there is more than one room in the revisionist house. Serge Thion presents a moderate—indeed antifascist—version, one capable of bringing tears to the eyes of Jean-Gabriel Cohn-Bendit. At stake is only a limited operation, aimed at eliminating from the list of Hitler's crimes one that, once submitted to critical reflection, seems impossible. "Let us reduce the question to its central articulation: striking a major crime from the catalogue of Nazi ignominies would be tantamount to rehabilitating the Third Reich, warping it 'leftward,' making it comparable to other political regimes. This proceeds from a confusion: one attributes to authors casting doubt on the gas chambers the intention of casting doubt on all the other horrors, which are far better known and documented. But that is merely a polemical ploy" (*Vérité* p. 39). In point of fact, there is neither confusion nor polemical ploy. It is Faurisson who stands within revisionist truth when he proffers his famous formula: "Never did Hitler either order or accept that anyone be killed for reason of race or religion" (*Vérité*, p. 91).[35] The "revisionists," in fact, all more or less share several extremely simple principles.

1. There was no genocide and the instrument symbolizing it, the gas chamber, never existed.[36]

2. The "final solution" was never anything other than the expulsion of the Jews toward eastern Europe, their "repression," as Faurisson elegantly puts it (*Vérité*, p. 90). Since "most of the Jews of France came from the East," it may be concluded that it was never anything more than their repatriation, a bit as when French authorities repatriated Algerians, in October 1961, in their "native douars."[37]

3. The number of Jewish victims of Nazism is far smaller than

has been claimed: "There is no document worthy of the name which has figured the total loss of the Jewish population during the last war to be more than 200,000. . . . We may also add that included in the total number of Jewish victims are cases of natural death," the German lawyer Manfred Roeder writes calmly, which would mean that demographically the death rate among Jewish communities was exceptionally low. Others, in their generosity, go as far as a million (Rassinier, Butz),[38] attributing a large fraction of those deaths to Allied aircraft. Faurisson, for his part, (almost) divides the million in two: a few hundred thousand deaths in uniform (which is a fine demonstration of valor) and as many killed "in acts of war" (*Vérité*, p. 197). As for the death statistics for Auschwitz, they "rose to about 50,000" (ibid.).

4. Hitler's Germany does not bear the principal responsibility for the Second World War. It shares that responsibility, for example, with the Jews (Faurisson in *Vérité*, p. 187), or it may even not bear any responsibility at all.

5. The principal enemy of the human race during the 1930s and 1940s was not Nazi Germany but Stalin's Soviet Union.

6. The genocide was an invention of Allied propaganda, which was largely Jewish, and specifically Zionist, and which may be easily explained by the Jewish propensity to give imaginary statistics,[39] under the influence of the Talmud.

Anyone can verify, through recourse to the relevant sources, that I am not inventing anything. Moreover, the revisionists convened a Los Angeles congress in September 1979, which allowed them to offer a reward of $50,000 to anyone capable of proving the existence of a gas chamber for the purpose of killing Jews.[40] It may be assumed that they themselves constituted the jury. They now possess a periodical, the *Journal of Historical Review*, whose first issue (Spring 1980) I have before me, and which features several of the masters of this ideological movement, notably Arthur Butz and Robert Faurisson. It contains the proceedings of the Los Angeles congress.

Here, for example, are several of the principles evolved by Dr. Austin J. App, a German-American who has taught in numerous colleges, both Catholic and secular:

> The Third Reich wanted to get Jews to emigrate, not to liquidate them physically. Had they intended liquidation, 500,000 concentration camp survivors [an imaginary statistic] would not now be in Israel to collect fancy indemnities from West Germany. Absolutely no Jews were "gassed" in any concentration camp. There were crematoria for cremating corpses who had died from whatever cause, including especially also the genocidic Anglo-American air raids. The majority of Jews who died in pogroms and those who disappeared and are still unaccounted for fell afoul in territories controlled by the Soviet Russians, not in territories under German control. Most of the Jews alleged to have met their death at the hands of the Germans were subversives, partisans, spies, and criminals, and also often victims of unfortunate but internationally legal reprisals.[41]

The various components of this ideological discourse can be easily discerned: German nationalism, neo-Nazism, anticommunism, anti-Zionism, anti-Semitism. These ingredients are to be found in differing forms and proportions, depending on the author (it is clear, for example, that German nationalism plays no direct role in the work of the French pacifist Paul Rassinier). The share of anti-Semitism—of a pathological hatred of the Jews—is enormous. The operation's aim is obvious: it is a question of depriving, ideologically, a community of what represents its historical memory. For here we find ourselves forced, in the last analysis, to *prove* what happened. We who, since 1945, *know* find ourselves obliged to be demonstrative, eloquent, to use rhetorical weapons, to enter into the world of what the Greeks called *Peithô*, persuasion, which they had made a goddess who is not our own. Is there a realization of what this means?

But let us return to our "revisionists." It will be suspected that—to parody the formula ascribed to Colonel Bigeard (since then a general and a minister)—one does not arrive at such historical results by resorting to the procedures of a choirboy. What then are the rules of revisionist method? All things considered, they are rather simple. Let us pass over the most obvious tactics: out and out lies,[42] forgeries, the appeal to imaginary documents. Those are common practices, but if need be a revisionist could make do without them. We shall mention, instead, since Butz (not without reticence, pp. 119–120, 128–130), Thion, and Faurisson (pp. 70, 88, 105–106, 156, 212n) make him one of their witnesses, the report written by Th. Christophersen, who was growing dandelions (for the production of synthetic rubber) in 1944, on a state farm, three kilometers from Auschwitz, a very real—but different—place. Nothing is missing, neither an imaginary "finding by the United Nations" explaining that "the undeniably regrettable losses of the Jewish people during the Second World War went as high as 200,000 and not six million" (*Mensonge d'Auschwitz*, p. 15), nor the idyllic description of a camp, or rather of a vacation resort in which women wore makeup and put on weight. It may be observed, since such a witness has been invoked, that the "revision," like the revolution of days gone by, is a block.

The principles of revisionist method can in fact be summarized as follows:

1. Any direct testimony contributed by a Jew is either a lie or a fantasy.

2. Any testimony or document prior to the Liberation is a forgery or is not acknowledged or is treated as a "rumor." Butz and Rassinier, for example, are totally unaware of the documents written by members of the Auschwitz *Sonderkommando*, which were hidden by them and then rediscovered after the war, documents giving a precise description and agreeing in all respects with what is known from other sources about the functioning of the gas chambers.[43] Faurisson is satisfied with an allusion (*Le*

Monde of January 16, 1979) to "manuscripts—miraculously—rediscovered," and whose inauthenticity he does not even attempt to demonstrate.

3. Any document, in general, with firsthand information concerning the methods of the Nazis is a forgery or has been tampered with. Thus Faurisson summarily categorizes as belonging to "forgeries, apocryphal, or suspect" works (*Vérité*, p. 284) the heroic "chronicle" of the Warsaw ghetto, which was kept by Emmanuel Ringelbaum and a team of whom I know one member personally. Upon inquiry, one discovers that the chronicle was indeed truncated—above all in its Warsaw edition of 1952—but the cuts consisted for the most part of a few passages damaging to Polish national pride.[44] They in no way modify the validity of the document concerning Nazi policy.

4. Any Nazi document bearing direct testimony is taken at face value if it is written in coded language, but unacknowledged (or underinterpreted) if it is written plainly, as in the case of such speeches of Himmler as that of December 16, 1943: "When I was obliged to give orders in a village to march against partisans and Jewish commissars—I say so to this audience, and my words are intended solely for those present—I systematically gave orders to kill the women and children of those partisans and commissars";[45] or this entry in Goebbels's *Diary* for May 13, 1943: "Modern peoples thus have no other solution than to exterminate the Jews."[46] On the other hand, any manifestation of wartime racism in the Allied camp (and they were not lacking, as may be imagined) is taken in the strongest sense.

5. Any Nazi testimony after the end of the war—in trials either in the East or the West, in Warsaw or Cologne, Jerusalem or Nuremberg, in 1945 or 1963, is considered as having been obtained under torture or by intimidation. I shall return to this important point, but note at this juncture that it is a bit surprising under such conditions that *no* SS officer has denied the existence of the gas chambers. More precisely, Rassinier "is of the impression" (*Ulysse trahi*, p. 132) that the last commandant of

Auschwitz, Richard Baer, "declared that there had never been any gas chambers at Auschwitz under his command." But Baer died, providentially, to be sure, in his prison cell in June 1963.

6. A vast pseudotechnical arsenal is mobilized to demonstrate the material impossibility of mass gassings. Concerning the validity of Faurisson's "chemical" arguments, a chemist's observations have been appended below. As for his considerations on gas chambers used for the execution of those sentenced to death in certain of the United States and the precautions surrounding their use (*Vérité*, pp. 301–309), they in no way prove that mass gassings are impossible. They amount to comparing realities that are incommensurate, as far from each other as the voracity of a starving man and a dinner at Maxim's. The act of gassing, like that of eating, can be performed under vastly different conditions.

7. Formerly, God's existence was proven by the notion that existence was contained in the very concept of God. Such was the famous "ontological proof." It may be said that for the "revisionists," the gas chambers did not exist because nonexistence was one of their attributes. Such is the nonontological proof. For example, the word *Vergasung* does indeed mean gassing when it appears in the negative in a letter from the historian Martin Broszat to *Die Zeit* (August 19, 1960): "*Keine Vergasung in Dachau*" ("no gassing in Dachau"); but *Vergasungskeller* means "carburation chamber" in a document of January 1943 cited by Georges Wellers (Faurisson, in *Vérité*, pp. 104, 109).

8. Finally, anything capable of rendering this frightening story acceptable or believable, of establishing its evolution or furnishing terms for comparison is either unacknowledged or falsified. Not a line in Faurisson and Thion recalls the exploits of the *Einsatzgruppen* (the famous ravine at Babi Yar, for instance). Not a line in Thion and Faurisson recalls that mentally ill Germans were exterminated from 1939 to 1941 and that certain of those in charge of the operation (e.g., F. Stangl at Treblinka) would soon try out their talents on the Jews.[47] Was

that episode an invention of the psychotic international? As for Butz, he is satisfied to affirm that there is nothing in common between the euthanasia of the mentally ill and the pseudo-extermination of the Jews (*The Hoax*, pp. 174–175). There are but a few lines in Butz (pp. 124, 130, 220) about the presence of Gypsies at Auschwitz. He does not even make an effort to refute what is taught in other quarters about their extermination. As for Faurisson, he limits himself to affirming that the Gypsies were interned not "for racial reasons, but for reasons of vagrancy and 'potential delinquency,'" which is quite simply false.[48] He specifies that numerous Gypsy children were born in Auschwitz, without saying what became of them (they were exterminated), and maintains that it was members of the Resistance who were responsible, when such was the case, for the disappearance of the Gypsies (*Vérité*, pp. 192, 212n53).

It will perhaps now be better perceived what such a historical method signifies: in our spectacle-oriented society, it is an attempt at extermination on paper that pursues in another register the actual work of extermination. One revives the dead in order the better to strike the living. Eichmann crossed Europe to organize the train transport system. Faurisson does not have trains at his disposal, but paper. P. Guillaume describes him for us: "a man thoroughly in possession of his subject (200 kilograms of working documents, representing research on several tons of texts)" (*Vérité*, p. 139); the worst part is that it is true, that Faurisson has indeed spent an incalculable number of workdays in the French or German archives in search not, as he pretends, of the truth,[49] but of falsehood, in quest of a way to destroy an immense system of indestructible proof, and which is indestructible precisely because it constitutes a system, not, as the attempt has been made to have us believe, a sheaf of suspect documents.

5. Moscow, Nuremberg, Jerusalem

S. Thion has written the following statement, which takes us to the heart of the false problem he is intent on debating:

What is thus most incredible for anyone preoccupied with this question is—given the enormity of the facts and the generality of their representation—the narrowness of the sources, once one is willing to eliminate the crowd of hearsay witness who in fact did not see. It is literally stupefying to observe that the centerpiece is the set of confessions before Allied tribunals by the heads of the German camps. Once one is prepared to imagine the situation of those defeated men, gambling with their own lives between the hands of their jailers, a paltry game in which truths and lies are the basic tokens in a tactic of survival, one will not be prepared to accept all their declarations as valid currency. (*Vérité*, pp. 33–34)

The analogy, for the "revisionists," is with the Moscow show trials (*Vérité*, pp. 29, 63, 82, 161) or with witchcraft trials, to which the Moscow trials are in fact compared (ibid., pp. 82, 183). We find distilled here the quintessence of the revisionists' paralogisms.

It is quite simply false. There is much more testimony, many other documents than the confessions of camp directors. I have enumerated some and I could cite many more. I have before me, for instance, a particularly moving booklet that was published in Geneva, in 1944, by the World Jewish Congress; it contains documents concerning Auschwitz and Treblinka (spelled "Tremblinki") that served as the basis for an American publication, in November 1944, by the Executive Office of the War Refugee Board.[50] It contains nothing that is not in essential agreement with both the documents of members of the *Sonderkommando* and the testimony of SS officers. I dare say as well that "hearsay witnesses who in fact did not see" also have something to teach us. When, for instance, a man is separated from the rest of his family and learns from former detainees that exit from the camp is by way of the smokestack, when there exists an immense amount of analogous testimony, when one knows that the interested parties never reappeared, such testimony is, all the same, deserving of some attention. But for the moment, the heart of the matter is not there. There is a confusion, under a single rubric, of witnesses who are in fact quite different. Kurt Gerstein, for instance, a principal witness of the extermination process at Belzec in 1942, a Christian anti-Nazi wearing an SS uniform, can not be compared with the commandant of Auschwitz, Rudolf Hoess. Yet his testimony, which was called into question for a variety of reasons, not all of which were bad (the manifestly erroneous nature of his statistics, the mediocre quality of his first publications) has victoriously survived the test. It was even confirmed by the Nazi professor W. Pfannenstiel, not only during his own denazification trial, at Darmstadt in June 1950, but, quite remarkably, during a visit he paid to Paul Rassinier in person. The fact that the confirmation was delivered in ignobly anti-Semitic terms does not in any way diminish (quite the contrary) its validity.[51]

But we must proceed further. To reason as though only lies and falsehoods could emerge from Moscow or Warsaw is to lapse into a fundamental error. If it is true that the Hitlerians could speak the truth about Katyn, it is no less the case that the Soviets can speak the truth about Auschwitz. It cannot be claimed, moreover, that they were particularly forceful in denouncing the Jewish dimension of the massacre, and it was not even through them that such reports began to circulate from 1942 to 1944. As for the share of the camp archives that they seized during the Liberation, it has not, if I can believe my informants in Poland, reappeared since.

Concerning Poland, from 1945 to the present, a country, that is, whose satellite status, however real, has not penetrated in any depth, a country whose intelligentsia has retained its backbone, with a flourishing historical school, it is a sheer absurdity to present the scholars working at the Oswiecim Museum as so many forgers. Their works are carefully executed and their publications—despite several perfectly obvious blind spots of a political nature (the U.S.S.R., the Communist party, Polish nationalism)—would do honor to any historical institute in the West.[52]

And if the historian Michel Borwicz, a Polish Jew who emigrated to the West, is credible for Faurisson in a case involving forgery (*Vérité*, p. 284), his testimony and historical analyses, which are based in large part on Polish publications, are equally valid when what is at stake is affirming the truth.[53]

But the essential question is not even there. Is there something in common between a Moscow trial (or one in Budapest, Prague, Sofia, or Peking) and two major (but not exclusive) sources of documentation such as the Nuremberg trials (1945–1946) and the Eichmann trial in Jerusalem? Is there something in common between the confessions of Hoess at Heide and Minden (English zone), at Nuremberg and Cracow, where he wrote his autobiography while awaiting execution, and the confessions of Bukharin, since that rather unfortunate comparison[54] has been made by militants close to La Vieille Taupe (*Vérité*, p. 148), or, better still, of Slansky? The Stalinist trials were a literary genre obeying extremely strict rules. The author of these pages, who took the trouble—in 1949, approximately at the time of the appearance of a memorable article by F. Fejtö in *Esprit* (November)—of deciphering, with his friend Charles Malamoud, the official record of the Rajk trial, believes he knows them rather well. Plainly, a show trial is easier to stage if the accused, the police, and the magistrates have in common what Dan Sperber calls a "shared knowledge,"[55] that is, if they are all communists, but that is a condition, with the invariable use of torture, which is not indispensable. The first rule is that the accused adopt entirely the language of his accusers; but that rule, if characteristic of all trials of the Moscow sort, is valid for them alone. The second rule, which is fundamental, is that absolutely everything that the accused says, either during the official investigation or publicly at the trial, must be politically significant, in accordance with party policy. The signification may not be immediately apparent; it may, for instance, augur a future trial, or the possibility of a future trial, but it always exists.

In the documentation on Auschwitz there is testimony that

gives the impression of having adopted completely the language of the victors. Such is the case, for instance, of SS Pery Broad, who wrote, *for the English* in 1945, a report on Auschwitz, where he had been part of the *Politische Abteilung*, that is, the Gestapo.[56] He speaks of himself there in the third person. But is it the case of the memoirs of Hoess?[57] Eichmann's lawyer in Jerusalem, Servatius, claimed as much: "Hoess's testimony is characterized by the fact of his total submission,"[58] but I doubt that any other reader of the autobiography would have that impression. Hoess proliferates autobiographical details, insignificant but authentic facts, personal comments, the most varied political commentaries (including a denunciation of the Soviet camps), anti-Semitic and anti-Gypsy accusations. Nothing in it suggests either fabrication or dictation.[59] Upon being arrested by the Allies, Hoess was beaten (and why should we disbelieve him?) several times; he disavows his first signed statement (p. 244); he was also mistreated by his Polish guards at the beginning of his incarceration in Cracow (p. 247). At Nuremberg, on April 15, 1946, he was first called as a *witness for the defense* by Kaltenbrunner's lawyer, Kauffmann, a fact which Faurisson, normally so garrulous on the subject of Hoess, omits mentioning.[60] "Is it the case," the lawyer asked him, "that you can not give the exact number of victims, since you were forbidden to count them?" The reply was affirmative and renders futile any speculation on the numbers given by Hoess. The most absurd cases, moreover, deal not with the figures for his victims, but with the number of Jews that he claims would have arrived at Auschwitz had Hitler's reign continued (for example, four million Romanian Jews, two and a half million Jews from Bulgaria [p. 287]). Hoess's testimony is, to be sure, valid only for what he saw. It is also deserving of criticism.[61] Faurisson makes a great deal out of an error, copied over several times, which, in testimony collected by the British, has him speaking of an imaginary camp called "Wolzek near Lublin" (most probably a confusion—and repetition—between Belzec and Maidanek). I fail to see what can be derived from such arguments. Errors, confusions, and even absurdities are to be found in all kinds of testimony, and even in many celebrated writers who were not forced to confess. Here is an example of a confusion at least as serious as the error over "Wolzek." A French author, speaking precisely of Hoess, tells us (p. 43) that he was incarcerated at the prison in "Krakau," and on the next page, places him in "Cracovie." But Krakau is the German name of the city called Cracovie in French. The author is Rassinier in his book *Le Drame des Juifs européens*.[62]

As for the Nuremberg trials, the principal target of the revisionists, it is possible to discover every imaginable fault in them: they were trials by the victors, who could also be reproached for war crimes. The statutes adopted in the inter-Allied agreement of 1945 present certain ambiguities, to the extent that the high court is placed partially under the authority of the controlling council of the four occupying powers. Article 21 requires the court to consider "as authentic evidence the documents and official reports of governments of the United Nations." Article 19 not only affirms, as Faurisson has said (*Vérité*, pp. 29, 71, 180), that "the Tribunal will not be bound by technical rules relative to the administration of evidence," but explains: "It will adopt and apply, insofar as possible, an accelerated and non-formalist procedure and will allow all means which it will judge to have probative value," which is tantamount to saying that it is master to decide what constitutes evidence and what does not.

But in point of fact, the statutes were of little importance.[64] The only question that counts, historically, is the following: according to which of the two competing models of jurisprudence did the tribunal function, the liberal (and primarily Anglo-Saxon) model or the Soviet model? The answer is not in doubt. The Soviets, who had detained Supreme Admiral Raeder and H. Fritzsche (a collaborator with Goebbels), who was subjected to Moscow-style interrogation, did not impose their law. They could neither impose the inclusion of the crime at Katyn among those attributed to the Nazis nor prevent a German lawyer (despite censorship of his arguments) from shedding a bit of light on their 1939 pact with Germany, nor prevent three acquittals (including Fritzsche's). The prosecution was far from always triumphant over the defense, and the principle of *Tu quoque*, which was officially forbidden, occasionally triumphed in practice, as when the German admirals were able to show that the American fleet under Admiral Nimitz had done exactly what *they* were being reproached with. The principle of collective guilt, which was officially in effect, was not retained in practice, and the tribunal did not make use of the concept of "crimes against humanity"—such crimes were treated as war crimes— and abandoned the notion of a conspiracy.[65] That the raw material accumulated and stocked at Nuremberg was not always of very good quality is a certainty. That a certain amount of sifting must be done is obvious. But sifting does not mean rejecting en bloc and speaking of witchcraft trials in a situation involving defendants who, in the immense majority of cases, contested point by point the charges against them, frequently pleaded ignorance or innocence, but never denied what was not deniable. As for the Jerusalem trial, it too was deserving of severe criticism,[66] but no such criticism, I believe, has ever called into question the administration of evidence. Eichmann presented himself as a second-rank bureaucrat, a kind of chief railway conductor, making the trains run; he above all tried to free himself from the crushing weight of the accusations lodged against him—in the hope of exculpating themselves—by his comrades in the SS; questioned according to Anglo-Saxon procedure by Captain Less, he specified that he had had direct and personal knowledge of the death trucks at Chelmno, the executions at Minsk, the gas chambers at Auschwitz (*Eichmann par Eichmann*, pp. 111, 115, 139). What force in the world—since he was not tortured— what "shared knowledge" with the German Jew questioning him could have constrained him to utter these sentences: "We were deep into the summer of 1941 when Heydrich asked me to come see him. 'The Führer has given the order to do away with the Jews.' Those are the exact words he uttered upon receiving me; and to confirm the effect produced, contrary to his custom, he paused for a long moment. I still remember it quite well."[67]

As for works written on the Hitlerian genocide, Eichmann, who was in a better position to judge their historical validity than the "revisionists," "often referred to the works of Léon Poliakov as an authority and the best source for the events" (A. Less, *Eichmann par Eichmann*, p. 12). Thus the true question raised by those who are troubled by the "revisionist" arguments—and some of those who are troubled are in good faith—is not that of the validity of one trial or another. In the last analysis, they would be willing to reject all such trials. What is difficult for them to admit is that the official truth, sanctioned by the decisions of the highest courts, by the discourse of chiefs of state, in both the West and the East, should also be, exceptionally, the truth pure and simple. There lies the true difficulty, which obliges us to look a bit more closely at the work of the true cultural hero of revisionism, a hero, moreover, who died in 1967: Paul Rassinier.

6. *The Fantastic Calculations of Paul Rassinier*

I am not here to "judge" Paul Rassinier. Lucien Febvre once assembled two studies "against the surrogate judges of the Valley of Josaphat."[68] Thion speaks of the "incredible slander whose victim he has been" (p. 60). He concedes "that there are verbal excesses and, occasionally, debatable affirmations to be found in his writings," but concludes: "One day, it will indeed be necessary to rehabilitate Paul Rassinier" (p. 165). As for Faurisson: "An authentic revolutionary, an authentic resistance fighter, an authentic deportee, [Rassinier] loved the truth as it should be loved: quite strong and above all else" (*Vérité*, p. 195). It will be appreciated that such praise, with that insistence on the love of the truth that characterizes all forgers, is not exactly of the sort to win my own sympathy.[69]

There is, in fact, something tragic in the fate of Paul Rassinier;

not so much a discontinuity in his career (of which there are many: Mussolini, Doriot) but a rift within his very being. What happened at the time of his death (July 28, 1967) symbolizes rather well his destiny. In Paris, the eulogy at his funeral was pronounced by Maurice Bardèche; in Bermont, near Belfort, where he was buried, a representative of the pacifist group La Voie de la Paix was the speaker.[70] A grade-school teacher, then a history and geography professor in a Collège d'Enseignement général, Rassinier was a Communist, then a Socialist, initially of the Marceau Pivert tendency, then of the Paul Faure tendency. A number of the militants of that tendency eventually made the transition to a pro-Vichy and anti-Semitic stance after 1940 (the emblematic Jew being Léon Blum). This was not the case for Rassinier. In favor of the Munich pact, he was nonetheless a member of the Resistance, arrested by the Gestapo in October 1943, and deported to Buchenwald, then to Dora. His experience as a deportee was less that of a political militant than of a petty convict. It was that experience which accounts for the value of *Passage de la ligne* [*Crossing the Line*] (1948), the first part of *Le Mensonge d'Ulysse* [*Ulysses's Lie*] (1950), and of his critique of the concentration camp bureaucracy and literature. *Le Mensonge d'Ulysse* also denounces French and colonial arbitrariness. It was prefaced in 1950 by an anarchist of the extreme right, Albert Paraz, an anti-Semite and a friend of Céline's. The foreword to the second edition of *Le Mensonge d'Ulysse* (1954) features a striking tribute to Maurice Bardèche (p. 235*n*6), who had begun his political campaign in 1948 with *Nuremberg ou la Terre promise* [*Nuremberg or the Promised Land*]. It is worthwhile reading that "admirable book" (Rassinier, *Véritable procès Eichmann*, p. 43). At the time Maurice Bardèche had not yet discovered that Hitler's genocide did not exist: "There was a will to exterminate the Jews, for which there is copious evidence" (p. 187). But that extermination does not concern us: "What transpired at Auschwitz, Maidanek, and other places concerns the Slavs; as for us, our business is the West" (p. 115).

Thus the real question for him is: "How many Frenchmen were at Auschwitz and Treblinka?" (p. 162). "There was no deportation of the French, but a deportation of the Jews; and if certain Frenchmen were deported along with them, it was because they had accepted or seemed to accept the defense of the Jewish cause." The book closes with a pithy formula: "Our choice is between having the SS on our side or in our homes." As of 1955, Rassinier was published by extreme right-wing firms, Les Sept Couleurs and La Librairie Française, which was run by the professional anti-Semite H. Coston. Today La Vieille Taupe declares: "Those who reproach Paul Rassinier for allowing himself to be published by an extreme-right firm are those who would have preferred that he not be published at all."[71]

Are those publications, and his writings for *Rivarol*, the result of a heroic "compromise," such as that, which some have advanced, of Lenin, who made his way back to Russia by way of an imperial Germany at war? Not quite. There are to be found in Rassinier's publications the wherewithal to assemble an anthology of the most stupid and shopworn cliches of anti-Semitism. In that endeavor, moreover, he was aided by quotations from an extremist Zionist of insane bent, Kadmi Cohen. Jewish power as the center of commerce and the world bank is to be dated to ancient times. Saul, David, and Solomon did in their day what Israel does today: the "counter-state" situated "along the most important commercial arteries of the modern world"; Saul, David, and Solomon, then, "attempted to install the Jewish people at the intersection of the two great commercial arteries of their time." The result was that at the end of ten centuries, "all the gold" of the Roman world was placed "periodically on galley-boats heading for Judea." Rassinier does not specify, however, whether those shipments were organized by the bank under the sign of *rubrum scutum*, "red shield" in English (in German, *Rothschild*). "If, on two occasions, Rome sent Titus (70 A.D.), then Hadrian (135 A.D.) to destroy the kingdom of Judea and to disperse its inhabitants throughout the Empire, among other reasons, there was the following one: the retrieval of what it considered to be its gold. Until Titus, it had been extremely well-disposed toward the Jews, the Berenice affair proves as much" (*Drame*, pp. 128–129). Is a historian of antiquity obliged to specify that all this, in its entirety, is grotesque? As for the idyll between Titus and Berenice, it occurred, in its essential phase, after the taking of Jerusalem. But all that concerns antiquity: Jewish greed remains a threat in the modern world as well. Should the international Zionist movement get its "hands on Wall Street," "the principal Israeli way station in the Diaspora would become not only the commercial roof of the Atlantic world, but (thanks to the oil factor) the command-post of all its industry as well." Thus, however imperfectly, would the Biblical prophecy be realized: "The women of Israel would continue, to be sure, to give birth in pain, but their men would win their bread and that of their children through the sweat of other people's brows" (*Drame*, p. 129). Mere "verbal excesses," as S. Thion would say. Need we specify that, according to Rassinier, Léon Blum's positions in 1938, which the author, who was a socialist at the time, deems pro-war, "were inspired by the frequently repeated stands of world Jewry."[72] Rassinier, in fact, is literally obsessed by the theme of the international Jewish conspiracy. The Centre de Documentation Juive Contemporaine (CDJC), the quite peaceful location of a library and archives in which Faurisson could work until 1978, becomes the Centre *mondial*, or World Center, de documentation juive and an "enterprise for the falsification and fabrication of historical documents" (*Drame*, p. 8 and passim), and that error compounded by slander crossed the Atlantic and is to be found in Butz (*The Hoax*, p. 248). The alliance of Jews and communists is a permanent datum of world politics. In 1950, Moscow, Tel Aviv, and Warsaw entered into coalition against a renascent Europe and the result was publications such as Poliakov's *Bréviaire de la haine* [*Breviary of Hatred*] (1951).[73] "Since then," according to Rassinier, "it has not stopped" (*Drame*, p. 9).

Rassinier's glory lay in being the first to demonstrate systematically that there was no genocide and in exonerating the Nazis of "the horrendous and libelous accusation" (*Drame*, p. 107). For the "drama of the European Jews . . . is not that six million of them had been exterminated as they claim, but only in the fact that they have made that claim" (*Drame*, p. 12). Rassinier's friends are on solid ground, to be sure, when they claim that what counts is not an author's sentiments but the scientific validity of his statements. I agree with them in theory, even though anti-Semitic paranoia is perhaps not the best preparation for a study of Hitler's policies toward the Jews. As Thion says, "It is important that such matters remain the concern of decent and honest people" (p. 45). Vouching for the scientific validity of Rassinier's work we have Serge Thion, a sociologist, a member of the Centre National de Recherche Scientifique, who holds a doctorate, and who must, then, know how to read. He tells us that, in *Le Drame des Juifs européens*, Rassinier "shatters the most solid statistical study of the number of those who disappeared from the Jewish communities of Europe, that by the American Hilberg" (*Vérité*, p. 164). Let's take a look.

I am not a specialist in historical demography, but I am nevertheless capable of following an elementary argument. I shall not say anything here about the number of those who disappeared, noting simply that according to the previously mentioned report by Richard Korherr, who was an SS inspector for statistical matters (and who is not mentioned a single time in Thion's work), by the end of March 1943, more than two and a half million Jews had already been "evacuated," which means, without any doubt, in the majority of cases, killed, and that that figure did not include "those deaths occurring . . . in the front zone," which may exclude from it victims of actions by the *Einsatzgruppen* (Wellers, *Mythomanie*, p. 43).[74] Rassinier, for his part, estimates the number of Jewish losses at around one million, more or less (*Drame*, p. 212). But how does he reason?

I must confess some slight astonishment at this juncture: for

Rassinier does not reason, or, more precisely, he pursues the following argument: I take an ink pad (*pâté*), add some lark pâté (with the habitual amount of horse) and finally one city block (*pâté*) of houses, and I arrive at the precise figure of 3,268,471 Jews allegedly exterminated by Hitler, but in fact having survived the war. How does Rassinier arrive at that figure? By adding up data of extremely different kinds. The crux of the problem is obviously the considerable mass of Jews living in Poland, a country partitioned in 1939, the Baltic states, the Ukraine, White Russia, and Bessarabia: more than five million human beings.[75]

In order to save, on paper, the majority of these Jews from extermination, Rassinier makes use of a single source: an article by the Soviet Jewish journalist David Bergelson, who, in a Yiddish newspaper in Moscow, *Die Einheit* of December 5, 1942, an article quoted, according to Rassinier, in a German newspaper in Buenos Aires, *Der Weg*, in January 1953,[76] affirmed that "a majority (80%) of the Jews of the Ukraine, of Lithuania and Lettonia were saved," thanks to the Red Army, we are to assume (*Drame*, p. 125). But the geographical dimensions of the rescue are expanded a bit later in the book, since we learn of "Polish, Baltic, and Romanian Jews who, in the years 1941–1942, were evacuated to central Asia, and who, if we are to believe the Jewish journalist David Bergelson, would have numbered between 2 and 2.2 million in 1942" (*Drame*, p. 218). As Thion says (p. 33), "there are good sources and poor ones, the trick being to gauge them well." It happens that this source is worth nothing at all, and those who speak at every turn of war propaganda should have been able to perceive that we have in this case a rather typical example (cf. Wellers, *Mythomanie*, p. 38). Bergelson was a writer who belonged to a Jewish committee created by the Soviet authorities precisely for propaganda purposes, and for targeting American Jews in particular. After the war, in 1952, his mission accomplished, he was executed. Rassinier does not mention this, and *not for a moment* does he wonder how Bergelson might have been informed and how the Red Army, surprised and trapped, would have been able to save so many Jews. It did save, to be sure, a few. How many? We do not know.

With that much established, it is futile to pursue the analysis and demonstrate how Rassinier "saves" another million and a half Russian Jews. As he himself writes (*Drame*, p. 221), "A demographic study could only be technical in nature." But a bit alarmed by the results of his own calculations, Rassinier proffers this disarming observation: "If they are no longer in Europe and not in Israel, these 3,268,471 Jews [not one less, not one more] who were quite alive in 1945 all the same have to be somewhere else—along with however many more they have naturally increased their numbers by!" (*Drame*, p. 217). For, as a songster put it after the Liberation in France, "the ovens were then only incubators." What is to be done with those excess Jews? They can, of course, be temporarily installed in central Asia, but they can't stay there indefinitely. Rassinier comes up with a solution. Between 1945 and 1961,[77] a clandestine escape network allowed more than a million of them, "at a great cost in dangers incurred, . . . to leave central Asia for the American continent" (*Drame*, p. 218), that is, by crossing China and the Pacific Ocean. In brief, "they are necessarily in the United States" (ibid.).

But other surprises are possible. Given the quarrel between Khruschev and Mao Zedong (Rassinier was writing in 1963), it goes without saying that Mao will help the Jews leave Soviet territory. "In that case, it is possible that the presence of a large number of Jews would suddenly come to light, one day, in all the countries of North and South America, perhaps in Israel as well" (*Drame*, p. 214). In the seventeenth century it happened that gazettes suddenly announced the reappearance of the ten lost tribes of Israel. Rassinier has carried off an exploit of the same type. But as he puts it, "We are dealing here only with conjectures, not certainties: a working hypothesis needed by all scholars as a starting point for their research" (*Drame*, p. 219). And it is on the basis of arguments of this sort—and there are many more—that Rassinier feels fully justified in writing of the Hitlerian genocide that it is, in truth, "the most tragic and most macabre hoax of all time."[78]

7. *The Jewish War*

Serge Thion, in the nuanced evocation of him that he gives (p. 14), notes in Faurisson "a certain propensity [which he shares] to side with the defeated, with those who have received the short end of the stick." But who are the defeated? The Germans, and more precisely the Nazis? To be sure, they were defeated, and the German people has suffered, frightfully, as have other peoples who were not defeated—the Russians, the Poles, the Yugoslavs, the Czechs, and the Greeks. The Jews, in Eastern Europe and in several other regions (in Holland, in Greece), were not defeated; they were annihilated. It is not always easy to comprehend what that means. One can feel it almost physically in the immense Jewish cemetery of Warsaw, near the ghetto where "the Marxist Brandt," as Butz calls him, one day came to kneel (*The Hoax*, p. 244): the gravestones suddenly disappear around 1942 only to reappear on an infinitesimal scale in 1945. Richard Marienstras has tried to articulate this: "Those whose civilization—whose respiration—was entirely defined by Yiddishkeit, those for whom every vital relation depended on the Yiddish world, those people, following the disappearance of their culture, can not modify and displace their allegiance to what no longer is and which can exist only in an obsessive and terrified memory. For them, there is no project and no deliverance; they do not forget when they say they have forgotten; they do not hope, even if what they have substituted for hope is strident—its stridency reveals the despair and the unhappiness of which it is made."[79] It was necessary to attempt to articulate what can barely be said, and if there are those who feel "redeemed" by the military victories of Israel, I, for my part, can only pity and even despise them.

It was not a war and, as I have already said, the State Council of the Polish Republic which, in April 1967, conferred military decorations on the victims of Auschwitz for having died "while struggling against Hitler's genocide" revealed that it had not understood or had not wanted to understand what had happened.[80] But, we are told, a war is precisely what it was. An Englishman, Richard Harwood (the pseudonym of the neo-Nazi Verrall) explained it to us in his famous pamphlet, which provoked the just outrage of P. Viannson-Ponté and prompted Faurisson to reenter the battle (*Le Monde*, July 17, 1977, and *Vérité*, pp. 65–92):

> On September 5, 1939, Chaim Weizmann, president of the Zionist Organization (1920) and the Jewish Agency (1929), who later became president of the republic of Israel, had declared war on Germany in the name of Jews the world over, specifying that "the Jews stand by Great Britain and will fight on the side of the democracies. . . . The Jewish Agency is prepared to take immediate measures to make use of Jewish manpower, Jewish technical competence and resources, etc." (*Jewish Chronicle*, September 8, 1939)

It is of little consequence, to be sure, that Weizmann had no power to speak in the name of Jews throughout the world, nor that he had no intention of doing so.[81] A Zionist leader with strong ties to Great Britain, despite the conflict provoked by the British policy of ceasing immigration to Palestine, he spoke, as did Ben-Gurion during the same period, in the name of his own followers and of a minority ideology. The feelings of American Jews, for example, were not in doubt, but no one could declare war in their name. Not content with merely repeating "Harwood," Faurisson adds a rather significant error: "In the person of Chaim Weizmann, the President of the World Jewish Congress, . . . the international Jewish community declared war on Germany on September 5, 1939" (*Vérité*, p. 187, repeated on p. 91). The president of the World Jewish Congress at the time was the American rabbi Stephen Wise. But, given the impossibility of invoking the spokesman of international Jewry, the best thing is to invent him. The "declaration of war," Faurisson specifies, was the consequence of the economic boycott of Nazi Germany decided on by "the international Jewish community in retaliation for the anti-Semitic measures taken by Hitler." It is all quite simple: "That fatal machinery was bound to lead, on both sides, to a world war" (*Vérité*, p. 187).[82] Once the wine has been poured, it will have to be drunk: the war came; "the German soldier engaged in fierce combat against the partisans, . . . including, if need be, against women and children mingling with the partisans." But, Faurisson specifies, "the army gave the most Draconian orders that no German soldier was to participate in excesses against the civilian population, including the Jews." Better yet: it may be said of the Wehrmacht, including the SS, "that it was, in certain respects, far less threatening for non-combatant civilians than many other armies" (*Vérité*, pp. 187 and 211*n*45). Apparently, the *Einsatzgruppen* did not exist.

From this point on, it becomes possible to explain and justify everything. The Jewish star? A military measure. "Hitler was perhaps less concerned with the Jewish question than with ensuring the safety of German soldiers" (*Vérité*, p. 190).[83] Many Jews spoke German and were suspected of practicing "espionage, terrorism, black market operations, and of arms trafficking." Children wearing the star at age six? Faurisson has an answer for everything: "If we remain in the framework of military logic, there are today a sufficient number of stories and memoirs in which Jews recall that already as children they were engaged in all sorts of illicit or resistance activities against the Germans" (*Vérité*, p. 190).

And on that same page, which one would do well to feature in an anthology of the obscene, Faurisson shows us, through a precise example, that the Germans were quite right to be distrustful: "They feared what was, moreover, about to take place in the Warsaw ghetto, where, suddenly, right behind the front, in April 1943, there was an insurrection. To their stupefaction, the Germans then discovered that the Jews had built seven hundred bunkers. They put down that insurrection and transferred the survivors to labor and concentration camps. This was a tragedy for the Jews." It is useful to read this page a bit more closely. All footnotes have charitably disappeared, but note 48 on page 211 allows us to learn Faurisson's source and to see him at work. His "informant," as the anthropologists say, is Reichsführer Heinrich Himmler himself, and more precisely his speech at Poznan on October 6, 1943: "I cleaned up large Jewish ghettos in territories of the rear. In a ghetto in Warsaw, we had street-fighting during four weeks. Four weeks! We demolished about seven hundred bunkers."[84]

Faurisson has commented on this text and that event on several levels, first of all by adding to Himmler's indication "in territories of the rear (*in den Etappengebieten*)" the little words "right" and "front," which make it coherent with his military logic. The reader may thus forget that the "front" was at the time quite distant, more than a thousand kilometers away, rather astonishing changes from someone as obsessed with footnotes and precision,[85] but the "front," after all, is a rather ambiguous notion. Concerning the event itself, which occurred at a time when the ghetto was already emptied of three-quarters of its population by massive deportations, the reader will learn nothing. Here, too, Faurisson's master is Himmler, who, on June 21, 1944, at Sonthofen, attempted to make the German generals assembled believe that he was forced to confront, in Warsaw, not a handful of insurgents, but "more than five hundred thousand Jews," whom he was obliged to liquidate "in five weeks of street-fighting" (*Geheimreden*, p. 170). There is a similar silence concerning the immediate context of the speech of October 6, 1943, which had Himmler protesting against the same economic tyranny so often invoked by the revisionists: "The ghetto manufactured fur coats, clothing, etc. Earlier, when one wanted to enter, one was told: 'Halt! You're interfering with the war economy! Halt! This is an arms factory!'" (*Geheimreden*, p. 170). Silence is maintained about all this, but there is a warning to the reader (in the same note 48, p. 211) concerning *Geheimreden*: "This work is to be used with precaution, particularly in its French translation." Why that precaution? We already know, from reading the speech at Poznan, that the reader might learn, *on the preceding page*, that Himmler had given the order to kill (*umbringen*) the men, women, and children of the Jewish people. It is clear that in *that* war, Himmler was not defeated.

8. On the Art of Not Reading Texts

If there is not, in the scientific sense of the term, a "debate" over the existence of the gas chambers, it is a fact that the "revisionists" claim that such a debate exists, or rather that it does not exist, since they are persuaded—with any necessary reservation for the acts of one or two madmen in the SS—that no such thing existed. But gas chambers did not exist in and for themselves; they were the endpoint of a process of triage which, upon entry into a camp or at a camp, summarily sorted out men and women whom the SS deemed capable of working from the rest.

The process is known both through Nazi administrative documents and the accounts of deportees. Here, for example, is a telegram addressed from Auschwitz to the central economic administration of the camps at Oranienburg on March 8, 1943. The document enumerated various convoys, including the following: "Transported from Breslau, arrived 3/5/43. Total: 1,405 Jews. Put to work: 406 men (Buna factories) and 190 women. Subjected to special treatment (*sonderbehandelt wurden*): 125 men and 684 women and children."[86] The sum is precise. Will anyone dare claim that these individuals were being brought to a rest camp?

As for the deportees, the tale has been told a thousand times and it is practically identical for all witnesses,[87] a fact that unfortunately does not mean that they were plagiarizing each other. The testimony of Primo Levi, at the time a young Italian chemist, is particularly austere. He left on February 22, 1944 in a train containing 650 deportees. Upon their arrival in Auschwitz, about ten SS officers "interrogated those disembarking with some indifference. 'How old? In good health? Sick?' In less than ten minutes, we, the healthy males, were regrouped. What happened to the others—women, children, and the aged—we were not able to ascertain, neither at the time nor thereafter: they were purely and simply swallowed up by the night." Sometimes, adds Primo Levi, who was forced to learn quickly, things were even simpler. Those who left the train on one side of the tracks were enrolled, "the others went to the gas chamber."[88] Such was the functioning of SS rationality. Auschwitz was, as has been repeated in every key (Butz, Faurisson, Thion) a great industrial center, specializing in the production of synthetic rubber. But no one has ever explained why babies were slated to go there, and no one has ever told us what became of those babies. The absolute inability of the "revisionists" to tell us where those who were not registered in the camp (and whose names nonetheless appeared on the convoy lists) went is proof of the mendacious character of their affirmations.[89] It is not for lack of effort on their part. Christophersen, *the* revisionist witness, writes calmly: "When, at roll call, detainees were asked whether they were prepared to accomplish the task at hand [in this case, the planting of rubber-yielding dandelions], and whether thay had ever done anything comparable previously, volunteers were almost always too numerous. Thus there was a selection; subsequently, that selection process has been completely distorted. It was natural to want to keep the detainees occupied and they did not ask for anything better. The selection process had no other purpose than to make use of them according to their tastes, talents, and relative health" (*Mensonge d'Auschwitz*, p. 22). A. R. Butz, normally so adroit, slips up and is content more or less to note that "industrial and other activities required that selections procedures take place for various purposes" (*The Hoax*, p. 111). His rather unique argument against the usual interpretation is that there were a large number of Jews in the hospital. This amounts, once again, to resorting to an imaginary rationality.

The heart of the question lies in knowing what happened during the "selection process" upon entry into the camp or, later on, during operations aimed, according to the going interpretation, at separating those who were still capable of working from those who were not. Might one, during the selection process, be rejected and show up subsequently? At Dora, Rassinier had a comrade who was selected and who did reappear. But there was no gas chammber at Dora, and the man had been sent to Bergen-Belsen, a so-called hospital-camp, though in fact a death camp, from which he had the good fortune to return (*Mensonge*, p. 170). Faurisson triumphantly published a photo of Simone Veil, who was alleged to have been gassed and who was quite alive. The mechanism of his error is extremely simple, and the indications furnished by Faurisson (*Vérité*, p. 328) allow one to reconstitute it easily. According to the Polish historian Danuta Czech, who set about reconstituting the camp calendar for the series *Hefte von Auschwitz*, convoy 71, arriving from Drancy (April 16, 1944) was treated as follows: 165 men were registered; the rest of the convoy was gassed (*Hefte von Auschwitz*, 7, 1964, p. 88). The camp archives, which are incomplete, did not include the names of women who were registered. The error has been rectified by Klarsfeld in his *Mémorial*: "The Auschwitz calendar does not mention any woman who was selected, but this is erroneous, since in 1945 seventy female survivors from the convoy were counted. There were also thirty-five male survivors."

Nevertheless, "good use" can also be made of the notion of selection, for instance, for argumentative ends. An optimist, as is known, says a glass is half full and a pessimist that it is half empty. One can also choose to see only the "positive" aspect of selection, if the word be permitted. Such was the tack of Hans Laternser, who was the lawyer of the German general staff at Nuremberg and defended, in Frankfurt, from 1963 to 1965, several defendants in the Auschwitz trial. Given the fact, he explains, that the aim of Himmler and Hitler was the annihilation of the Jews, those who "selected the Jews to gain them entry into the camp were thus posing an obstacle to the final solution."[90]

Such is not, it will be agreed, the interpretation of Robert Faurisson. He has nevertheless been led, at first spontaneously, then by the devastating objections of G. Wellers, to attend to another aspect of the selection procedure, that of the separation between sufferers from typhus and the healthy, since that is how he ultimately interprets the "special actions" and the selections.[91] The decisive text on this subject is a document whose authenticity has been contested by no one (even if Butz chooses boldly to maintain strict silence about it). From August 30 to November 18, 1942, Professor Dr. Johann Paul Kremer served as an SS physician in the camp at Auschwitz. The British arrested him in August 1945, and confiscated a diary in which he noted the different events of his life, including the "special actions" he participated in at Auschwitz. That diary has been published in part.[92]

In order to interpret it,[93] I shall appeal exceptionally to a rule of exegesis posited by Faurisson. He has formulated it in various ways with reference to literary texts. Here is one of the oldest: "For one not to search for a meaning and a single meaning in an utterance, whether in prose or poetry, in high or low literature, grave reasons, which have yet to be discovered, would be called for."[94] And, more schematically: "One must look for the letter before looking for the spirit. Texts have only one meaning or they have no meaning at all" (*Nouvelles litteraires*, February 10–17, 1977; *Vérité*, p. 54). With reference to poetry, which Faurisson interprets professionally, the principle is palpably absurd: poetry perpetually plays on polysemy; but the rule has value when referring to plain language such as: I am going out to buy a French bread.

Kremer's *Diary* is incontrovertibly of the latter sort. His observations inform us of the physician's personal and professional life. Thus, on October 9, 1942: "I have sent to Munster a first package containing nine pounds of soap worth 200 RM. Weather rainy"; on September 21: "I wrote today because of Otto to the Police Headquarters in Cologne (the judiciary police service). Duck shooting in the evening. Dr. Meyer informed me of the hereditary transmission of a trauma (nose) in his father-in-law's family." Many of the remarks bear on life in the camp, the illnesses present there, and the precautions taken. For example, on September 1, that is, two days after the doctor's arrival: "I have ordered in writing from Berlin an SS officer's hat, a belt, and suspenders. In the afternoon, I was present at the disinfection of a block in order to delouse it with a gas, Zyklon B." From the day of his arrival, Kremer was struck by the importance of exanthematous typhus; he was vaccinated the following day, revaccinated on September 7 and 14. The tone does not change when it is a question of extracting experimental matter from the prisoners; for instance, on October 3: "Today I proceeded to preserve living matter taken from the livers and spleens of men as well as from the pancreas." Nor does it shift when Kremer is present at physical punishments or executions. Thus, on September 9: "Later in the morning I attended as a physician the administering of blows with a stick to eight detainees and one execution with a small-calibre firearm." There is a similar calm on October 13 and 17, even though the executions are far more numerous: seven Polish civilians in the first case, eleven victims in the second: "I was present at the administering of punishment and at eleven executions [*bei einem Straffvollzug und 11 Exekutionen zugegen*]."

The tone changes only in a single series of circumstances, and then occasionally (not always) to take on an emotional cast that is quite remarkable. I refer to what the text calls special actions (*Sonderaktionen*). Kremer attended eleven of these operations, which he numbered and that took place, on occasion, twice a day. In seven cases—September 5 (the second action); September 6 and 10, September 23 (two actions), September 30 and October 7, the tone remains commonplace. In the four other cases, which include the first and last "actions" in the series (showing that Kremer never quite managed to acclimatize himself) Kremer shows signs of violent emotion and even a certain fear. On September 2: "I attended a special action for the first time, outdoors, at three o'clock in the morning. In comparison, Dante's Inferno seems almost a comedy to me. It is not for nothing that Auschwitz is known as an annihilation camp (*Umsonst wird Auschwitz nicht das Lager der Vernichtung genannt*)."[95] On September 5 (first action): "Today, at noon, I was present at a special action in the FKL[96] (Muslims): the epitome of horror. *Hauptscharführer* Thilo was right to say to me today that we were here at the *anus mundi*." On October 12, after noting that as a result of a vaccination against typhus he had a fever, Kremer added: "Despite this, I attended during the night a special action for people coming from the Netherlands (1,600 persons). Frightful scenes in front of the bunker! It was the tenth special action." October 18: "This Sunday morning, in very cold rainy weather, I attended the eleventh special action (Dutch). Horrid scenes with three women begging to save their lives."

This coincidence between the coded terms (special action) and the emotional language is, all the same, remarkable. A second observation should be made: Kremer, in five out of eleven cases, gives several specifics concerning those targeted by the "special actions." In three cases (2, 10, and 11), we are dealing with Netherlanders, in two others (1 and 9), respectively with male and female "Muslims" and with persons coming from outside (*Auswärtige*). We will not be departing unduly from the letter of the text if we recall that in the argot of the camps "Muslims" were detainees who had arrived at the final stages of debilitation. But perhaps this would constitute too serious a contradiction of "witness" Christophersen?

The customary interpretation of these texts consists of affirming that a "special action" corresponded to a selection, a selection for arrivals coming from without, and also a selection for exhausted detainees. Each, when sent in the "wrong" direction, would take the path to the gas chambers.

Faurisson has contested this interpretation,[97] and proposes the following one, which I shall quote in its entirety:

The physician Johann Paul Kremer's diary should be quoted correctly. It will thus be observed that when he speaks of the horrors of Auschwitz, it is an allusion to the typhus epidemic of September-October 1942. On October 3, he wrote: "At Auschwitz, whole streets have been annihilated by typhus." He himself would contract what he calls "the Auschwitz disease." Germans would die of it. The sorting out of the ill from the healthy was the "selection" or one of the forms of the "special action" performed by the physician. The sorting out took place either within buildings or outdoors. Never did he write that Auschwitz was a *Vernichtungslager*, that is, according to a terminology developed by Allies after the war, an "extermination camp" (by which we are to understand a camp endowed with a gas chamber). In reality, what he wrote was: "It is not for nothing that Auschwitz is called the camp of annihilation (*das Lager der Vernichtung*)."[98] In the etymological sense of the word, typhus annihilates those whom it strikes. Another seriously mistaken quotation: for the date of September 2, 1942, Kremer's manuscript reads: "This morning, I was present, outdoors, for the first time, at a special action." Historians and magistrates customarily suppress the word "outdoors (*draussen*)" in order to have Kremer say that the action took place in a "gas chamber."[99] Finally, the atrocious scenes in front of the "last bunker" (this was the courtyard of Bunker 11) were executions of prisoners sentenced to death, executions the physician was obliged to attend. Among those sentenced were three women who had arrived in a convoy from Holland."[100]

Georges Wellers has observed that Faurisson made use of Kremer's confession in 1947 to interpret the notations in his diary for October 18, 1942 as though they referred to only three executions, but that he pretended to be unaware that on the same day in 1947 Kremer spoke of the gas chambers at Auschwitz (*Le Monde*, February 21, 1979; *Vérité*, pp. 332–334). To which

Faurisson retorted that he retained from Kremer's confession only what was credible, and not what was not. Since Kremer had once said that the gas chambers were reopened "a moment" after the death of the victims, his statement constitutes, he tells us gravely, "a flagrant physical impossibility" (*Vérité*, p. 112).

Let us leave aside what, in this interpretation, is to be attributed to pedantry or subjectivity (what is a *moment*?). It comes up against a series of absolutely decisive objections:

1. There is not a single passage in the *Diary* in which Kremer speaks about typhus in connection with the "special actions."
2. One is hard put to understand why typhus outbreaks would necessarily coincide with arrivals from outside the camp. (Was there at the time a typhus epidemic in Holland?)
3. It is hard to understand why an execution, a commonplace occurrence for Kremer, and also everything concerning typhus, should suddenly take on a tragic aspect when connected with a special action.
4. The fact that Auschwitz was the *Lager der Vernichtung* has no relation to typhus epidemics. Indeed, Faurisson, who is so concerned with precision when it comes to translation, did not perceive that Kremer, in speaking of typhus, did not use the verb *vernichten*. He wrote on October 3: "In Auschwitz whole streets have been stricken down by typhus (*In Auschwitz liegen ganze Strassenzüge an Typhus darnieder*)." The difference in verbs (*darniederliegen* instead of *vernichten*) is significant, and Faurisson allowed himself to be fooled by the translation of the Polish publisher. Finally, a detail which I mention to show how Faurisson reads texts: it is false that Kremer had typhus and that what he called the Auschwitz illness is typhus. The indications in the diary for September 3, 4, and 14, show clearly that the Auschwitz illness is diarrhea with a moderate fever (37.8 degrees C. on September 14). Kremer was, in fact, vaccinated against (exanthematic) typhus and against typhoid fever. Faurisson's interpretation is thus not admissible, and the explanation—so dear to those revisionists, like Butz, prepared to admit that there was a

lot of dying at Auschwitz—of the death rates at Auschwitz by typhus stands condemned along with it. One must return to what is to be learned from the camp archives and from Kremer's confessions: that the "special actions" corresponded to the arrival of convoys of deportees (who were, as a rule, duly registered in the camp archives); that deportees not enrolled in the camp were gassed in the bunkers of Birkenau (small houses located in the forest);[101] that those suffering from illnesses in the camp (and specifically from typhus) as well as male and female "Muslims" were also gassed; and that at the last moment, there were occasionally painful scenes, such as that of October 18, 1942, with the three "young and healthy" Dutch women who "did not want to enter the gas chamber and cried to save their lives" and who were shot,[102] scenes that disturbed the SS-imposed order.

When Kremer spoke of *the* camp of annihilation, he was not, it is true, referring to a juridico-administrative concept, which did not figure, as is also true, on the official rolls of the Third Reich. He was simply speaking about what he saw. On the level he most cherishes, that of philological precision and accurate translation, Faurisson's interpretation is incoherent; on the level of intellectual ethics and scientific probity, it is bogus.[103]

9. On Plato, Lies, and Ideology

Arthur Butz has referred to historians who have attempted to reconstruct the progress of the genocide as "mythologists of extermination" (*The Hoax*, p. 248 and passim). In forging that expression, it is clear that he has defined what he himself and the other "revisionists" have accomplished: a discourse replacing reality by fiction. Rejecting on principle all firsthand testimony and accepting as decisive only the testimony of those who, by their own admission, saw nothing at all, such as the delegates of the International Committee of the Red Cross, is thus an unmistakable sign.[104] Replacing history by myth is a procedure that would hardly be dangerous if there were an absolute criterion allowing one to distinguish at first sight between the two. It is the distinguishing feature of a lie to want to pass itself off as the truth. To be sure, that truth may not always aspire to universality. It may be the truth of a small sect, a truth not to be placed at everyone's disposition. Such is the case of the publishers of Christophersen's "testimony," who must have few illusions concerning the credibility of their witness, since they have appended an epigraph from Theodor Storm: "Never conceal the truth. Even if it brings you suffering, it will never bring you remorse. But since it is a pearl, make sure not to cast it before swine."[105]

There are "truths" that are just as deceitful, but more elaborate; and if a prize for mendacity were to be given, I would say that Butz's tome, *The Hoax of the Twentieth Century*, represents, at times, a rather hair-raising success: the reader is persuasively led by the hand and brought little by little to the idea that Auschwitz is a tendentious rumor that skillful propagandists have gradually transformed into a truth. Such are the "good tidings" whose clumsy evangelist Faurisson has become. It is Butz and not he who might be defined in Zola's terms as the "diabolical craftsman of the judicial error." Ought one to refute Butz? It would be possible, of course, and even easy, assuming one knew the archives, but it would be long and tedious. As was just observed with a few precise examples, to demolish a discourse takes time and space. When a fictitious account is well prepared, it does not contain elements allowing one to destroy it on strictly internal grounds.

This is an old story that could be traced, should one so choose, to ancient Greece. The poets knew that they could speak both truth and falsehood and combine one with the other by virtue of their resemblance. The Muses, "truthful daughters of great Zeus," address Hesiod as follows: "We know how to tell lies entirely similar to realities; but when we want to, we also know how to proclaim truths."[106] That proximity, that disquieting resemblance was fought by philosophy, then being born, which separates and confronts truth and appearance. History, too, intervenes in the debate. Whereas in Israel it appears as the expression of human ambiguity,[107] in Greece it plays on the opposition between truth and falsehood. "I write," says the first historian, Hecataeus of Milet, "what I believe to be true, for the words of the Greeks, it appears to me, are numerous and ridiculous." But from Hecataeus to Herodotus, and from Herodotus to Thucydides, each generation of historians attempts to disqualify the preceding one, as the truth might disqualify the mythical and mendacious. With Plato, philosophy itself enters into the fray and advances matters decisively. For although Plato retains from Parmenides the opposition between appearance and reality, his discourse deals primarily with the world of men, and thus with appearance, an appearance that surrounds the truth on all sides and serves as its counterpoint and deceptive imitation. Between the sophist and the one he imitates, there are resemblances, "as between a dog and a wolf, indeed as between the wildest beast and the tamest pet. In order to be certain, it is above all against resemblances that one must be on perpetual guard. It is indeed an extremely slippery genre" (*Sophist*, 231a). The entire dialogue of *The Sophist* is a meditation on the virtual impossibility of distinguishing the true from the false, and of the necessity, if one is to ferret out a liar, of according to nonbeing a certain form of existence. But he who disposes of the truth is also he who has a right to lie. Plato, in *The Republic*, produces a theory of the beautiful lie. In Book III of *Laws*, he writes a historical fabrication from Athens, in which the battle of Salamis, since it was waged on sea by the democratic sailors, is eliminated from the narrative of the second Median war. In the prologue to the *Timaeus* and in the *Critias*, he achieves his masterpiece in the genre: inventing out of thin air a lost continent, Atlantis, the adversary of an ancient and perfect Athens. It is a truthful story, Plato says and repeats, an emblematic falsehood in reality, which the philosophical reader can easily learn to decipher. But Plato's affirmations concerning the reality of Atlantis, after more than twenty-three centuries, still create dupes (and those who profit from them) today.

Such a discourse, to be sure, becomes dangerous only when it gains support from the power of a state and achieves monopoly status. Plato did not impose laws in any Greek city-state, but it is true that the Lower Empire, whether pagan or Christian, from the time of Diocletian on, became, in its own manner, Platonic. Let us allow the centuries to elapse. At present we are living in an "era of ideology."[108] How would Auschwitz elude the conflict of interpretations, the devouring ideological rage? But even then, the limits of that permanent rewriting of history characteristic of ideological discourse should be marked. "Zionists and Poles already give us quite divergent versions of Auschwitz," according to Faurisson (*Vérité*, p. 194). That is true. For the Israelis, or at least for their ideologues, Auschwitz was the inevitable and logical culmination of life in the Diaspora, and all the victims of the death camps had a vocation to become citizens of Israel (which is a twofold lie). As for the Poles, it is not always easy to distinguish in their writings what is in the order of "obligatory truth"—for example, reverence toward the official decisions of the Soviet Investigatory Commission following the Liberation—from what is (above all nationalist) ideology. The Polish historian Danuta Czech writes the following (which is rather surprising): "Konzentrazionslager Auschwitz-Birkenau served to achieve the program of the biological extermination of populations, above all the Slavic populations and among them particularly the Polish people and the peoples of the U.S.S.R., as well as the Jews and those considered Jews according to the Nuremberg decrees."[109] But neither the Poles nor the Israelis, to be sure, transform in any profound way the reality of the massacre.

What occurs with the works of Butz, Faurisson, and the other ideologues of "revisionism" is of an entirely different nature: a total lie, as is to be found in abuundance among sects and parties, including, to be sure, state parties. If the *History of the Communist (Bolshevik) Party* of Stalin's time is a lasting monument to the most murderous of historical lies, there exist as well liberal and scholarly versions of Stalinist history. *The Great Conspiracy Against Russia* by M. Sayers and A. E. Kahn[110] was a model for the genre, with its play of references and bibliographical notes, using on occasion works forbidden in the Soviet Union, such as *My Life* by Trotsky, but in the service of an entirely orthodox view of Russian history, with, for example, pearls, such as the following: "The death of Leon Trotsky left only one living candidate for a Napoleonic role in Russia: Adolf Hitler" (p. 112). Immediately following the war and the popular front among states, I witnessed the effectiveness of this kind of discourse.

In France, the Dreyfus Affair gave birth to even more consummate successes. In 1905, "Henri Dutrait-Crozon" (the pseudonym of two members of Action Française, F. Delebecque and Colonel G. Larpent) published, with a preface by Charles Maurras, a "revisionist view" of the first two volumes of the history of the Dreyfus Affair by J. Reinach,[111] which, as a literary genre, strikes me as being at the origin of contemporary "revisionism." All its formulations (or almost all) were not inaccurate; it was the whole alone that was mendacious, the false (such as the "confession" of Dreyfus) being accepted as true. That historical enterprise would nonetheless result in a genuinely scholarly book of more than 800 pages, with thousands of references, and which for an entrenched sectarian minority of French public opinion was to represent scripture concerning the captain's guilt. It matters little that new documents appear (such as Schwartzkoppen's *Notebooks*), which reduce that thesis to ridicule; they too are digested and integrated: "But what is the value of such testimony? It is a question that very few have taken the trouble to research."[112] And, to be sure, it was demonstrated, irrefutably, that for clear physical, moral, and intellectual reasons, such testimony could only be false.

Anyone can observe this kind of discourse functioning in his environment, and Thion's book, like several other works of similar style, offers a particularly refined example of it. Thion, taking up the title of a lecture by Rassinier,[113] opposes "historical truth" and "political truth." The first, I assume, is the result of faithful inquiry, the second was imposed, as demonstrated by Rassinier, Butz, and Faurisson, starting in 1942 by a Zionist and communist pressure group which ended up mobilizing all the resources of the Allied propaganda apparatus. The whole process ended with the creation of the state of Israel and reparations payments by Germany.

The process constituting this "truth" is the opposite of the one just described. Take the case of Thion. Like a number of militants of Third World causes, he undoubtedly encountered among his adversaries representatives of Zionist ideology, and even of the state of Israel, and it is that confrontation that he has transposed into the past, without realizing that the "Zionist lobby" was far from having the power ascribed to it, but transforming today's "political truth" into yesterday's historical truth.

A caricatural example of such insane reasoning is furnished by the Australian John Bennett, the former secretary of the Victorian Council for Civil Liberties, who participated in the Los Angeles Colloquium and whom Thion has quite properly cast as one of the leadng figures of "revisionism" abroad (*Vérité*, pp. 160–162). Bennett started out with an entirely legitimate struggle against the control exercised by Zionist circles over the dissemination of information, and specifically against their attempt to forbid a radio station broadcasting Palestinian positions. Harking back from the present to the past, he allowed himself to be convinced by Butz's book that the Australians had been "brainwashed." He undertook to denounce that lie and the support given to Israel, whose consequences he regarded as politically and economically dangerous: "Uncritical support of Israel by the West has led to a sixfold increase in oil prices; it has alienated eight hundred million Muslims, and could lead to a world war. . . . Until the West can appraise Israel on its merits, unclouded by Zionist Holocaust propaganda, our economies will be threatened by further oil price rises, and our very survival will be threatened by world war."[114]

As may be seen, "historical truth," in this case, is the pure product of "political truth"—or, rather, economic truth. But what is most extraordinary is that Bennett, in developing his argument in a long memorandum,[115] has placed at the beginning of his text George Orwell's famous line: "Whoever controls the past controls the future. Whoever controls the present controls the past." There is no better condemnation of his own reasoning.

And yet, beyond all ideological insanity, there is the sheer enormity of the fact, the immensity of the crime, with its technical dimensions, the work not (as in the genocide of the Armenians) of a presumably backward state but, on the contrary, of a state governing a hypercivilized, hypercultivated nation. Unbelievable? Yes, it is true. On the subject of witchcraft trials and the criticism they began to receive in the seventeenth century, Lucien Febvre liked to quote an admirable formula of Cyrano de Bergerac (which was, no doubt, inspired by Montaigne): "One should not believe all things concerning a man, because a man can say all things. One should believe of a man only what is human." And Lucien Febvre commented: "A fine text, a bit late: it is from 1654. But it allows us to salute—at long last—the birth in France of a new sense . . . the sense of the impossible."[116] The human? Impossible? The whole question is to determine whether those two words still have a meaning.

10. *Living With Faurisson?*

It is not easy to conclude. If the "revisionist" endeavor in general, and Faurisson's enterprise in particular, are in the order of a fraud, of an apologia for a crime in the form of a concealment of that crime, we have not yet finished explaining it by establishing the fraud. First, because no demonstration, however rigorous it may be, will completely convince everyone (there are still anti-Dreyfusards); and then, because we will have to pose the question of the meaning of the phenomenon and of its explosion in France at the end of 1978 and 1979. The only ones to be astonished, it is true, are those who will not have understood the commotion surrounding *Holocaust*, the last stage in the commodification of Auschwitz.[117] That it is possible to do something different and better is beyond doubt. There is still research to be done, men to be questioned, and I hope that Claude Lanzmann's film will be commensurate with its immense subject.[118]

But that is not the question, for we are observing a transformation of memory into history, and, as a film by Resnais and Jorge Semprun put it, "the war is over." My generation, now fifty years old, is more or less the last for whom Hitler's crime still remains a memory. That one must fight against the disappearance—or, worse yet, the debasement—of memory seems to me obvious. Neither a statute of limitations nor a pardon seems conceivable to me. Can one imagine Dr. Mengele visiting the Auschwitz Museum or presenting his card to the Centre de Documentation Juive Contemporaine? But what are we to do with this memory, which is ours, and not the memory of all? Legal action against the surviving perpetrators of the crime seems to me simultaneously necessary and ludicrous. So many crimes have occurred since then! There is really no common measure between the crimes of France in Algeria, of the United States in Vietnam, and actual genocides, those of the Armenians, the Jews, the Gypsies, the Khmers, the Tutsis of Rwanda; but, to restrict myself to the case of France, if Messieurs Lacoste, Papon, Massu, and Bigeard are petty criminals compared to Eichmann, they are not paper criminals. The Israels killed Eichmann, and they did well to do so, but in our spectacle-oriented society, what are we to do with a paper Eichmann?

It is not easy for me to expatiate on this point. I grew up with an exalted—some will say a megalomaniacal—conception of the historian's work. That is how I was raised, and it was during the war that my father had me read Chateaubriand's famous article in the *Mercure* of July 4, 1807: "When, in the silence of abjection, all one can hear is the slave's chains and the traitor's voice, when all tremble before the tyrant and it is as dangerous to incur his favor as to fall from his grace, the historian appears, charged with the vengeance of peoples." I still believe in the necessity of memory and attempt, in my own way, to be a memory-man, but I no longer believe that the historian is charged with the vengeance of peoples. It must be admitted that the war is over, that the tragedy has been, in a way, secularized, even if it entails for us, by which I mean us Jews, the loss of that discursive privilege that we have in large part enjoyed ever since Europe discovered the great massacre. And that is not in itself bad, for if there is anything that is unbearable, it is surely the pose of certain individuals who, draped in the grand sash of a major extermination, believe they in that way elude the banal pettinesses and cowardices that are part of the human lot.

For reasons of principle some have rushed to Faurisson's defense. A petition, circulated abroad and signed by several hundred, among the first of whom were Noam Chomsky and Alfred Lilienthal, has protested the treatment Faurisson has received—as though he had been interrupted by persecution in the middle of his historical research: "Since 1974, he has been conducting extensive independent historical research into the 'Holocaust' question." Following which he would have been denied access to public libraries and archives. What is scandalous about the petition is that it never raises the question of whether what Faurisson is saying is true or false, that it even presents his conclusions or "findings" as the result of a historical investigation, one, that is, in quest of the truth. To be sure, it may be argued that every man has a right to lies and falsehood, and that individual freedom entails that right, which is accorded, in the French liberal tradition, to the accused for his defense. But the right that the forger demands should not be conceded to him in the name of truth.

As for the "bans" whose victim Faurisson has been: the fact that the staff of the Centre de Documentation Juive Contemporaine, challenged in its fundamental activity, that of the memory of the crime, should—after years of forbearance—refuse to serve Faurisson seems perfectly normal to me. But can we proceed a step further? Neither illusion nor fraud nor mendacity are foreign to academic and scientific life. What an extraordinary anthology one could prepare of Stalin's U.S.S.R. as a place where contradiction had disappeared, under the tutelage of professional historians and geographers, some of whom, moreover, were far from mediocre teachers. There is something paltry and base in the way in which the Faurisson affair has been treated both within and without academia. For the university to have claimed that he did not publish anything—if indeed it did make that claim and was followed by the cabinet[119]—strikes me as deplorable. Faurisson's publications are what they are—try reading Nerval in Faurisson's "translation"[120]—but they exist and are situated within the order of the university. No one is forced to speak to him.

To live with Faurisson? Any other attitude would imply that we were imposing historical truth as legal truth, which is a dangerous attitude available to other fields of application. Anyone can dream of a society in which Faurissons would be unthinkable and even attempt to work toward its realization. But they exist just as evil exists—around us and in us. Let us be happy if, in this gray world that is ours, we can accumulate a few parcels of truth, experience a few fragments of satisfaction.

Appendix

Zyklon B

Ask those around you. I did, including a number of more or less young Jews and even orphans of deportees. Practically half of them had never heard of Zyklon B; others recalled the name in connection with the gas chambers (they had seen *Holocaust* on television or had read the relevant articles in *Le Monde*), but none knew exactly what kind of product it was.

Let them look it up in the dictionary, then: neither Cyclon nor Zyklon are to be found in *Le petit Larousse illustré* (1979 edition), *Le petit Quillet-Flammarion* (1963 edition), or even in the three-volume *Larousse* (1965 edition) or the twenty-volume *Encyclopaedia Universalis* (1968–1975 edition).

This, of course, makes the task of those who would like to deny that gas chambers existed in the Nazi concentration camps far easier. A Paul Rassinier can pinpoint "contradictions": "an insecticide: no *gas* had then been planned for exterminating"(!) and further on: "Zyklon B appears in the form of *blue granules* from which the *gas* emanates"; or: "This famous gas which has, until now, been presented to us 'in *tablets* from which the gas emanated upon contact with the air,' 'upon contact with water vapor,' in fact existed in the form of bottles filled with a highly volatile liquid."[121]

A Robert Faurisson is free to wax ironic on "gas crystals,"[122] or to insist repeatedly on the fact that Zyklon B adheres to surfaces and is difficult to ventilate, etc.[123]

The following note will attempt to clarify matters by explaining, among other things, the indispensable chemical terms.

I first thought it necessary to research the definition of Zyklon B in a classic work of industrial chemistry, which was published in Germany in 1954.[124]

> Hydocyanic (or prussic) acid is a powerful poison for the blood of all higher animals. The DL(50) [lethal dose in 50 percent of cases] for human beings is as high as 1 milligram per kilogram of body weight. In Germany, the most common application of hydrocyanic acid is Zyklon B, a mixture of liquid hydrocyanic acid with chloride and bromide derivatives as catalytic agents and silica as a support.

There follows a chart of the principal properties of several gases and vapors used as insecticides, in which the following may be read: "Blausaure—Formel HCN—Kp 25,6 C—Dichte (Luft = 1) 0,93," that is: "Hydrocyanic acid—(Chemical) formula HCN—Boiling point 25.6° Centigrade—Density (Air = 1) 0.93."

It will thus be seen that:

— Hydrocyanic acid is an extremely volatile liquid, since it boils at 25.6° Centigrade under atmospheric pressure and its "vapor tension" is already 360 mm of mercury at 7° Centigrade and 658.7 mm of mercury at 21.9° Centigrade.[125]

The characteristics of hydrocyanic acid may be envisaged by considering a more common and less toxic substance: ordinary ether, for example, boils at 34.6° Centigrade; try opening a flask of it on a table and you will see how easily such a "liquid" is transformed into a gas.

— But hydrocyanic acid has a higher boiling point than certain other gaseous insecticides mentioned in the same chart; thus sulphur dioxide (SO_2) boils at −10° Centigrade, methyl bromide at 3.6° Centigrade, or ethylene oxide at 11.6° Centigrade (Faurisson mentions the last compound under the name of Cartox; cf. *Vérité*, p. 310). It will thus be understood why Degesch, a Hamburg firm, speaks of the "long-lasting volatability" of Zyklon B.

— Finally, hydrocyanic acid is used in Germany in "adsorbed" form on a solid support ("Diatomit," which is a kind of siliceous soil). And that explains why a number of witnesses could speak of "solids used in the 'gas' chambers."

R. Faurisson's principal "technical" arguments in support of his thesis of the nonexistence of gas chambers in the deportation camps are:[126]

1. It is impossible to fit 2,000 persons in an enclosure of 210 cubic meters (or 236.78 cubic meters according to the documents).

2. Working crews intervened without gas masks.

3. In order to insert Zyklon B from outside, the SS guards

would have had to ask their future victims to kindly open the windows, and then to close them carefully.

4. It would have been impossible to enter the gas chamber to remove corpses without having first ventilated them.

5. Finally, since hydrocyanic acid is an inflammable explosive, it could not be used in proximity to a stove.

Now it happens that one of the first written documents that I had the opportunity to read about the gas chambers—it was in Switzerland in 1944, where I was privileged enough to begin my studies in chemistry—was a rather precise description of the gassing process and of the precautions taken after gassing (ventilation, etc.). I believe it useful at this juncture to quote it almost *in extenso*:[127]

> At the end of February 1943, at Birkenau, the new gassing installation and its modern crematorium, whose construction had just been completed, were inaugurated. . . . [There follows a description of the A crematoria and the B preparation hall.]
>
> From there, a door and a few steps led to the gas chamber, which was narrow and very long, and was situated at a slightly lower level. The walls of the chamber were covered with curtains, producing the illusion of an immense shower room. Three windows opened on the flat roof, and could be hermetically closed from without. Rails ran across the hall leading to the oven chamber.
>
> Here is how the "operations" took place:
>
> The unfortunates were brought into Hall B and told that they were to take a shower and that they were to undress in the room in which they were. To persuade them that they were actually being taken to the showers, two men dressed in white gave each of them a piece of soap and a towel. Then they were pushed into the gas chamber. About two thousand persons could fit, but each disposed of no more space than was necessary to remain standing. To get such a mass into the room, there

were repeated gun shots in order to force those who were already inside to squeeze still closer. When everyone had entered, the heavy door was bolted. There were a few minutes of waiting, probably for the temperature in the chamber to reach a certain degree; then SS guards, wearing gas masks, climbed onto the roof, opened the windows, and threw in the contents of several tin cans: a preparation in powder form. The cans were marked "Zyklon" (insecticide); they were manufactured in Hamburg. The contents were probably a cyanide compound, which turned into a gas at a certain temperature. In three minutes all the inhabitants of the room were killed. Until now, upon reopening the gas chamber, there has never been a single body showing any sign of life, something which, on the contrary, occurred quite frequently at Birkenwald because of the primitive methods used there. The room was thus opened and ventilated, and the Sonderkommando began transporting corpses on flat carts towards ovens, where they were burned.

I will not say that I was not "shocked" at reading this, but it was at a human level and not for reasons of technical plausibility. On rereading it today, I find it, on the one hand, remarkably consistent with the characteristics of Zyklon B mentioned above and, on the other, virtually a "reply" to Faurisson's arguments: people squeezed together; SS guards wore gas masks; the windows were on the roof and could be hermetically closed from without; the room was ventilated before the Sonderkommando entered; and the gas chamber was separated from the incinerating ovens since carts on rails were used to join the two.

I will add that this report by two young Slovakian Jews who had escaped from Birkenau[128] was published in Geneva in 1944. It was, that is, neither "a late addition," nor "composed under the surveillance of Polish jailers," nor "vague and brief," nor "miraculously rediscovered"—as Faurisson claims of all the testimony with which he is confronted.[129] It strikes me, on the contrary, as astonishingly precise and written without passion by individuals from whom, at the time, a certain lack of composure might have been forgiven.

Let us examine now a bit more closely other "scientific" affirmations by R. Faurisson. I shall take only two examples:

1. Concerning corpses transformed into soap during World War I, he writes:[130] "This absurd legend (ask any anatomist, chemist, or specialist about it) was taken up anew, but without great success, concerning the Second World War." I shall not debate the truth or falsity of this "legend"[131] in this forum, but I fail to see its "absurdity." Since soap is regularly prepared from beef or mutton fat and from pork lard,[132] why not from other higher animals?

2. On the subject of gas emanating from hydrocyanic salts upon contact with water, he writes:[133] "For the first time in the history of chemistry, a salt added to water gave off a gas." Without being "historians of chemistry," many readers, I take it, know (and may even have seen) how a commonplace acetylene generator works, in which calcium carbide (a "salt" and a solid) is decomposed by water and produces a gaseous form of acetylene.[134]

In conclusion, I would like to refer to an incident which unfortunately occurred quite recently in Switzerland:[135] on the night of May 15, 1980, there were a number of graves covered with swastikas and graffiti, one of which read: "Mehr Zyklon B für Juden (More Zyklon B for the Jews)." Its author must not yet have read the works of R. Faurisson.

Pitch Bloch, Ph. D.
Chemical Engineer
Federal Polytechnical School of Zurich

On Faurisson and Chomsky

(1981)

Pursuing his crusade—whose theme may be summarized as follows: the gas chambers did not exist because they can not have existed; they can not have existed because they should not have existed; or better still: they did not exist because they did not exist—Robert Faurisson has just published a new book.[1]

This work is neither more nor less mendacious and dishonest than the preceding ones. I am not at the disposal of R. Faurisson, who, moreover, has not devoted a single line to attempting to respond to my dismantling of his lies in a text that he clearly is familiar with if we may judge from certain editorial details (such as the rectification of all too obvious cases of falsification).[2] If every time a "revisionist" trotted out a new fable it were necessary to respond, all the forests of Canada would not suffice. I shall simply observe the following point: Faurisson's book is centered on the diary of the SS physician J. P. Kremer, a text I dealt with at length, showing that *not once* in the diary do the "special actions" in which the doctor participated have any relation with the struggle against typhus. Faurisson is unable, and for good reason, to supply a single argument, a single response on this subject. I have said as much, and will repeat it: his interpretation is a deliberate falsehood, in the full sense of the term.[3] If one day it becomes necessary to analyze the rest of his lies and his falsifications, I shall do so, but such an operation seems to me to be of little interest and would be futile in the face of the sect whose prophet he has now become.

More troubling, because it comes from a man whose scientific stature, combined with the just and courageous fight he waged against the American war in Vietnam, have granted him great prestige, is the preface to Faurisson's book, which is by Noam Chomsky. An extraordinary windfall indeed: to maintain that the genocide of the Jews is a "historical lie" and to be prefaced by an illustrious linguist, the son of a professor of Hebrew, a libertarian and the enemy of every imperialism is surely even better than being supported by Jean-Gabriel Cohn-Bendit.

I read the text carefully and with an increasing sense of surprise. Epithets came to my pen, expressing, progressively, the extent of my surprise and my indignation. Finally, I decided to remove those adjectives from my text. Linguists, and even non-linguists, will be able to restore them without difficulty.[4] I shall proceed in order.

1. The preface in question partakes of a rather new genre in the republic of letters. Indeed, Noam Chomsky has read neither the book he prefaced, nor the previous works of the author, nor the criticisms addressed to them, and he is incompetent in the field they deal with: "I have nothing to say here about the work of Robert Faurisson or his critics, of which I know very little, or about the topics they address, concerning which I have no special knowledge." [5] These are indeed remarkable qualifications. But since he needs to be able to affirm a proposition and its opposite, Chomsky nonetheless proclaims, a few pages further on, his competence. Faurisson is accused of being an anti-Semite: "As noted earlier, I do not know his work very well. But from what I have read—largely as a result of the nature of the attacks on him—I find no evidence to support [such conclusions]" (Preface, p. xv). He has also read his critics, specifically my article in *Esprit* (September 1980), and even the personal letters I sent to him on the subject, "a private correspondence which it would be inappropriate to cite in detail here." A fine case of scruples, and a fine example as well of double language, since Chomsky did not realize that the book he was prefacing

contained unauthorized reproductions of a series of personal letters,[6] and he himself does arrogate the right of summarizing
(while falsifying) my own letters. I shall simply say to him:
"Kindly publish—I give you my authorization—the entirety of
that correspondence. It will then be possible to judge whether
you are qualified to give me lessons in intellectual honesty."

2. Chomsky-the-Janus-faced has thus read Faurisson and not
read him, read his critics and not read them. Let us consider the
issues in logical order. What has he read of Faurisson which allows him to bestow so fine a certificate? For is he not "a relatively apolitical liberal of some sort" (pp. xiv–xv)? Since Chomsky refers to *nothing* in support of this, it is impossible to know,
and I shall simply say: Faurisson's *personal* anti-Semitism, in
fact, interests me rather little. It exists and I can testify to it, but
it is nothing compared with the anti-Semitism of his texts. Is it
anti-Semitic to write with consummate calm that in requiring
Jews to wear the yellow star starting at the age of six "Hitler was
perhaps less concerned with the Jewish question than with ensuring the safety of German soldiers" (*Vérité*, p. 190)? Certainly
not, within Faurisson's logic, since in the final analysis there is no
practical anti-Semitism possible. But within Chomsky's logic? Is
the invention of an imaginary declaration of war against Hitler,
in the name of the international Jewish community, by an imaginary president of the World Jewish Congress,[7] a case of anti-
Semitism or of deliberate falsification? Can Chomsky perhaps
press linguistic imagination to the point of discovering that there
are false anti-Semites?

Let us now pose the other side of the question. What does
Noam Chomsky know of the "criticisms" that have been addressed to Faurisson, and specifically of the study that he refers
to, which I published in *Esprit* and which attempts to analyze
"historically" the "method" of Faurisson and of several others?
The answer is simple. "Certain individuals have taken Faurisson's defense for reasons of principle. A petition with several
hundred signatories, led by Noam Chomsky, protested against

the treatment Faurisson has received by presenting his 'conclusions' as though they were in fact discoveries (*Vérité*, p. 163). That petition seems to me to be scandalous."[8]

The content of those lines leaves no doubt about Chomsky's motives. It is not a question of the gas chambers; it is very little a question of Faurisson, and only secondarily of freedom of speech. It is above all a question of Noam Chomsky. It is as though, by anticipation, Jacques Prévert were speaking of him, and not of André Breton, when he wrote in 1930: "He was, then, quite thin-skinned. For a press clipping, he would not leave his room for eight days."[9] Like many intellectuals, Chomsky is scarcely sensitive to the wounds he inflicts, but extremely attentive to whatever scratches he is forced to put up with.

But what is his argument? He signed, we are told, an innocent petition "in defense of Robert Faurisson's freedom of speech and expression. The petition said absolutely nothing about the character, quality, or validity of his research, but limited itself quite explicitly to defending elementary rights which are "taken for granted in democratic societies." My mistake, he contends, stems from my having made an error in English. I believed that the word "findings" meant "discoveries," whereas its meaning is "conclusions." I will not quibble on this last—insignificant—point, concerning which Chomsky's position is all the stronger in that he had received my own admission in a letter. But he forgot to specify that the error in question, which had appeared in my original manuscript, had been corrected prior to publication. The text that appeared in *Esprit* does not include it, and if Chomsky, rather bizarrely, reproaches me for it, it was because he was drawing on my correspondence with him. Moreover, the error was infinitesimal: *findings* is a scientific term, and it was legitimate for me to play on its etymological meaning, which is indeed "discoveries." Here, in addition, is what was written to me on this minuscule subject by a professor of Cambridge University, who is a native New Yorker, and who presumably knows the language spoken in Cambridge, Massachusetts: "Chomsky's bad faith in playing with words is alarming. To be sure, if one opens a dictionary to the word *findings* one will find, among other meanings, that of *conclusions*. And yet *no one*, and Chomsky knows this perfectly well, would ever make use of *findings*, or *discoveries*, or even *conclusions*, in this context, in the strictly neutral sense now invoked by Chomsky. Those words, and particularly the first two, imply absolutely that they be taken seriously as designating the truth. There are more than enough neutral words at the disposal of whoever needs them: one might, for example, use *views* or *opinions*."

But let us return to the heart of the matter. Is the petition an innocent declaration in favor of a persecuted man that everyone, and first of all myself, could (or should) have signed?

Let us read:

> Dr. Faurisson has served as a respected professor of twentieth-century French literature and document criticism for over four years at the University of Lyon 2 in France. Since 1974 he has been conducting extensive independent historical research into the "Holocaust" question. Since he began making his findings public, Professor Faurisson has been subject to a vicious campaign of harassment, intimidation, slander, and physical violence in a crude attempt to silence him. Fearful officials have even tried to stop him from further research by denying him access to public libraries and archives.

Let us pass over what is excessive or even openly false in the petition. Faurisson has been forbidden from neither archives nor public libraries.[10] Does the petition in fact present Robert Faurisson as a serious historian conducting genuine historical research? To ask that question is to supply an answer.[11] The most droll aspect of it all is that one finds the following adage, which has become something of a motto, preceding works published by La Vieille Taupe: "What is terrible when one sets out after the truth is that one finds it." For my part, I maintain—and prove—that with the exception of the quite limited case of the *Diary of*

Anne Frank,[12] Faurisson does not set out after the truth but after falsehoods. Is that a "detail" which does not interest Chomsky? And if one is to understand that poorly informed, he signed on trust a genuinely "scandalous" text, how are we to accept his willingness to underwrite today the efforts of a falsifier?

3. But there is more still: regarding himself as untouchable, invulnerable to criticism, unaware of what Nazism in Europe was like, draped in an imperial pride and an American chauvinism worthy of those "new mandarins" whom he used to denounce, Chomsky accuses all those who hold a different opinion from his own of being assassins of freedom.

That issue of *Esprit* (September 1980) must have driven him mad. Along with my five lines in which Chomsky's name was mentioned with reference to Faurisson, there were twelve pages by Paul Thibaud,[13] who took the liberty of criticizing the inability of Chomsky (and Serge Thion) to gauge, in the case of Cambodia, the dimensions of the totalitarian phenomenon. Those pages are commented on as follows by Chomsky: "I omit discussion of an accompanying article by the editor that again merits no comment, at least among people who retain a commitment to elementary values of truth and honesty" (Preface, p. x). But would not an "elementary respect for honesty and the truth" have obliged Chomsky to indicate the following fact, which is also elementary: Thibaud's article (of twelve pages)[14] was a response to an article by Serge Thion, which was seventeen pages and entirely devoted to the defense and illustration of the theses of . . . Noam Chomsky? Is that how the editor of *Esprit* revealed his intolerance and dishonesty?

"I do not want to discuss individuals," Chomsky writes, and immediately thereafter, in accordance with the same double discourse with which we are beginning to be familiar, he attacks an imaginary "person" who "does indeed find the petition 'scandalous' [which was indeed the word I used], not on the basis of misreading, but because of what it actually says" (p. xi). An elegant way of not saying—and, at the same time, saying—that I assault the freedoms of my enemies. For Chomsky goes on to say: "We are obliged to conclude from this that the individual in question believes that the petition was scandalous because Faurisson *should* in fact be deprived of the normal right to self-expression, that he should be harassed and even subjected to acts of physical violence, etc." It happens that what I wrote was precisely the opposite, and that in the very page on which Chomsky did such a poor job of deciphering the five lines that so disturbed him. Was it really impossible to read that page through? The conditions under which Faurisson was brought to request leave of Lyon and enter the National Center of Broadcasted Instruction were certainly regrettable, and I have said as much, but his freedom of expression, subject to extant law, has not been threatened at all. He was able to be published on two occasions in *Le Monde*. Thion's book, in which his theses are vented, was not the subject of any lawsuit, and if Faurisson is the target of a civil suit, brought by various antiracist associations, which do not all have freedom as their primary goal,[15] such lawsuits do not prevent him from writing or being published. Is not the book prefaced by Chomsky—with the exception of instances of libel toward specific individuals that it may contain—proof? Would he like a law passed by the republic requiring that Faurisson's works be read in public schools? Is he asking for all history books to be rewritten in accord with his discoveries—I mean, conclusions (*findings*)? Is he requesting at the very least that they be advertised and sold at the entrance to synagogues? Is every French intellectual required to assume in turn the roles of his exegete, like Serge Thion, his psychiatrist, like Pierre Guillaume, or his buffoon?

The simple truth, Noam Chomsky, is that you were unable to abide by the ethical maxim you had imposed. You had the right to say: my worst enemy has the right to be free, on condition that he not ask for my death or that of my brothers. You did not have the right to say: my worst enemy is a comrade, or a "relatively apolitical sort of liberal." You did not have the right to take a falsifier of history and to recast him in the colors of truth.

There was once, not so long ago, a man who uttered this

simple and powerful principle: "It is the responsibility of intellectuals to speak the truth and to expose lies." But perhaps you know him?[16]

Postscript (1987)

This text, which was written six and a half years ago, could be prolonged indefinitely. Barely had I completed it when the affair took a rather droll turn, since, in a letter of December 6 addressed to Jean-Pierre Faye, Chomsky somehow disavowed not his text but the use that had been made of it with his agreement as a preface to Robert Faurisson's book. The book was nonetheless printed with the preface in question, which was dated October 11, 1980. On that same December 6, he wrote to Serge Thion concerning the same text: "If publication is not under way, I strongly suggest that you not put it in a book by Faurisson," which did not prevent him from maintaining his fundamental position.[17]

Let us restate the point with due calm: the principle he invokes is not what is at stake. If Chomsky had restricted himself to defending Faurisson's right to free speech, from my point of view there would not be any Chomsky problem. But that is not the issue. Nor is the issue for me one of responding to the innumerable proclamations, articles, and letters through which Chomsky, like some worn-out computer reprinting the same speech, has spewed forth his outrage at those who have been so bold as to criticize him, and specifically at the author of these pages.[18]

It will suffice for me to observe: 1) that he went considerably further than was generally believed in his personal support of Faurisson, exchanging friendly letters with him,[19] accepting even to be prefaced by the leader of the revisionist league Pierre Guillaume[20] (while claiming—mendaciously—that he had not written a preface for Faurisson),[21] characterizing Guillaume as "libertarian and antifascist on principle"[22] (which must have provoked some hilarity from the interested party, since he regards antifascism as fundamentally mendacious); 2) that he has not remained faithful to his own libertarian principles since he—whom the slightest legal action against Faurisson throws into a fit—went so far as to threaten a publisher with a lawsuit over a biographical note concerning him in which several sentences had the misfortune of displeasing him. And in fact, he succeeded in having the biographical note in question assigned to a more loyal editor.[23]

To be sure, it is not the case that Chomsky's theses in any way approximate those of the neo-Nazis.[24] But why does he find so much energy and even tenderness in defending those who have become the publishers and defenders of the neo-Nazis,[25] and so much rage against those who allow themselves to fight them?[26] That is the simple question I shall raise. When logic has no other end than self-defense, it goes mad.

THREE

On the Side of
the Persecuted

There is a well-known bit of Jewish folklore: in a village in Siberia, two old Jews are seated on a bench. One of them is reading a newspaper and suddenly says: "Sao Paulo just beat Rio de Janeiro in soccer." The other replies: "Is it good for the Jews?"

That is a question we have often had the occasion to ask ourselves in the course of the last few months; but the answers are perhaps not the ones given or heard by many.

A series of anti-Semitic acts culminated on October 3, 1980, with the bomb in front of the synagogue on rue Copernic. Who can doubt that all this is bad for the Jews? I am certainly not about to deny that the government and its police force were not up to their duty. But among certain Jewish groups the response was degrading: manhunts, the throwing of acid at real or imaginary Nazis, the most brutal recourse to physical force were among the methods employed. And it is of little consequence whether the victims did or did not hold Hitlerite opinions. In this case, the means used to combat them seem inspired by fascism and Nazism.

A Catholic publicist[1] published on the first page of *Le Monde* an "Open Letter to My Jewish Friends" in which what appeared was above all his radical incomprehension of who—and what— his interlocutors are. The space accorded to that short polemic may legitimately offend, and for my part, I was in fact shocked by the publication of that text in such a venue. But the reaction, on the Jewish side, was disproportionate. Was there really a need to speak of eventually boycotting *Le Monde*?

An adept of the hypercritical paranoid method, to plagiarize a phrase of Salvador Dali, strains to demonstrate that Hitler's gas chambers never existed. The attempt is absurd, but as may occur in the case of other absurdities, a small sect is constituted around a professor desperate for a bit of excitement and publicity. It joins together, like other sects, a few madmen, a few perverts, and several flagellants, not to mention the usual proportion of dupes and imbeciles to be found in this sort of body. A famous linguist grants the principal author of this nonsense some manner of support. Immediately thereafter he is criticized, which is normal, but the quality of his linguistic theory is also called into question, which is absurd. Have we not seen a hundred cases of famous scientists becoming known for the foolishness of their reactions outside of their field of specialization?

Let us speak of this affair with some seriousness. I am not one of those who minimize its importance. To see such absurdities printed even in serious newspapers is something that hurts. But how is one to react in a way that is "good for the Jews"? Confronting an actual Eichmann, one had to resort to armed struggle and, if need be, to ruse. Confronting a paper Eichmann, one should respond with paper. There are several of us who have done so, and will continue to do so. In so doing, we are not placing ourselves on the same ground as our enemy. We do not "debate" him; we demonstrate the mechanisms of his lies and falsifications, which may be methodologically useful for the younger generations. It is precisely for that reason that a tribunal should not be charged with enunciating historical truth. It is precisely because the truth of the great massacre is in the order of history and not religion that it should not take the revisionist sect too seriously. It will be necessary to get used to the fact that such a sect exists. All things considered is it any more dangerous than the sect of the Reverend Moon?

In any event, here too violence is the worst of methods. Last February 6, four individuals destroyed a few hundred books of the revisionist sect in the offices of the distibutor of its publisher,

La Vieille Taupe. That act should be radically condemned. Burning books is what the Nazis—or the Red Guards during the so-called Great Proletarian Cultural Revolution—did. These are abject methods, which, moreover, can only consecrate as martyrs the very people who must indeed be fought. Nothing would be worse than to transform the head of the sect into a kind of expiatory victim of the crimes of another age. Certainly *that* would not be good for the Jews.

And since many of those potential persecutors invoke the Jewish tradition, allow me to refer them to a text, which I excerpt from a *midrash* (or ancient rabbinic commentary) of Leviticus 27:5. Rabbi Huna is speaking in the name of Rabbi Joseph: "God is always on the side of the persecuted. One can find a case where a just man persecutes a just man, and God is on the side of the persecuted; when an evil man persecutes a just man, God is on the side of the persecuted; when an evil man persecutes an evil man, God is on the side of the persecuted; and even when a just man persecutes an evil man, God is on the side of the persecuted."

To reflect on such a text and its implications: that, surely, would be good for the Jews.

FOUR

Theses on Revisionism

(1985)

1. From One Revisionism to Another

I shall call "revisionism" the doctrine according to which the genocide practiced by Nazi Germany against Jews and Gypsies did not exist but is to be regarded as a myth, a fable, or a hoax.[1] I shall speak of "revisionism" in the absolute sense of the word, but there are also relative revisionisms of which I shall say a few words.

The word itself has a history which is strange and would merit elaboration. The first modern "revisionists" were, in France, the partisans of a "revision" or judicial review of the trial of Alfred Dreyfus (1894), but the word was quickly turned around by their adversaries,[2] and that reversal should be considered as symptomatic. The word has subsequently taken on a meaning that is at times positive, at times negative, always implying the critique of a dominant orthodoxy. Bernstein and his friends were revisionists in relation to orthodox Marxists, and the term has been transmitted to the Maoists who use it to characterize their Soviet enemies. In relation to traditional Zionism, the disciples of Vladimir Jabotinsky, currently in power in Israel, were also "revisionists," as are the American historians who contest the officially and traditionally received version of the origins of the Cold War.

The revisionists of Hitler's genocide, however, invoke as their predecessor, not without being partially justified, a different

American historical school, which may be epitomized by the name of H. E. Barnes (1889–1968).[3] A "radical" historian and sociologist (in the American sense of the term), at least at the beginning of his career, an anti-imperialist and anticolonialist,[4] Barnes rose up against the historical orthodoxy that ascribed blame for World War I solely to the central European empires. Although not totalitarian, that orthodoxy was no less real in France and England than in the United States. The French "yellow book" of 1914 removed the most embarrassing episodes and occasionally resorted to out and out fraudulence, as in the case of its presentation of the Russian general mobilization (July 30, 1914) as following the Austro-Hungarian mobilization (July 31). During the war, for the first time, propaganda was employed in a massive way.[5] In both camps, historians entered the fray. In 1919, for example, an American historian published a collection significantly and paradoxically entitled *Volleys from a Non-Combatant*.[6] In the liberal world, the orthodoxy was not imposed as it was and had to be in the totalitarian world, but existed no less. In 1935, the French historian Jules Isaac, the author of well-known manuals for lycée students, chose to submit as a thesis topic to the Sorbonne the Poincaré ministry (January 1912–January 1913), which, in the historiographical context of the day, would have raised the problem of Poincaré's responsibility in the origin of the war. The Sorbonne requested that "for reasons of appropriateness," the name of Poincaré not be mentioned in the subject description. Isaac refused that compromise and wrote to the Dean of the Faculté des Lettres: "If, 'for reasons of appropriateness,' the Faculté forbids me from mentioning the name of Poincaré in the title, 'for reasons of appropriateness' the Faculté can also ask me not to bring into full relief, in the course of my work, the personal role of Poincaré."[7] What was true after the First World War remained true after the second. On December 22, 1950, President Truman addressed a convention of the American Historical Society and asked it to help him in implementing a federal historical curriculum for the fight against communism.[8] It was, to be sure, a matter of opposing lies with the truth, but is truth so easy to cast in federal terms?

H. E. Barnes unfortunately was not satisfied with destroying the orthodoxy of the Entente and their American allies. He reversed it. His book, *The Genesis of the World War*,[9] discovered—or rather invented—a "Franco-Russian plot which caused the war." He did not hesitate to "reveal," for example, that Jaurès was assassinated "by instigation of the Russian secret police."[10] Jules Isaac could say of him, with due moderation, that he was "audacious, and extremely capricious in his application of historical method."[11]

Barnes's book still has a lesson for us. Addressing the French public, the patriarch of American revisionism invoked the Dreyfus Affair; by recalling the example of the Affair, he ends up whitewashing Germany entirely of any responsibility in the genesis of the world conflict—which is as absurd as the opposite thesis.[12] The Affair was thus a reference, and as paradoxical as it may seem, it would remain so for a number of revisionists of the Nazi genocide.[13]

It is in fact a valid point of reference, but in an entirely different sense. Hannah Arendt quite properly saw in it one of the first stages of the genesis of modern totalitarianism.[14] Mutatis mutandis, the evidence for Dreyfus's guilt, despite the "proof" that flooded the case and which the anti-Dreyfusards strained to turn around, remains, for the anti-Dreyfusard core, as central a dogma as the innocence of Hitler, accused of genocide, is for the revisionist of today. The exculpation of Hitler in the name of Dreyfusard values, and with the obstinacy of the most narrow-minded nationalists, is a modern refinement worthy of interest.

The Dreyfus Affair, the struggle against the nationalist versions of the 1914–1918 war,[15] the struggle against the "lies" of the Second World War, and against the greatest of all "lies," Hitler's genocide, that "hoax of the twentieth century":[16] such are the three elements that allow one to grasp the "good conscience" of the revisionists and particularly of the "radical" or "*gauch-*

iste" revisionists, of Paul Rassinier and Jean-Gabriel Cohn-Bendit.[17] Rassinier's case is quite remarkable: a socialist, a pacifist who was nonetheless in the Resistance, a deportee, he is the true father of contemporary revisionism.

> Rassinier, with a kind of obstinacy whose enigmatic character one is hard put to dispell, remained faithful within that absolute novelty, the world of the concentration camps, to the lesson of 1914. If he described his experience in all its details, worked to conceptualize and thematize it, it was not in order to convey it, but rather to reduce its experiential character, cleansing it of all that seemed repetitious in it. He did not magnify the SS out of fascination or by virtue of who knows what masochism. He banalized them with the sole aim of fitting *one war into the other*, and of crediting the behavior of all concerned—that of the victim and that of the executioner, that of the German soldiers and that of their adversaries—to the account of a common "unreasonable abjection."[18]

Denying—for a long time in isolation—the Hitlerian genocide, Rassinier took himself simultaneously for Romain Rolland "above the melee" in 1914 and Bernard Lazare, the solitary fighter for truth and justice in 1896. His example would influence H. E. Barnes and would contribute to the transition from the older revisionism to the modern variety.[19] It was necessary to reconstitute this context, and we shall attempt to delineate it with greater precision. Need we, however, refute the "revisionist" theses, and specifically the most characteristic of them, the negation of the Hitlerian genocide and its preferred instrument, the gas chamber? At times it has seemed necessary to do so.[20] Such will certainly not be my intention in these pages. In the final analysis, one does not refute a closed system, a total lie that is not refutable to the extent that its conclusion has preceded any evidence.[21] It was once necessary to prove that the *Protocols of the Elders of Zion* was a fabrication. As Hannah Arendt has said, if so many believed the document to be authentic, "the historian's job is no longer [only] to detect the hoax. Nor is his task to invent explanations concealing the essential historical and political fact: a forgery was believed in. That fact is more important than the (historically speaking, secondary) fact that one was dealing with a forgery."[22]

2. On Myths of War and the Advance of Truth

Propaganda, or, *bourrage de crâne*, "skull-cramming," as it was called during the war of 1914–1918; propaganda and *bourrage de crâne* during the war of 1939–1945. The great Hitlerian slaughter is placed on the same level as the "children with their hands cut off" of 1914; we would quite simply be dealing with a maneuver of psychological warfare. That central theory of "revisionism" has the merit of recalling for us two fundamental elements of the world conflict. On the whole, Allied propaganda made very little use of the great massacre in its psychological war against Nazi Germany. In general, information about the genocide, when it began to filter through (which was quite early on), encountered huge obstacles, not the least of which was—precisely—the precedent of 1914–1918. In a sense it may be said that the first "revisionists," and there were a number of Jews among them, had been recruited during the war in the intelligence agencies of the Allied powers. All this, for example, has been established beyond refutation in a recent work by Walter Laqueur.[23]

In the flow of information coming from the occupied territories were to be found the true, the less true, and the false. The general meaning of what was occurring left no doubt, but as far as the modalities were concerned, there were frequently grounds for hesitating between one version and another. Concerning the camp at Auschwitz, for example, it was not until April 1944, following a number of escapes, that it became possible to establish a firsthand description—which proved remarkably precise—of the extermination process. Those "protocols of Auschwitz" were to be made public by the American War Refugee Board only in November 1944.[24] Starting in May 1944, the deportation and massacre of Hungarian Jews constituted events announced by the Allied and neutral press virtually on a daily basis.[25]

I spoke of the "true" and the "false." That simple opposition accounts rather inadequately for what occurred. From errors concerning architectural form to confusions about distances and numbers, all kinds of imprecision existed, as did a number of phantasms and myths. But they did not exist in isolation, like some creation sui generis or "rumor," a hoax hatched by a specific milieu, such as the New York Zionists.[26] They existed as a shadow projected by—or prolonging—reality.[27] Consider as well that the most direct and authentic reports, when they arrived at Allied intelligence services, needed to be deciphered, since they were written in the coded language of the totalitarian systems, a language that most often could not be fully interpreted until the end of the war.

We shall give an example of both these phenomena, starting with the second. British secret services had deciphered the codes used by the Germans for their internal communications. Among the police documents that came to be known in this manner there were statistics: entries and exits of human raw material for a certain number of camps, including Auschwitz, between the spring of 1942 and February 1943. One of the columns indicating "departures by any means" was interpreted to mean death. But there was no mention in such texts of gassings.[28] Thanks to an official Polish publication, we are quite familiar with this kind of document. For instance, this statistic entered on October 18, 1944 in the women's camp at Birkenau, which adds up various "departures" diminishing the number of those enrolled in the camp: natural death, transit, and "special treatment," which was subsequently deciphered as meaning gassing.[29]

One of the crucial documents discussed in Laqueur's book[30] is a telegram sent from Berne to London, on August 10, 1942, by G. Riegner, the secretary of the World Jewish Congress. That telegram, written on the basis of information conveyed by a German industrialist, announced that there were plans at Hitler's headquarters to assemble all of Europe's Jews "to be at one blow exterminated." Among the means studied: prussic acid. There is a remarkable share of error and myth in the document. The decision to proceed with exterminations had been taken months before; the use of prussic acid (Zyklon B), which was inaugurated in September 1941 for Soviet war prisoners, had been common at Auschwitz since the spring of 1942, and the utilization of gas obviously contradicts the notion of an extermination in a single blow, which would have required a nuclear weapon, and which did not exist at the time. In Freudian terms, we may say that there was a condensation and displacement of information.

But a condensation of what? One of the most remarkable debates provoked among historians by Hitler's extermination policy pitted Martin Broszat against Christopher Browning in the same German scholarly journal.[31]

Refuting a semi-revisionist book by the British historian David Irving,[32] which had exonerated Hitler—in favor of Himmler—of responsibility for the great slaughter, Broszat saw in the "final solution," which was indeed an extermination, something that was partially improvised and developed, as it were, on a case-by-case basis. To which Browning responded that the information communicated by Hoess (according to Himmler) and by Eichmann (according to Heydrich) had to be taken quite seriously:[33] it was during the summer of 1941 that Hitler took the decision to exterminate the Jews. That such an order, communicated to a few individuals, and having begun in quick order to be executed, should become through condensation the "one blow" of Riegner's telegram is not at all implausible.

But how would one not also insist on the crucial role of different phases in a process developing in time, phases concerning which Broszat has contributed important clarifications? Various phases or stages included: the model ghetto at Theresienstadt and the "family camp" at Auschwitz; the ghettos with their privileged social strata, whose members believed they would escape, by virtue of those privileges, a common fate that they helped to implement; at the very sites of extermination, the situation of those who were not selected for the gas chamber. Only gradual phases or stages of every sort allowed the extermination policy to be pursued with relative smoothness. All these stages of a process, these phases of a murder serve as so many arguments for the revisionists. Because Jewish weddings were celebrated at Maidanek, near Lublin, it will be pretended that the camps were, if need be, places of rejoicing.[34] But who does not perceive that such phases were the temporal and social conditions necessary for the proper functioning of the killing?

3. That There Are Several Abodes . . .

Revisionism is to be found in multiple and various forms: tracts, "scholarly" volumes, common propaganda, mimeographed pamphlets, apparently distinguished journals, video cassettes. Examining a collection of such documents on the shelves of a library,[35] noting the number of translations of a single text,[36] reading the numerous scholarly references to newspapers or to obscure volumes, one has the impression of a single vast international enterprise. Such a conclusion may be excessive, although undeniably there exists in California the center of a revisionist International, which receives and distributes all this literature.[37] There is nothing surprising about all this: it is simply the result of the planetary circulation of information and the dominant position of the United States in the world market.[38] In point of fact, the "information" is often disseminated, on very different levels, by the same individuals. Take the case of Dietlieb Felderer, who was born at Innsbruck in 1942, moved to Sweden, is a Jehovah's Witness, and thus belongs, through conversion, to a group that was persecuted, but not exterminated, during the Hitler period.[39] A collaborator of the *Journal of Historical Review*, a periodical with scientific pretentions,[40] he also publishes—in Täby, Sweden—a truly obscene anti-Semitic mimeographed periodical, *Jewish Information*,[41] distributes numerous tracts, and organizes (theoretically each summer) "revisionist" trips to Poland. Taking such new-style tourists to Auschwitz or the remains of Treblinka and explaining to them that nothing very serious happened there is, all the same, a rather unprecedented idea, and surely furnishes a number of exceptionally piquant sensations. Revisionism occurs at the intersection of various and occasionally contradictory ideologies: Nazi-style anti-Semitism, extreme right-wing anticommunism, anti-Zionism, German nationalism, the various nationalisms of the countries of eastern Europe, libertarian pacifism, ultra-left-wing Marxism. As may be easily anticipated, these doctrines at times appear in a pure state, and at others—and even most frequently—in alloyed form. Let us give a few rather unfamiliar examples. A Hungarian publishing firm in London has brought out, in addition to an English translation of the *Protocols of the Elders of Zion*, a book entitled *The World Conquerors*, in which, through a remarkable reversal, it is explained that the real war criminals of World War II were the Jews.[42] The book is also violently anticommunist, accusing all Hungarian communists, and even all Spanish communists of being Jews. Such a reversal is characteristic of this ideology. In *The Jew Süss* (1940), it was the Jews who were the torturers.

Whereas traditional (Maurrassian) French anti-Semitism tends to be pro-Israeli, *all* revisionists are resolute anti-Zionists. Some make the transition from anti-Zionism to anti-Semitism, which is the case for a certain extreme left.[43] Others follow the same path in the other direction. The absolute necessity of anti-Zionist discourse for revisionism is easy to explain. It is a matter of anticipating the creation of the state of Israel. Israel is a state that employs violent means of domination. That being the case, by proceeding as though such an entity already existed in 1943, it is possible to overlook the fact that the Jewish communities were unarmed. Pressing things to an extreme, one can even explain Nazism as a (no doubt phantasmatic) creation of Zionism.[44]

Once that is established, German nationalism can very well be combined with the defense of Arab positions.[45] There is a Palestinian revisionism that has, moreover, a number of staunch adversaries.[46] There are also, even in Israel, several Judeo-revisionists, though they appear to be quite few in number.[47]

Generally speaking, the thematic of all these works, and particularly those inspired by (old- or new-style)[48] German national socialism, is quite impoverished. One has the sense that all these volumes are pre-programmed, that their pages pile up without contributing anything new. The reader regularly relearns the same facts: that the Jews declared war on Hitler's Germany as of 1933, as is infallibly documented in some obscure journal or another from the Midwest;[49] that the losses they endured during the war and which, moreover, were quite moderate, were solely due to the random effects of the partisan resistance effort; that there were no extermination facilities; that deaths in the camps were due almost exclusively to typhus. I shall limit myself here to observing a point of method and to pointing out several deviations.

It is a fundamental practice of revisionism to refuse to distinguish between words and reality. During the world war, there were declarations by Allied leaders directed at the Germans that were horrendous, as well as acts that were no less so and that constitute war crimes in every sense of the term. But it is striking to observe that the revisionists, although they mention these acts (the bombing of Dresden, the dramatic evacuation of Germans from regions becoming Polish or becoming Czechoslovakian again, etc.), always put the accent on rather hysterical texts, smacking of the crudest wartime racism and which never even began to be applied. Since one Theodore Kaufmann, who is baptized for the occasion a personal adviser to Roosevelt, published a wartime pamphlet entitled *Germany Must Perish*, predicting the sterilization of the Germans, that pamphlet is placed on the same level as the speeches of Hitler and Himmler, which had every chance of being implemented.[50]

Nadine Fresco has suggestively compared the revisionist method with a well-known Freudian joke, that of the kettle:[51] "A borrowed a copper kettle. Upon its return, B complains that the kettle has a big hole, making it unusable. Here is A's defense: '1. I never borrowed the kettle from B. 2. The kettle had a hole in it when I borrowed it from B. 3. I returned the kettle in perfect condition.'"

There are numerous examples. Concerning the "Wannsee agreement" (January 20 1942), which shows a number of functionaries at work on the "final solution," it will simultaneously be said—or suggested—that since it is unsigned, it is hardly a trustworthy document, and that it contains nothing very surprising.[52] A kind of record is reached on the subject of Himmler's secret speeches, in which the theory and practice of mass murder are set forth with relatively little dissimulation.[53] It will be claimed *simultaneously* that these texts, published under a title not agreed to by their author, have been tampered with, that words that are not present in the original have been interpolated (such as *umbringen*, "to kill," which no doubt has replaced some other term, such as "to evacuate") *and* that their meaning is in fact benign: the extermination of Judaism (*Ausrottung des Judentums*) is not the extermination of the Jews.[54] But the joke about the kettle may be extended beyond Freud. Why wouldn't A say: *I* was the one who loaned the kettle to B, and it was in perfect condition. There is an entire literature proving that the true murderers of the Jews and above all of the Germans were Jews: Jewish kapos, Jewish partisans, etc. The collective murder, which never took place, was thus fully justifiable and justified.[55]

This is a transcending, through excess, of the revisionist norm. There are also transcendences through lack. The British historian David Irving believes that the final solution was elaborated by Himmler and kept secret from Hitler, despite a formal order, given by the German chancellor in November 1941, not to exterminate the Jews.[56]

4. On an Explosive Mixture

Let us return to the geography of revisionism and raise the question of its political and intellectual bearing. I do not dispose of all the necessary elements, and the few hypotheses I shall formulate are of necessity tentative and schematic. Several markers can nevertheless be established. Two countries dominate—by far—revisionist production: Germany and the United States. In the first, such books are numerous and enjoy a certain success if one may judge from the reprintings a number of them have gone through. They are tightly bound to a specific milieu: an extreme right-wing that sees itself as heir to Nazism and dreams of its rehabilitation.

Revisionism in the strict sense has not won any adepts in the extreme or ultra-left, or very few. Small terrorist groups, to be sure, have made the transition from anti-Zionism and aid to the Palestinian liberation movement to outright anti-Semitism, but without invoking the revisionist argument.[57] The declaration of the German terrorist Ulrike Meinhof is often quoted: "Six million Jews were killed and thrown onto the dungheap of Europe because they were money-Jews (*Geldjuden*).[58] Reading that statement in context, one sees that it is but a variation on the theme of Bebel's formula: "Anti-Semitism is the socialism of fools." It remains that a transition is possible and has occasionally occurred.

In the United States, revisionism is above all the specialty of a Californian group, W. A. Carto's Liberty Lobby, which draws on venerable and solid anti-Semitic, anti-Zionist, and anti-black traditions and also draws—or attempts to—on the nationalism of Americans of Germanic origin.[59] It does not appear that gestures toward libertarians, despite the patronage of H. E. Barnes, have met with much success.[60] In academic and intellectual circles, a work like Arthur Butz's is almost completely unknown.[61]

In several countries, on the contrary, revisionism is the specialty not of the racist and anti-Semitic extreme right, but of several groups of individuals coming from the extreme left. This is the case in Sweden following the intervention on Robert Faurisson's behalf of the extreme left-wing sociologist Jan Myrdal, whose intervention was on behalf not merely of the man but, in part, of his ideas;[62] in Australia, following the action of the former secretary of the Victorian Council for Civil Liberties, John Bennett;[63] and even in Italy, where a small Marxist libertarian group invokes its debt to Paul Rassinier.[64]

And yet it is the French case that seems the most interesting and complex. Let us observe first of all this curious fact: to the extent that the international press has dealt with the revisionist problem, discussion, over the last three years, has centered on the case of Robert Faurisson. It was on his behalf that Noam Chomsky wrote a text that served as a preface to one of his books;[65] and it was on the basis of his "theses" that newspapers the world over, in Germany as in America, published the most detailed analyses.[66] This observation is all the more surprising in that in those two countries there were and still are revisionists of greater stature than Faurisson.

Not that his revisionism was of a particularly daunting sort. His originality has consisted in posing the problem on a strictly technical level. And even in that domain, he owes a lot to Butz. Certain of his formulations that provoked scandals were in reality mere translations or adaptations of German texts.[67]

To be sure, Faurisson's social status, that of a university professor in a large city, in a country in which such credentials afford one access to the media more readily than elsewhere; his native talent for scandal, which is longstanding; the lawsuits brought against him;[68] and the presentation of his work by an honorable sociologist, Serge Thion,[69] have all played a role. It is equally remarkable that whereas in England, the country that invented freedom of the press, revisionists have not had access to the popular press,[70] in France, in certain liberal or libertarian dailies (*Le Monde, Libération*), there have appeared the rudiments of a debate, with the reader occasionally being left with the impression that he is dealing with two equally valid positions between which one might very well hesitate.[71]

Like other countries, France has always known—and still does know—a neo-Nazi tendency, symbolized by Maurice Bardèche and his journal, *Défense de l'Occident*, and recently revived by the New Right. Revisionist themes were featured in it very early on.[72] With Paul Rassinier (1906–1967), a communist, then a socialist, a deportee to Buchenwald and to Dora, a lifelong anticolonialist, but a friend of Bardèche and a writer for *Rivarol*, we are dealing with something else: the alliance of a pacifist and libertarian extremist left and an unabashedly Hitlerian extreme right.[73] Anti-Semitism, intimately connected, in this case, with anti-Zionism, constitutes the bridge between the two. That alliance would be renewed in the next generation through the dissemination accorded revisionist positions in general and Faurisson's positions in particular by the Marxist group La Vieille Taupe and several adjacent ones (La Guerre Sociale, La Jeune Taupe, etc).[74]

What is the political aim of this group, an aim in large part facilitated by the sacralization of the Jewish people over a period of several decades, by the belated remorse that gripped the West afer the discovery of the great slaughter, and consequently by the protection the Israeli venture has enjoyed—even in its most debatable aspects? The central theme is perfectly clear: it is a matter of shattering the antifascist consensus resulting from the Second World War and sealed by the revelation of the extermination of the Jews. To the mind of the extreme left, the importance of Nazi crimes should be diminished and the guilt of the West and of the communist world augmented in order to reveal a common oppression.[75]

What would be needed, in brief, would be to change enemies. Is this completely unprecedented? Such ideologies have roots in France. At the end of the nineteenth century, the liberal consensus united peasants, workers, and bourgeois republicans in a common hostility to the "feudal" landholding aristocracy. Edouard Drumont, the author of *La France juive* [*Jewish*

France], who was a great man and an important sociologist in the eyes of more than one socialist,[76] also proposed a shift of enemies: no longer the lord's castle, with its torture chambers, but the mysterious lair where the Jew developed his riches with Christian blood. And he lashed out at official history: "The French historical school," wrote Drumont, "once again has passed by all this without seeing it, despite investigatory techniques it claims to have invented. It paused naively before dungeons that, according to Viollet-le-Duc himself, were latrines, before *in-pace* that were cellars; it did not enter the mysterious *sacrificarium*, the den more bloody than Bluebeard's, in which the childlike victims of Semitic superstition lie bloodless, their veins parched."[77] A strange alliance indeed . . .

5. On the Nations and Israel

Just as the ancient city-states set up "treasures" at Delphi and Olympia that expressed their rivalry in the cult of Apollo and Zeus, the nations victimized by Hitler—or at least certain of them—have erected pavilions at Auschwitz recalling the misfortune befalling their citizens. Misfortunes also know competition. Among those pavilions, incongruously, there is a Jewish pavilion. For lack of an underwriting authority, it was erected by the Polish government and proclaims above all the martyrology of Poland.[78]

A word should be said at this point about these "practices," specifically about those nations of eastern Europe from which the immense majority of the Jews who were murdered came and that currently constitute "socialist" Europe. It goes without saying that "revisionism" is totally banned there. But history? Let us simply say a few words—after a necessarily brief investigation—about historiography in three socialist countries: the U.S.S.R., because of the leading role it has within the system and because its armies liberated Auschwitz; the German Democratic Republic, in so much as it is heir to part of the territory and population of the national socialist state; and finally Poland, because it was on its territory that a majority of the exterminations took place.[79]

To my knowledge, there is, in the strict sense, no Soviet historiography of the genocide of the Jews. A few books or booklets, either reports or propaganda, were published at the time of victory.[80] The study of the German concentration camps appears to have been quite rudimentary—for reasons that seem obvious—and the only volume in Russian on Auschwitz I was able to locate was translated from the Polish and published in Warsaw.[81]

To be sure, *The History of the Great Patriotic War (1941–1945)* by Boris Tepulchowski, which passes as being representative of post-Stalinist Soviet historiography, mentions the gas chambers and the extermination as it was practiced at Auschwitz, Maidanek, and Treblinka, but the victimized populations do not include the Jews, whereas the murder of six million Polish citizens is mentioned. Two lines explain that the entire Jewish population on occupied Soviet soil was exterminated.[82] A Jewish nationality exists in the Soviet Union, but it is in some respects a negative nationality. Such is the situation reflected in Soviet historiography.

The case of the German Democratic Republic is rather different. According to official ideology, there has been an absolute break with the capitalist and Nazi period. Anti-Semitism and the exterminations are a legacy that must not be assumed in any manner whatsoever, neither by paying reparations to Israel, nor by sending a head of government to kneel at the site of the Warsaw ghetto. It is believed in East Berlin that the Federal Republic, on the contrary, should assume the heritage of Hitler's Germany, and for a long time, there was a pretense of believing that it was a continuation of it. The result is that studies of the extermination, although far from nonexistent as is sometimes erroneously claimed,[83] are to a great degree instrumental and are a reaction less to the imperatives of knowledge and historical reflection than to the need to complete and rectify what is being written or done in the Federal Republic or to engage its leaders in polemics.[84]

The revisionists appear not to have commented on a small but significant fact: although Poland, since the end of the war, has endured several political earthquakes, which have led to considerable emigration, including an emigration of militant nationalists not normally known for any excessive tenderness toward either the Jews or the communists (who, in revisionist ideology, were the first great fabricators of the "lie" of the extermination), there has not been a single Pole who has come forth to contribute anything to the revisionist cause.

In fact, the history of the death camps is in large part based on works published in Poland, through either documents reproduced in the Auschwitz Museum series, works of the Polish Commission on War Crimes, or volumes of the Jewish Historical Institute of Warsaw.

Obviously, such literature is in need of periodic correction. Polish nationalism, which is by tradition violently anti-Semitic, combined with Communist censorship, has intervened on numerous occasions. It is frequently the case that publications attach greater importance to the anti-Polish repression, which was ferocious, than to the extermination of the Jews. There is also frequently a posthumous naturalization as Poles of Jews, a naturalization that occurred only rarely during the period in question.[85]

One nationalism can detect with relative ease the deformations due to another nationalism. The Polish historiography of the genocide and, in general, of the occupation period is taken quite seriously by Israeli historiographers, is debated, at times condemned, and that confrontation is a reflection of the great Judeo-Polish drama.[86]

There is certainly not *an* Israeli historiography. A glance at the collection entitled *Yad Vashem Studies*, for example, reveals that it is shot through with tensions and is capable of integrating work from abroad; at times not without resistance. The great syntheses coming from the Diaspora, those of G. Reitlinger and R. Hilberg, and fundamental discussions such as Hannah Arendt's have been greeted with attacks of great violence. Among the more delicate points: the questions of Jewish "passivity," of Jewish collaboration (the collaboration of the rope and the hanged man), of the nationality of Hitler's Jewish victims, of the unique character of the slaughter, and finally that of the "banality of evil," which Hannah Arendt opposed to the demonization of Eichmann and his masters.[87] These are genuine problems raised by the writing of history. Between a historiography that insists, to the point of absoluteness, on specificity, and one straining to integrate the great massacre into the movement and trends of history, which is not always a matter of course, the clash can only be violent.[88] But, concerning Israel, can one limit the debate to history? The Shoah (Holocaust) exceeds it, first, by virtue of the dramatic role it played in the very origins of the state, then by what must indeed be called the daily use made of the great slaughter by the Israeli political class.[89] The genocide of the Jews abruptly ceases being a historical reality, experienced existentially, and becomes a commonplace tool of political legitimation, brought to bear in obtaining political support within the country as well as in pressuring the Diaspora to follow unconditionally the inflections of Israeli policy. Such is the paradox of a use that makes of the genocide at once a sacred moment in history, a very secular argument, and even a pretext for tourism and commerce.[90]

Need it be said that among the perverse effects of this instrumentalization of the genocide, there is a constant and adroitly fueled confusion of Nazi and Arab hatreds?

No one can expect the years 1939–1945 to fall into place in the (not always) peaceful realm of medieval charters and Greek inscriptions, but their permanent exploitation toward extremely pragmatic ends deprives them of their historical density, strips them of their reality, and thus offers the folly and lies of the revisionists their most fearsome and effective collaboration.

6. History after Auschwitz

In concluding, can we attempt to state the test to which revisionism puts the historian? Meditating, after the war, on the theme of "negative dialectics," Adorno wondered to what extent it was possible to "think" after Auschwitz. What the Lisbon earthquake had been for Voltaire and the grave of theodicy for Leibniz, the genocide was—a hundredfold—for the generation that lived through it: "With the massacre by administrative means of millions of individuals, death became something which had never previously had to be feared in that form. . . . Genocide is the absolute integration, everywhere underway, in which men are leveled, trained, to use the military term, until, fused with the concept of their utter inanity, they are literally exterminated. . . . Absolute negativity is foreseeable; it no longer surprises anyone."[91] Absolute negativity? Does such a concept have any meaning for a historian? Auschwitz has become a symbol, which it was not immediately after the war[92]—the symbol of an enormous silence. But even that symbol can be challenged. Auschwitz juxtaposed an extermination camp (Birkenau), a work camp (Auschwitz I), and a factory-camp for the production of synthetic rubber (Auschwitz III Monowitz). The site of absolute negativity would rather be Treblinka or Belzec, although one can always conceive a crime more absolute than another.[93] A historian, by definition, works in relative terms, and that is what makes any apprehension of revisionist discourse so difficult for him. The word itself has nothing shocking about it for a historian: he instinctively adopts the adjective as his own. If he is shown that there was no gas chamber functioning at Dachau, that *The Diary of Anne Frank*, as it has been published in various languages, raises problems of coherence if not of authenticity, or that Krema I, that of the Auschwitz camp, was reconstructed after the war by the Poles,[94] he is prepared to yield.

Events are not things, even if reality possesses an irreducible opaqueness. A historical discourse is a web of explanations that may give way to an "other explanation,"[95] if the latter is deemed to account for diversity in a more satisfactory manner. A Marxist, for instance, will attempt to argue in terms of capitalist profitability, and will wonder whether simple destruction in gas chambers can or cannot be made to enter easily into such an interpretative framework. Depending on the case, he will either adapt the gas chambers to Marxism or suppress their existence in the name of the same doctrine.[96] The revisionist enterprise, in its essence, does not, however, appear to me to partake of that quest for an "other explanation." What must be sought in it is rather that absolute negativity of which Adorno spoke, and that is precisely what the historian has such a hard time understanding. At stake is a gigantic effort not even to create a fictive world, but to eradicate from history an immense event.

In this order of thought, it must be admitted that two revisionist books, Arthur Butz's *The Hoax of the Twentieth Century* and Wilhelm Stäglich's *Der Auschwitz Mythos*, represent a rather remarkable success: that of the *appearance* of a historical narrative, better still, of a critical investigation, with all the external features defining a work of history, except for what makes it of any value: truth.

One can, to be sure, search out and find precedents for revisionism in the history of ideological movements. Under the Restoration, for pedagogical reasons, did not the Reverend Father Loriquet delete the Revolution and the Empire from the history he taught his pupils? But that was no more than "legitimate" deception, which, as we know from Plato on, is an inseparable part of education—an innocent game in relation to modern revisionisms.

To be sure, if I can speak at this point of absolutes, it is because we are dealing with pure discourse, not reality. Revisionism is an ancient practice, but the revisionist crisis occurred in the West only after the widespread broadcast of *Holocaust*, that is, after the turning of the genocide into a spectacle, its transformation into pure language and an object of mass consumption.[97] There lies, I believe, the point of departure for considerations that will, I hope, be pursued by others than myself.

Assassins of Memory

1. The Destruction of the Helots of Sparta

We are in 424/423 B.C., the eighth year of the Peloponnesian War, opposing Athens and Sparta, along with their respective allies. The situation is perilous for the Lacedemonians. The Athenians are installed on the island of Cytherea, to the south of Laconia, and at Pylos (present-day Navarin) on the west coast of the Peloponnesus. Sparta attempts a diversionary tactic, by sending an expeditionary force to Athens' (shaky) allies on the Calcidian peninsula, in northeastern Greece. Here is what the historian Thucydides relates at this juncture and the episode through which he comments on the crisis threatening Sparta:

> Athens at the time posed an immanent threat to the Peloponnesus and especially to the very land of the Lacedemonians. The latter nevertheless had a hope: to deter the Athenians by sending an expeditionary force to one of their allies, which would trouble them [the Athenians] in turn. The allies were prepared to receive it and to defect as soon as it appeared. At the same time the Lacedemonians were looking for a pretext for expediting Helots to a foreign theatre lest they take advantage of the presence of the Athenians at Pylos to foment revolution. Fearing their youthful ardor and their number (for the Lacedemonians, the central issue in their relations with the Helots had always been to keep them under surveillance), they had, on a previous occasion, already resorted to the following measures. They had let it be

known that all those [among the Helots] who felt that through their conduct in the face of the enemy they were so deserving should have their credentials for emancipation inspected. It was, from their perspective, a test: those who demonstrated sufficient pride to believe they should be first to be freed were thus the prime candidates for a future rebellion. About two thousand of them were selected: adorned with a crown, they ran the circuit of sanctuaries as free men. Shortly thereafter, they were made to disappear, and no one knew in what manner each of them had been eliminated.[1]

A strange text indeed, written in a partially encoded language. The Helots "disappear," are "eliminated" (one might also translate "destroyed"), but the words designating murder or death are not pronounced, and the weapon remains unknown.

To understand this episode, concerning which George Grote (1794–1871), the British founder of the positive history of ancient Greece,[2] wrote that it revealed "a refinement of deception and cruelty rarely equaled in history,"[3] is it enough to know who the Helots were? They constituted the servile category of Lacedemonian society. Unlike the slaves of Athens, they were neither bought nor sold abroad. They cultivated the land of the upper stratum of the city-state, the peers (*homoioi*), those who formed the warrior elite. To explain their origin, the ancients had concocted various theories among which moderns still lose their way.[4] The Helots formed two subclasses, which were in certain respects quite distinct. Some were Laconians quite naturally aspiring to juridical equality with their Spartan masters. Athenian peasants had been emancipated at the dawn of the sixth century B.C.. Their case was not theoretically out of the question as a model. The others were foreigners, Messenians, relatives of the Lacedemonians, speaking a Doric language like them, and conquered by Lacedemonia (the city-state whose capital was Sparta) in the course of three harsh wars. A significant portion of them emigrated, some to Messina in Sicily, others to Naupacta on the coast facing the Peloponnesus. The Helots of Messina aspired to reconstitute their ancient city, and they succeeded in doing so, moreover, after the Theban Epaminondas destroyed the power of Lacedemonia at Leuctra in 370–369 B.C. The Messenians then proclaimed a "law of return," and invited with varying degrees of success the Messenian diaspora to return to the homeland of their memories.

That much established, whether Laconians or Messenians, the Helots were in some cases submissive, adopting the values of the ruling class, and in others rebellious, and quite frequently so as of the fifth century B.C.. A general rebellion of the lower classes almost erupted in 397 B.C.. According to Xenophon, an informer working for the Spartan rulers was able to say at the time: "Each time the subject of the Spartans came up among these people [the lower classes] none of them could conceal that it would not displease him to devour them, and even raw."[5]

Another difference with the slaves of Athens was that the Helots were normally part of the Lacedemonian army, serving as weapons carriers. It even happened that some experienced combat and benefited from a kind of emancipation. But even when freed they did not become first-class citizens. The ruling Spartan elite thus faced an insoluble contradiction. Sparta could not do without Helots—neither, it goes without saying, for the cultivation of the soil nor even for waging war. Yet (even lightly) armed Helots represented an obvious danger for them. The solution adopted by Sparta had been to lock the Helots into a scorned status, a phenomenon of which history offers numerous examples. No one has better epitomized this status than Myron of Priena, a historian of the third century B.C., who writes: "The Helots are made to perform the most ignominious and degrading tasks. They are forced to wear a dogskin cap and to dress in animal hides; each year they receive a certain number of blows, without having committed any infraction, in order to remind them that they are slaves; worse yet, if there are any who exceed in strength the measure appropriate to slaves, they are punished by death, and their masters receive a fine for not having impeded their development."[6]

It happened, however, that the yoke would break or threaten to break. The city then proceeded to perform on a grand scale, while adding a measure of fraud, what the masters were doing on a lesser one: killing the most valiant of them. This is what happened in the episode narrated by Thucydides. Instead of emancipating *or* killing, it emancipated *and* killed. Chosen Helots would run the circuit of sanctuaries, as young apprentice warriors in Athens might, after which they disappeared.

But when precisely did this dramatic and sinister adventure occur? Earlier, says Thucydides. But did that mean a recent past? In the nineteenth century, historians were divided between two hypotheses, and the same situation holds at present.[7] No one, to my knowledge—although I could, of course, be wrong—has maintained that we are dealing here with a case of pure fiction or suggested that this explosion of ruse and hatred had been invented by some intimate of the victims.[8] But did Thucydides know more than he said? Apparently the Spartans kept their secret rather well. Only a slim thread of memory has come down to the Athenian historian.

2. History and Stories

In the Thucydides text I have just commented on, there is a little word that has not, to my knowledge, attracted the attention of the exegetes: the word *each*. When the Spartans opted to do away with the Helots who had distinguished themselves, their decision concerned a collectivity whose boundaries they themselves had fixed, with the participation of the victims, but each death was obviously individual. Each victim had his own history, and we will never know how death was administered,[9] individually, collectively, or in small groups. That last hypothesis is, nevertheless, the most plausible, since it is best suited to the artisan-like and nonindustrial techniques of the age. Whatever the case, the sources at the historian's disposal can not be bypassed, and it will remain for him to interpret them.

For the history of the (partially successful) attempt to exterminate the Jews and the Gypsies during the Second World War by the German National Socialist regime, we, of course, have at our disposal an infinitely richer store of documentation than for the horrendous episode in Spartan history that I recalled above. But the fundamental problems, upon closer inspection, are not that different. To be sure, the comparison, which is frequently made, with the Helots has its limits. In all probability, the latter represented the majority of the Lacedemonian population. This is suggested by an indication in Herodotus (among other sources): during the battle of Platea (479 B.C., during the Second Median War) every hoplite was accompanied by seven Helots.[10] When the attempt was made to capture in a single word the status of Jews in the Middle Ages and in the modern period, above all in Europe, the term *pariah*—following Max Weber—rather than *Helot*, tended to be chosen.[11] But the two notions occasionally come into contact. An institutionalized contempt, which may very well be accompanied, in certain cases, by privileges (court Jews, for example), characterizes the status of both communities: one need but think of the famous "distinctive signs."

The pariah status of the Jews was called radically into question by the French Revolution and its sequels extending, with occasional regressions, through the nineteenth century and even our own. The Russian Revolution of 1917 as well as the German Revolution of 1918–1919 are part of that heritage, and there was no trace of that pariah status either in the U.S.S.R. at the beginning of the 1930s (despite the Stalinist regression) or in Weimar Germany. It has even been possible to speak of that era as a "golden age" of European Jewry.[12] *Mitteleuropa*, and particularly Poland and Romania, were, to be sure, exceptions to the rule, and it was principally central and eastern Europe that, since the beginning of the nineteenth century, had fueled the Zionist movement, which was an index of persecution and unrest as well as a national movement and a belated colonial enterprise. This was not the only imaginable (or imagined) response to humiliation—one has but to think of the Bund—but events determined the outcome.

The "golden age" was followed, with Hitler, by a colossal regression that, as Nazism gradually made its way through Europe, everywhere annulled what had been achieved in the wake of the French Revolution. The condition of Jews again became that of pariahs or, if one prefers, Helots, as may be seen from various legislative measures, such as the "Nuremberg laws" (September 1935) or the Statute on Jews in France, promulgated on its own initiative by Vichy (October 1940).[13] But a legal status, although it may have murderous consequences, is not itself a murder. The massive murder, which took the form initially of actions by the *Einsatzgruppen*, and then of gassings, did not begin before the war against the Soviet Union, which, after long preparations, began on June 22, 1941. It was in December, at Chelmno, in Poland, that gas trucks were used for the first time.

How might all this be told or explained (since history is both a narrative and a quest for intelligibility)?[14] I shall not attempt to summarize here the very extensive historiographical debates.[15] Let us, nevertheless, raise a few questions.

For the facts to be ascertained with all possible precision and for the historian to purge as best he can his work of all that is fabricated, legendary, or mythical is the very least to be expected and obviously constitutes a never-ending task. There is no such thing as a perfect history, any more than there exist exhaustive histories. However "positivist" he is intent on being, however desirous of "letting the facts speak for themselves," as the ingenuous say, the historian cannot evade his own responsibility, that of his personal choices or values.[16] For my part, I have no scorn for the genre of the chronicle, which is said to constitute the degree zero of historical narration. It has the merit of imbuing history with novelistic experience. But, aside from concealing their presuppositions, chronicles evade all concern for intelligibility.[17]

Ever since the disaster was acknowledged and came to be investigated, the history of the Hitlerian genocide has oscillated between two extremes, frequently epitomized by the terms *intentionalism* and *functionalism*.[18] For Lucy Davidowicz, for example, the extermination was preformed in Hitler's brain as of

1919, just as the destiny of humanity, according to certain biologists of the eighteenth century, was preformed in the person of Adam. In the last analysis, the "war against the Jews"[19] occurred independently of the successes and failures of Hitler's foreign policies and of the war itself. We need hardly specify that in such a "history," there is no discussion of either the mentally ill or the Gypsies, of Bolshevik functionaries or non-Jewish deportees, who also underwent, in varying degrees, the process of extermination. On this level, we are still dealing with history only to the extent that the raw material has been borrowed from reality. The structure is not that of a historical process, composed of advances and setbacks, of chance and necessity; it is that of the self-enclosed structure of myth.

At the other extreme, the extermination appears to be such only at the end of the process, as a sort of retrospective illusion. The "Genesis of the Final Solution"[20] occurred, so to speak, on an ad hoc basis, as the camps, for instance, gradually became overcrowded and it became necessary to make space by getting rid of encumbering human material. I do not deny that this explanatory model accounts for a certain number of details, but how is one to exclude from consideration a murderous ideology, which, with the war in the East, had taken on unprecedented virulence?

Pure functionalism dissolves the genocide as a complex within a greater diversity. As Franz Neumann wrote in 1944:

> National-Socialism, which claims to have abolished the class struggle, needs an adversary whose very existence can serve to integrate antagonistic groups within a common society. That enemy can not be too weak. If it were too weak, it would be impossible to present it to the population as its supreme enemy. Nor can it be too strong, for that would commit the Nazis to a difficult struggle against a powerful enemy. It was for that reason that the Catholic church was not promoted to the rank of supreme enemy. But the Jews fit the bill admirably. As

a result, such an ideology and such anti-Semitic practices entail the extermination of the Jews, the only
means to achieve an ultimate aim: the destruction of institutions, beliefs, and groups still remaining free.[21]

On January 30, 1939, the Führer had proclaimed (and his words
have quite properly remained famous): "If international Jewish
finance, in Europe and elsewhere, again succeeds in precipitating
peoples into a world war, the result will not be the Bolsheviza-
tion of the world and with it the victory of Judaism, but, on the
contrary, the annihilation of the Jewish race in Europe." More
important than having uttered those words is the fact that he
constantly referred to them, in public and private, implicitly or
explicitly, even when confused about the date of his speech,
throughout the war.[22]

Intention or function: the dilemma can take many other
forms. It is tempting, but dangerous, to write history as a classical tragedy whose resolution is known in advance. The scholars
who are most careful about respecting its various phases do not
always elude that danger. This is the case of the American historian K. A. Schleunes, whose book on the "twisted road"[23] leading
to Auschwitz, a study of anti-Semitic policies between 1933 and
1939, proclaims that as of 1938, the path to annihilation was
clear.[24] As though Hitler from then on was definitively shielded
from all accidents,[25] as though other methods had not been tried
out before the final one. As opposed to this, Claude Lanzmann,
in the grandiose historical film entitled *Shoah* (1985), begins his
narrative in December 1941 at Chelmno. That tactic may appear
brutal, but it is justified.[26] Even after the exploits of the *Einsatzgruppen* in occupied U.S.S.R., the decision to kill not directly,
but through use of gas, marked the crucial turning point in the
mechanical slaughter.

The first gassing using Zyklon B at Auschwitz took place, according to Rudolph Hoess, the commandant of the camp that
thus became an extermination camp, on September 3, 1941, and
the victims were Soviet war prisoners.[27] Those two dates, that of

Auschwitz and that of Chelmno, raise two fundamental questions in the debate over continuity or discontinuity.

It was not the first time in Hitler's Germany that gas was used for the extermination of human beings. As of September 1, 1939 (the date assigned retrospectively), Hitler in person, as the war began, authorized Reichsleiter Bouhler and Dr. Brandt to "grant merciful deaths." This was the beginning of Operation T4, and gas chambers were one of the instruments used for the euthanasia of incurables and the mentally ill.[28] The operation, however, came up against the firm reaction of the Christian clergy, and specifically the Catholic church. The bishop of Münster, Clemens August, Count of Galen, was brave enough to file an official complaint on July 28, 1941, and to denounce such murders publicly in a sermon delivered on August 3. Operation T4 was stopped officially on August 24, 1941; it was nevertheless continued on a much smaller scale and with increased secrecy. It had around 100,000 victims. The links between Operation T4 and the extermination of the Jews are twofold and contradictory.[29] Specialized personnel had thus been trained (and would prove their full efficiency at Treblinka), but in—theoretically—putting a halt to the extermination of incurables,[30] Hitler was also in a better position to unite the country, with a single enemy, "Judeo-Bolshevism." That was a crusade in which pastors and bishops—including the Count of Galen—were happy to participate, to the extent that they saw it, precisely, as a crusade. In that sense, the stopping of one operation allowed for the realization of the other in an atmosphere of sacred union.

There can be no doubt that with the invasion of the U.S.S.R, the war changed in nature. There were now two categories of enemy: one, the Slavs, was for the most part slated for slavery (which had already been tried out in Poland); the other, "Judeo-Bolsheviks" against whom a war of extermination was declared.[31] The destruction of the Jews and that of "Communism" were thus twin operations.

The question is not one of judging what indeed the Stalinist regime was. The word *totalitarianism*, which is applied by many specialists to the two antagonistic dictatorships may be used to describe an outcome. In certain respects, one may even speak of a more deep-seated system in the case of Stalin than in that of Hitler: the Dimitrov trial was not characterized by the abject confessions of the Moscow trials, and although Leon Trotsky, in August 1937, could accuse a Nazi prosecutor in a Danzig trial brought against a Trotskyist group of drawing his inspiration from Vishinsky,[32] that prosecutor did not obtain the confession of imaginary crimes. That being the case, the historical process was totally different depending on whether one was in one or the other of the two regimes temporarily allied from August 1939 to June 1941. For the Hitlerians, the Stalinist regime represented absolute subversion as well as Jewish gangrene. Inversely, for a Europe occupied by Hitler, Stalin and the Red Army represented the hope of liberation. Those images were all the more forcefully striking in that it was indeed the Red Army that liberated Auschwitz.

For most historians, however, one question remains difficult to resolve. If the extermination of the Jews was inseparably bound up with the war in the East, it remains to determine in what state of mind—the enthusiasm of early victories, or the growing sense of failure at the end of the fall of 1941—the fatal decision was taken. The sparse testimony we have brings us to the end of the summer,[33] but the debate continues unresolved. In any event, there is no doubt that it was the ideological war against the U.S.S.R. that served as the motor of the final solution throughout all of Europe.

There remains a final dilemma for the historian: the relation between the extermination of the Jews and the Gypsies, and the exploitation by forced labor, which concerned both "racial" deportees and "ordinary" interns, the convicts of Dora or Ravensbrück, be they political or common-law prisoners, homosexuals or Jehovah's Witnesses. The question is not simple, and evolved a great deal from the prewar period to the phase of total war.

The camps were created by the Nazi regime with the purpose not of forcing men and women to work but of isolating them. No doubt they were obliged to work, but, in Arno Mayer's phrase, their labor was "Sisyphean" and not "productive."[34] A concern for production would gradually appear, above all as of 1940, under the auspices of the WVHA,[35] the Central Office of Economic Administration, an increasingly important sector of the SS state. There was no common measure between such production and "free" work, even as performed by those workers drafted from all over Europe to replace mobilized Germans. Concentration camp labor *also* served the ends of exhaustion and control. In relation to "free" labor, concentration camp labor, the work of slaves, also had the characteristic of being indefinitely replenishable. What was the situation in the case of the Jews? It is clear that at sites devoted to extermination pure and simple (Chelmno, Sobibor, Belzec, Treblinka), the only available work was the maintenance of the killing machine and the retrieval of possessions from the victims. Himmler, moreover, on the subject of the Warsaw ghetto, echoed the conflict between the "economists" and the exterminators, whose chief he was.[36] But Maidanek and (above all) Auschwitz, which were enormous industrial centers, were living proof that extermination could go on side by side with exploitation by forced labor. The immediate elimination of the weak, the aged, women, and children left only a labor force. There, too, slaves were infinitely available, and it was futile to want to ensure the replenishment and renewal of the labor force through "normal" channels. Between exploitation and extermination there was a tension, never a break.

It is thus the historian's task to delimit this field of forces. He can not, however, say *all*, and what he can no doubt *least* communicate is death as it was experienced by the victims once the doors closed. It is easier to write the history of Buchenwald than of Auschwitz, and easier to write that of Auschwitz than of Treblinka. As Thucydides said, we will never know how *each* one disappeared.

3. Discourse-Memory-Truth

"We are living through the shattering of history." That formula figures on the back cover of volumes in a famous collection entitled—precisely—*Bibliotheque des histoires*. Among the transformations that do indeed seem to be calling the unity of the genre into question, pride of place is accorded the attention paid to discourse, not merely to "discursive practices," as they give way to each other in the course of centuries (in Michel Foucault's undertaking), but to the discourse of the figure offering himself as the untouchable bestower of truth, the historian himself. When the Greek Herodotus describes barbarians, what, in fact, is he describing if not Greeks—transformed or inverted Greeks? The Other is constructed on the basis of the Same. One expects to read of the customs and laws of the Persians and Scythians, to discover their physiognomies, and one is confronted with a painting analogous to those of the baroque painter Arcimboldo, who constructed portraits with vegetables, fruits, and flowers.[37]

The historian *writes*; he conjures up a place and a time, but he himself is situated in a place and time, at the center of a *nation*, for example, which entails the elimination of other nations. As a writer, he has depended at length solely on written texts, which has simultaneously entailed the elimination of oral or gestural manifestations, the booty of the anthropologist.[38]

The historian *writes*, and that writing is neither neutral nor transparent. It is rooted in literary forms, even rhetorical figures which distance allows one to detect. Thus in the nineteenth century, Michelet is an author of realist novels, Ranke of realist comedies, Tocqueville of realist tragedies, and J. Burckhardt of realist satires. As for Marx, he is a philosophical apologist for history in the mode of metonymy and synecdoche.[39] Who can regret the historian's loss of innocence, the fact that he has been taken as an object or that he takes himself as an object of study? It remains the case nonetheless that if historical discourse is not connected—by as many intermediate links as one likes—to what may be called, for lack of a better term, reality, we may still be immersed in discourse, but such discourse would no longer be historical.

Writing is not the only historical mode.[40] Why is *Shoah* a great work of history rather than a collection of tales?[41] It is neither a novelistic recreation like *Holocaust*,[42] nor a documentary—only a single document from the period is read in it, concerning the trucks at Chelmno—but a film in which men of today speak of the past. With Jewish survivors expressing themselves in a space that was once that of death, while trains no longer leading to the gas chambers roll on, and former Nazis sketching their past exploits, the witnesses reconstruct a past that was all too real; testimonial accounts overlap and confirm each other in the barest of voices and diction. We are, in brief, given absolute proof that the historian is also an artist.

Within this shattered realm of historical discourse, how is one to situate the "revisionist" enterprise? Its perfidiousness lies precisely in its seeming to be precisely what it is not, an attempt to write and think through history. It is not a matter of *constructing* a true narrative. Nor is it one of revising the alleged accomplishments of historical science. There is nothing more natural than the "revision" of history, and nothing more ordinary. Time itself modifies the perspective not only of the historian but of the lay individual as well. *La Bataille du rail* is a film produced in 1946 as a true discourse about the resistance of the railway workers. Anyone viewing it again today[43] recognizes in it the description of an ideal world in which everyone, from engineers to lampmen, are united in the effort to dupe the enemy. The history of the deportation also has its share of dross. Mythical thinking and propaganda played their role, as well at times as a certain rivalry between non-Jews and Jews (once analyzed by O. Wormser-Migot), with the former claiming equality of suffering with the latter.[44]

But denying history is not the same as revising it. The case of Faurisson is not new in this regard. In 1690, the Reverend Father

Jean Hardouin (1646–1729), a great scholar, began denying the authenticity of the majority of the extant works of Greek and Latin literature, whether classical or Christian. Both Virgil's *Aeneid* and the works of Saint Augustine were said to be forgeries fabricated in the fourteenth century by heretical monks. The grounds for that "hypothesis": the great heresiarchs, Wyclif in the fourteenth century and Luther and Calvin in the sixteenth, all drew on Saint Augustine. His disappearance would entail Virgil's. Revisionism would progress in the service of ideology.[45]

The method of today's "revisionists," the deniers, has often been analyzed. As Nadine Fresco and Jacques Baynac have written:[46] "Curious historians indeed these individuals who instead of attempting 'to know the precise unfolding of events,' act as judges of 'criminal evidence' in a trial taking place only because they deny the existence of the object of litigation and who, when a verdict is due, will be led to declare false every trace of evidence contrary to the a priori from which they refuse to budge."[47]

It is perhaps not without use to return to those methods and to demonstrate how Faurisson, an expert on literature, works to strip discourse of its reality.

The diary of the SS physician Johann Paul Kremer,[48] who practiced at Auschwitz from August 30 to November 18, 1942, is certainly not, as Faurisson's publishers write, "the final argument of those for whom the 'gas chambers' would have existed,"[49] but it is an important, authentic, firsthand document concerning that relatively early period of the extermination at Auschwitz. Kremer mentioned the gassings only once directly, on March 1, 1943, when he was already back in Münster: "Having returned to register at the shop of the shoemaker Grevsmühl, I saw a tract of the German Socialist[?] party there, which had been sent to him and in which it was said that we had already liquidated two million Jews by shooting or by gassing." This is in no way challenged by him, and he was in a good position to know.[50] At Auschwitz, he wrote in the semi-coded language prevalent in the SS administration of the camp. He spoke not of gassings, but of "special actions." But he did not conceal his horror. Auschwitz is said to be worse than Dante's Hell; it is the "camp of annihilation," the *anus mundi*, that is, the place at which all the world's excrement is unloaded.[51]

On two occasions,[52] Faurisson attempted to explain that Hell, annihilation, and anus of the world in terms of typhus alone. Kremer, however, had explained his text with perfect clarity, during his trials in both Poland and the German Federal Republic. "Special actions" included gassings. Concerning Faurisson's "explanation," I have written the following,[53] which I repeat: "On the level he most cherishes, that of philological precision and accurate translation, Faurisson's interpretation is incoherent; on the level of intellectual ethics and scientific probity, it is bogus." A great advocate of public debates, Faurisson, however, when he claimed to answer me, did not try to challenge my reasoning, concluding that he had already said enough on the subject in *Mémoire en défense*, which had been published in the interim.[54] But in his own camp, or rather in his own sect—I have received more than one proof of this—not every one reached the same conclusion. Thus the ingenuous Jean-Gabriel Cohn-Bendit, who, contrary to his friends, proclaimed himself an "exterminationist," but said he did not believe in gas chambers.[55] The core of his intervention concerned the meaning of the word *Sonderaktion*, "special action," which is normally interpreted as designating selection for the gas chamber, an interpretation all the more natural in that it is the one given by Kremer himself. Here, for instance, is his entry on October 12, 1942 in the German original and in Faurisson's *almost* literally correct translation:[56]

2. Schutzimpfung gegen Typhus; danach abends starke allegemeinreaktion (Fieber). Trotzdem in der Nacht noch bei einer Sonderaktion aus Holland (1 600 Personen) zugegen. Schauerliche Szene vor dem letzten Bunker (Hössler)! Das war die 10. Sonderaktion.

Which translates:

2. Preventive typhus vaccination; after that, in the evening, a strong general reaction (fever). Despite this, that night, I was present at still another special action on people coming from Holland (1,600 individuals). Terrifying scenes in front of the last bunker (Hössler)! It was the tenth special action.

For J.-G. Cohn-Bendit, the crucial word is *aus*, "out of": he interprets "*eine Sonderaktion aus Holland*" as "a convoy *coming from* Holland." And it is that little word that allows him to justify Faurisson and his defender Chomsky: this "Sonderaktion" would have no connection with gas chambers. But then why need he be present (*zugegen*) for a convoy? Why is a convoy an action? And why would a "special action" be performed on women coming from the camp itself? J.-G. Cohn-Bendit extricates himself from this last difficulty by imagining that the women were being transferred to another camp; but why transfer women who had reached the last stages of physical debilitation—that is the meaning of the word *Muslims* used by Kremer—to another *Lager*, whereas the logic of murder is fully coherent? J.-G. Cohn-Bendit's interpretation thus collapses. But what is interesting is that Faurisson supported this interpretation, which is so different from his own.[57] In former times, cosmologies were concerned with "saving the phenomena," accounting, for example, for the apparent movement of the sun. The revisionists, for their part, who are so willfully "materialist," are concerned with saving nonphenomena. Any interpretation will do provided it is a denial. They function in a realm of empty discourse.

Precisely the same problem is raised by the doctoral thesis defense at Nantes on June 15, 1985, by Henri Roques, concerning the "Confessions" of Kurt Gerstein.[58]

The intention of the dissertation's author—a retired agrarian engineer, a militant of the anti-Semitic extreme right, and a disciple of Faurisson more than of the professors who "directed" and judged his thesis—was enunciated by him with utter clarity on the day of his defense.

Céline, our great Louis-Ferdinand Céline, came up with
a magnificent adjective to characterize the gas chambers.
In his post-war correspondence (perhaps with Albert
Paraz), he spoke of the "magical gas chambers." Indeed,
to penetrate the world of the gas chambers, a master ma-
gician was needed, and Kurt Gerstein fit the bill perfectly. With him, as with others, the gas chambers became immaterial and the fascination they exercised grew
with their immateriality. I have attempted to break that
magic circle. I have considered and examined the Gerstein document in six versions like any other document
to which one would ascribe historical value.[59]

But that is precisely what Henri Roques does not do. In a thesis
that is in the order of literature (or, as Faurisson would say, the
"criticism of texts and documents"), he lays out, to be sure, the
six versions of the testimony, which are crammed with implausi-
bilities and contradictions, but does not ask the only important
question: are there or are there not testimony and documents
attesting to Kurt Gerstein's actual presence at a gassing at Belzec? Now such—direct or indirect—testimony exists and is perfectly cogent. Such is the case in particular of the testimony,
which was supplied on several occasions, of his traveling companion, the (Nazi) professor of medicine W. Pfannenstiel.[60] The
problem is so clear that even the Germanist Jean-Paul Allard,
who chaired the thesis jury with evident sympathy for the candidate,[61] could not forgo questioning him on the subject.

But the matter should be stated clearly: in itself, a narrative
account does not contain proof that it is (partially or totally)
truthful or mendacious. Even testimony as direct and factual as
Dr. J. P. Kremer's diary must be interpreted in light of its context.
A few years ago, a deciphering of the diary of the architect
H. A. A. Legrand, who died insane in Limoges in 1876, was published. That diary, which is written in a script of the author's
invention, contains a meticulous reproduction and transcription
(including the postage stamps) of the author's correspondence
with the circle of women who loved him.[62] Those women bore

illustrious names and titles. It has not been possible to identify, even at a far more modest level, a single one of them. The most plausible hypothesis is that this "love circle" is purely and simply phantasmatic. This is not at all the case, however, for Gerstein, who, to be sure, was not the ideal witness dreamed of by criminal court judges, but whose account has been amply verified.[63] Once again, "revisionism" appears as a concerted derealization of discourse, and its literature is a pastiche, a parody of History.[64]

4. The Sect

At the core of contemporary "revisionism" in France, there have, of course, been personalities such as Paul Rassinier[65] or Robert Faurisson and, since 1978, there has above all been the relentless and pathological work of an extreme-left-wing revolutionary group, La Vieille Taupe. It was initially a bookstore, from 1965 to 1972, and an excellent resource for those seeking rare brochures of ancient or modern revolutionary dissent, having acquired the estate of Marx's prewar publisher Costes. The bookstore—founded by Pierre Guillaume, a former militant of Socialisme ou Barbarie, who moved to the subgroup Pouvoir ouvrier (along with J.-F. Lyotard and P. Souyiri)—became in turn, in September 1967, a new informal subgroup.[66] La Vieille Taupe had a turbulent history, but managed to attract such traveling companions as La Jeune Taupe or La Guerre Sociale, all of which are convinced they are more or less sole heirs to the revolutionary tradition.

The history of revolutionary sects in France has not been written, but it may be surmised that of all of them, the most important, through the influence it exercised, was that which crystallized around Socialisme ou Barbarie (SOB), from 1949 to 1965.

SOB was born as a tendency of the (Trotskyist) Internationalist Communist party, a tendency led above all by Cornelius Castoriadis and Claude Lefort, and which broke with Trotskyism on the basis of a radical critique of Soviet bureaucracy.[67] It became absurd to criticize Stalinism ferociously and at the same time to call for an unconditional defense of the U.S.S.R., "a bureaucratic deformation of a worker state." The U.S.S.R. was a class society, even if the bureaucracy, the ruling class of a totalitarian society, was not to be confused with a bourgeoisie it had effectively destroyed.

SOB lived the life of all sects, traversed by tensions, marked by breaks and reconciliations. What were the stakes? It may be said that the group, an "organ of criticism and revolutionary orientation," was at once a "philosophical society," a place for the theoretical analysis of contemporary societies—and in this domain its role was incomparable—and, in purpose, the core of a Leninist-style revolutionary party—and in that it could only fail, any sect with dreams of becoming a church and of creating a new orthodoxy being "destined as a result to provoke a new reformation."[68]

It was around those issues that the most violent forms of dissidence within the group occurred: the "anti-party" tendency of Claude Lefort in 1958; the "proletarian" dissidence of Pouvoir ouvrier, after the majority's break with Marxism in 1963. The ideas of SOB, those of worker-run factories, for example, of the break with political apparatuses, of the analysis of the opposition between the "rulers" and the "ruled," exploded in May 1968 after the disappearance of the journal.[69]

What does La Vieille Taupe owe to its prehistory? Certainly the retrospective refusal, which came from Trotskyism, of the antifascist consensus on which the resistance to Nazism had been based (the Trotskyists resisted, but on their own, and according to internationalist principles that were rather difficult to apply); certainly as well, and this was specific to Socialisme ou Barbarie, the idea that the revolutionary struggle had to be fought against bureaucratic terrorism as well as against capitalist domination. But on two levels they innovated. First, by seeking—unlike SOB, which had functioned in sectarian solitude, and unlike those members of the extreme left who isolate themselves in scientific and critical thought[70]—to penetrate the jungle of the mass media.[71] And then, in 1970, La Vieille Taupe rallied to the positions of Paul Rassinier.[72] From this it derived the most radical deductions. In the view of La Vieille Taupe, there was no specificity to the Hitler experience among the gallery of modern tyrannies: the concentration camps could only be exploitation camps, in the economic sense of the word, and, as a result, the extermination camps could not have existed since, in all due logic, they should not have existed.

On this were grafted two theoretically adventitious elements that were to end up being crucial. The first is the perverse and megalomaniacal personality of an individual, Pierre Guillaume, who was convinced that he understood the secrets of world revolution and, in addition, of world capitalism, since he attempted to make a financial killing for his group in Brazil, which he regarded as the heart of capitalist growth,[73] and above all the will to publicity through scandal, which was a break with the practice of revolutionary "groupuscules." On that terrain, P. Guillaume and his friends encountered a man who could not care less for world revolution, but who, in the service of a mad anti-Semitic passion, entertained personal dreams of scandalous glory: Robert Faurisson.

But the audience addressed by La Vieille Taupe through various media and tracts, periodicals, cassettes, and comic books that it distributed and continues to distribute is also totally uninterested in world revolution. Only a few young people, concerned lest they be fooled by what they assumed was "official" propaganda, could in any way be sensitive to the revisionist thesis. To work at the level of the mass media, they had to ally themselves theoretically and practically with the only groups for whom such a position had ideological interest: the anti-Semitic far right (of either fundamentalist Catholic[74] or paleo- or neo-Nazi[75] stripe) and the fraction of the Arab Islamic world struggling—for good or bad reasons—against Israel. In both cases an alliance was attempted and sealed. In 1986, after the Roques affair, the Front National was the only important political group to support that Nazi intellectual and his analyses. The publication in 1986 of W. Stäglich's Nazi volume *The Myth of Auschwitz* sealed the first alliance, and the indefatigable activity of Vincent Monteil[76] has contributed what it can toward the establishment of the second.[77]

On occasion La Vieille Taupe has issued a reminder that it is not anti-Semitic, that it has published two works by Bernard Lazare, the first of which, *L'Antisémitisme, son histoire et ses causes*, has regularly been used by anti-Semites, but the second of which, *Contre l'antisémitisme*,[78] escapes that accusation. It has indulged in grandiloquent proclamations that leave no doubt as to the megalomania of their author: "The proletarians of La Vieille Taupe, without any pleasure, have been obliged to become historians, jurists, sociologists, psychologists, anthropologists, publishers, distributors, and militants, all functions alien to them, but which have allowed them to accomplish a labor it would have taken the employees of the university years to assimilate." It has also issued solemn declarations: "At present the myth is dead. . . . We have no calling to continue activities that have been imposed on us by necessity."[79] With the exception of a brief intervention at the time of the Polish crisis in December 1981, it does not appear to have been engaged in anything else.

But ideological positions have their own logic. That of a delusion concerning a plot (by the Jews, to be sure). In 1980 Faurisson was prepared to write that there was no conspiracy:[80] "It would seem more precise to say that a myth was forged, a kind of patriotic religion in which truth and falsehood were combined in varying doses by the victors of the last war."[81] He has just put his name to a tract (in the spring of 1987) in which he explains that the "lie of Auschwitz" was born in April 1944 in central Europe and that there are "five principal parties"—all of them Jews, to be sure—who bear responsibility. "For details, contact Robert Faurisson."[82] A tract that is perhaps not directly the work of La Vieille Taupe, but that was plainly inspired by it as well as by the work of the late Paul Rassinier, calmly explains that the Jews were responsible for the Second World War, that through the agency of Israel they will provoke a third one, and that so fictitious is the tale of their extermination that they can be seen in every quarter: "Every 'miraculous' escapee is proof that their story about the extermination is garbage."[83] At the head of all its publications, La Vieille Taupe reprints the maxim: "The terrible thing about looking for the truth is that one finds it." What is terrible, in fact, is that La Vieille Taupe has glaringly revealed the truth about itself.

5. History and the Nation

Let us now take the problem up at a higher level, that of nations.

In the nineteenth century and during a large part of our own century, history has been one of the modes of expression of nation-states.[84] In France that organic relation has practically disappeared. The consensus expressed in both (small and large) editions of Lavisse's *Histoire de France*[85] has ceased to exist, and the teaching of history in primary school along with it. But if such is the case for France and a few other countries, it is far from being the general case, and an instrumental exploitation of history that, to be sure, is not limited to the nation is common among "scholars" as well as professional propagandists. History seems to be a vast storeroom of props in which one is free, when the need is felt, to come up with authorization to fish out one file or another, with an implicit ban on producing any others. It is even the case, moreover, that this very pragmatic conception of history has been amply justified in theory.[86]

The worst of all historiographies is plainly state historiography, and governments rarely confess to having been criminal. Perhaps the most painful case of this sort is that of Turkish historiography concerning the Armenian genocide of 1915. Nothing could be more normal than for the Turks to insist on the wartime situation, on the support many Armenians voiced for the Russian offensive, on the local conflicts between Armenians and their neigbors, in which the Armenians did not always behave like the lamb in La Fontaine's fable. But the Turks do not stop there: they offer the very exemplar of a historiography of denial. Let us put ourselves in the position of Armenian minorities throughout the world. Imagine now Faurisson as a minister, Faurisson as a general, an ambassador, or an influential member of the United Nations; imagine Faurisson responding in the press each time it is a question of the genocide of the Jews, in brief, a state-sponsored Faurisson combined with an international Faurisson, and along with it, Talaat-Himmler having his solemn mausoleum in the capital.[87]

The Israeli case, on the other hand, presents several complex features. Although more than one present-day leader of Israel who was of age (and in particular Prime Minister Y. Shamir) belonged to a group—the Stern gang—which preferred fighting the British and even offering the Hitlerians their collaboration rather than fighting against Nazism, Israel has made instrumental use of Hitler's genocide—spatially, since Mount Herzl, topped by the grave of the founder of Zionism, is the site of the monument, library, synagogue, and research center of Yad Vashem, devoted to the genocide; and temporally, since one of its holidays is the Day of the Shoah.[88] That is merely one aspect of the commemoration of the slaughter. A country at once ancient and young (*Altneuland*, in Herzl's word), a people "chosen" for glory and suffering and which Zionism has not succeeded—as planned—in "normalizing," Israel has witnessed a proliferation of what, in the United States, are called "memorial foundations," some of which, to be sure, are dedicated to the victims of the genocide. But the issue is not there, nor is it in the scientific character of Israeli historiography. The research conducted at the Yad Vashem Institute is as good as any in the world, albeit with an occasionally nationalist orientation.[89] In Israel there are ways other than holidays, monuments, volumes of history, and museums[90] to commemorate the great massacre:

trials—Eichmann's and more recently J. Demanjuk's[?]—also serve the organization of memory. But above all the Shoah serves as a perpetual self-justification in all domains, in legitimizing the slightest border incident as marking a renewal of the massacre, in assimilating the Palestinians (toward whom the Israelis, all the same, are guilty of undeniable wrongs) to the SS. The result has been effective—even though the great majority of Israel's inhabitants has had no direct experience of Nazi persecution—but some prefer to hear no more of those tragic days, and one can even find here and there in Israel a Faurisson disciple! On the other hand, in the Diaspora Israel is frequently judged only in the light of the Nazi experience, which is not a particularly lofty perspective for the state. Visiting a camp for Palestinian prisoners at El Ansar in 1983, Bernard Kouchner and Monique Donabedian observed: "At El Ansar, there is no gas chamber, and prisoners know that they will leave it alive."[91] Such a justification seems rather weak.

Germany, or rather the German empire during the Hitler period, was, par excellence, a place of torture. Since 1945, it has been a place, par excellence, for the *Schuldfrage*, the question of guilt, as Karl Jaspers called it in 1946.[92] Germany, or rather the Federal Republic. Austria, from the outset, considered itself an innocent victim, exactly like the other countries invaded by Hitler, a circumstance that has had such far-flung consequences as the Waldheim affair.[93] As for the DDR, it has concluded that the 1945 split, characterized by the destruction of the power of the traditional ruling classes and their replacement by a bureaucracy, has freed it from assuming its share of the Hitlerian legacy.[94]

There has been nothing comparable in the Federal Republic; instead Auschwitz, taken as a symbol, has provoked widespread reflection in all domains—cultural,[95] artistic, and historical. The Institute for Contemporary History in Munich is presently the world center for the study of the Third Reich and Hitler's genocide. This may be easily explained. Between Germans and Jews, from 1933 to 1945, the relation had not simply been one of persecutors and persecuted, or of destroyers and those destroyed, as was the case for the Gypsies. What the Nazis wanted (and this is perfectly expressed by the ideology of the SS)[96] was to replace the Jews in their mythological role as chosen people, which had been a subject of fascination for nations on the rise ever since the time of the Enlightenment. In that sense, Nazism may be said to be a *perversa imitatio*,[97] a perverse imitation of the *image* of the Jewish people. It was a matter of breaking with Abraham, and consequently also with Jesus, and searching for a new lineage among the Aryans. Intellectually, the New Right in France today does not argue any differently.[98]

The fact that German nationalism, of either traditional or Hitlerian stripe, should react to the obsessive presence of the *Schuldfrage*, that it should contest a historiography that it regarded as merely prolonging the propaganda of the anti-Hitlerian émigrés[99] was only to be expected. Since the "revisionists" have decided that only Nazi books were worthy of being believed, on condition that they not be by repentant Nazis, let us open up Stäglich's volume, which is far more adroit, to be sure, than Faurisson's, and that in addition has the merit of being frank. It was written against those "groups which, through their financial power, control a large sector of the news," the Elders of Zion, of course. It evokes that period "when the German people, impelled by most dire necessity, attempted to forge an autonomous path toward the future," which was the path of national socialism, of course. As for those historians who have disseminated the "*official* image of Auschwitz," "they are all Jews, which would explain the partiality of their works."[100] This is only an extreme example of a "revisionist" literature that, for obvious reasons, is the most significant in the world and that enjoys the most extensive printings.[101] Its central theme is simple and clear: from Versailles to Nuremberg,[102] the German people has been subjected to an immense injustice that it is now a manner of righting by cleansing that people of the slander heaped upon it. This is the thesis of the dagger in the back, but extended to infinity. All this, in fact, is logical and merely transcribes the simple "truth" expressed by one of the witnesses questioned in L. Boekel's film, *The Spy Who Came in from the Far-Right*, on his reaction to the semi-revisionist works of the British historian David Irving: "I think it is good for Germany." What has been transpiring in Germany since 1985—forty years after the surrender—and more specifically since President Reagan's symbolic visit to the military cemetery of Bitburg in May of the same year is quite different in significance. Authors like Stäglich and Kern are merely preaching to the already convinced, combat veterans desperate for national honor, for example.

The "Quarrel" about which I will now say a few words is a quite different affair. To my knowledge, it is unparalleled in contemporary German historiography. Its participants are the elite of the German intelligentsia. It concerns not merely historians, but at least one philosopher, J. Habermas, and a number of political personalities. It has made its way into both scholarly works and the popular press. It is still evolving, in both Germany and in the world of letters, whence the necessarily tentative aspect of the following remarks.

It appears that the powderkeg was ignited by Ernst Nolte, a well-known historian of fascism, in an article about "A Past That Will Not Pass Away," which appeared in the *Frankfurter Allgemeine Zeitung* of June 6, 1986, and was an abbreviated journalistic version of an extended study that had appeared in English the previous year.[104] At the same time two essays were published in a book by the historian A. Hillgruber: *A Double Disappearance: The Destruction of the German Reich and the End of the Jews in Europe*.[105] The debate was further complicated by an article by Martin Broszat, the head of the functionalist school, which was billed as a "Plea for a Historicization of National-Socialism."[106] The debate itself was in fact initiated by Habermas, an heir to the Frankfurt School. He denounced a "kind of liquidation of damages: the apologetic tendencies in German historiography relative to the contemporary period."[107]

What were the stakes of this debate? In fact, they were numerous. Let us say straightaway that none of these authors is a "revisionist" in the sense shared by Faurisson and Stäglich. All accept the great massacre of the Hitler period as an uncontestable given. The question raised is first of all that of the relativity of the crime, and that has been done principally by Nolte. Historical relativity: the entire history of the revolutionary and socialist left (since the French Revolution) has been that of the projected annihilation of its political and social adversary. The reaction from the right was no more than a reaction to what the left had effectively achieved, from Lenin's seizing of power to the liquidation of the kulaks, from the gulag to the mass murders perpetrated by Pol Pot and his regime in Cambodia.

As for the Hitlerian genocide, that "Asiatic" undertaking, according to Nolte and his disciples, is to be explained, and ultimately even justified, in terms as much of a contagion spreading from the East as of a fear of the Bolshevik threat: did not Hitler identify Jews with Bolsheviks? Germany was a victim at the same time it was an executioner: that is a constant theme of nationalist literature that, to be sure, goes further than Nolte and speaks of crimes suffered and not crimes perpetrated. But already in 1983, the Greens, in their "Accusation Against the Nuclear Powers," forgetting that the destruction of Coventry dated from 1940, had accused the Western Allies of having decided, on January 14, 1943, "to proceed with the indiscriminate bombardment of German cities, thus revoking the rule of conduct, which had been the basis of international law previously respected [sic], stipulating that civilian populations were to be spared."[108] Hiroshima and future Hiroshimas would thus allow us to forget Treblinka, even as the crimes of Stalin would justify those of Adolf Hitler.

The question raised is finally one of German identity, German history, and its continuity or discontinuity. The problem is at once historical, ethical, and psychological: how is one to reintegrate twelve years under Hitler, during which—as Martin Broszat has properly noted—the Germans not only slaughtered but lived their lives? Can a country without history live? Such was the question raised by M. Stürmer already before the Quarrel. It was Habermas, in his first article, who explained that the constitutional pact of 1949, which had tethered Germany to democracy, was the basis for contemporary patriotism. All these questions are worth raising. Some of them, all the same, are troubling. Ever since Thucydides, it has been common to explain war as a result of fear.[109] Nazi fear in the face of the communists was indeed real,[110] but it was also completely insane given Stalin's foreign policy, which sought to avoid war. It is a serious matter for a historian such as Nolte to make use of perfectly worthless items from the revisionist arsenal. Like Rassinier, Faurisson, and Kern, he draws on a wild bit of polemic by an American, T. Kauffman, published "in 1940" and entitled *Germany Must Perish*, as well as on an alleged declaration of war by Chaim Weizmann, in the name of world Judaism, in September 1939.[111] No one has ever suggested that the American army, following Kauffman's proposal, ever sterilized a single German; to place on the same level a fantasied crime and a real one, the Marquis de Sade and Adolf Hitler, is a sophism unworthy of a historian.

This does not mean that German history is not to be written anew, like any other national history; nor does it mean that the genocide of the Jews should not be inserted into a history that would be simultaneously German,[112] European, and worldwide, and thus compared and confronted and even, if possible, explained. But from there to justifying it? . . .

6. *Auschwitz and the Third World*

There is nothing more common, nothing more sadly banal in human history than massacres. The Assyrians perpetrated theirs while piling heads into pyramids. The Israelites, on order from Yahweh, declared enemy peoples anathema: "Therefore go forth and strike Amalek, declare him anathema along with all he possesses; be without mercy for him; kill men and women, children and infants, cattle and sheep, camels and donkeys."[113] Moreover,

King Saul (in the eleventh century B.C.) was punished by Yahweh for not having completed the task. Thus it is that the "chosen people" is occasionally credited with having invented genocide, and Hitler probably had that image in mind. It is also the case that contemporary historians malignly reinvoke that tradition of extermination.[114] They forget that the practice was reciprocal in the region. What Yahweh commanded the Israelites was ordered by Camos to his people at the expense of the Israelites: "And I killed everything, seven thousand men and children, and free women, and girls and slaves, whom I consecrated to Astor-Camos."[115] But the Bible remains part of our culture. It is of little use to continue, recalling Tamerlane or, above all, the extermination of the American Indians during the sixteenth century, through direct slaughter or bacterial contagion, the tragic consequence of the unification of the planet.

These parallels are of relatively little weight, because, with the possible exception of the American Indians, they are part of our culture, not of our memory. But already the example of the Indians and that of the black victims of slavery reveal that Auschwitz or Treblinka may not be perceived in all quarters as they are by us.

It nonetheless remains the case that—quite normally in our country and in the nearest Third World communities, those of North Africa, but also in the "Third World that begins in our suburbs," according to Alain Geismar's formula—the image of Auschwitz and of Hitler's massacres cannot but have evolved. Let us attempt to indicate a few stages and a few memories.

I personally entered the fight against the Algerian war and specifically against torture[116]—which was not, as we soon came to realize, the worst part of it—with a constant point of reference: the obsessive memory of our national injustices—particularly the Dreyfus Affair—and of the Nazi crimes of torture and extermination. The reference to other crimes, those of colonialism, only came later, as part of a growing historical awareness.

That reference to Nazism remained in effect throughout the

war. For instance, the day after the Paris pogrom of October 17, 1961 (I still regard use of that term as appropriate), a certain number of intellectuals, including myself, at the behest of *Les Temps modernes*, Jean-Paul Sartre's journal, signed a manifesto, in which one could read: "By remaining passive, French citizens would become complicitous in the racist explosion whose theatre Paris has now become; we refuse to make any distinction between the Algerians piled up at the Palais des Sports while waiting to be 'dispatched' and the Jews stored at Drancy before their deportation." Needless to say, if the crimes committed on October 17 and the following days were abominable, the formula was absurd: repatriated in the "douars of their homeland," the Algerians did not go to Treblinka. But the logic of the protest was understood. I recall the refusal of one would-be signatory, the former minister René Capitant. The Algerians, he told us, were militants. The Jews were pure victims. Fundamentally, it was he who was right.

In the two camps confronting each other at the time, fantasies of extermination were given free rein, but they were only fantasies. Thus a Paris city councilor, Monsieur Alex Moscovitch, could declare, on October 27, at the Hotel de Ville: "All these agents of the enemy should be expelled from the territory of metropolitan France. We have been requesting permission to do so for two years already. What we need is quite simple and quite clear: authorization, and enough boats. The problem of sinking those boats is, alas, not within the jurisdiction of the Paris City Council."[117] That project, at least, was not executed. I prefer, nevertheless, to have been in the opposite camp.

What were the arguments at the time of lawyer Jacques Vergès, who was already what he is today: a cynical intermediary between the worlds of terrorism and the courts? Along with the members of his collective, he demanded, at the very least, *Nuremberg for Algeria*.[118] In November 1961, he wrote publicly to Dr. Servatius, who had just defended Adolf Eichmann in Jerusalem:[119] "In arrogating to yourselves the right to judge Eichmann, you are creating a precedent for those colonized peoples interested in judging their former masters, you told the judges of Israel. But did you think that so numerous a new clientele was already in the offing—that of the neo-colonialists? You certainly did, since despite the 45,000 fresh corpses in the Constantinois, you did not think of making that comparison in 1946."[120] The allusion to the massacres of 1945, which had occurred amidst the enthusiasm of victory, is significant, but it is also remarkable that the Jerusalem trial served as a point of reference. In Vergès's eyes, Israel, at the time, was the symbol not of colonialism but of decolonization.

In those days, in any event, the word genocide often was heard, particularly from the mouths of the Algerian lawyers Maîtres Oussedik and Ben Abdallah, and everyone saw in it an allusion to the genocide of the Jews. I myself did not employ the word, but I could quote texts that I signed or declarations I made in which the idea surfaced.

The Vietnam War followed the Algerian war as a point of fixation for intellectual and student protest—we approach the period in which the street slogan "CRS-SS" could be heard. On December 1, 1967, the Russell Tribunal, meeting at Roskilde (Denmark) condemned the United States for genocide of the Vietnamese people. As a founder (along with Laurent Schwartz, who was one of the judges) of the National Vietnam Committee, I unsuccessfully intervened to try to prevent a decision that I did not find reasonable. In the December issue of *Les Temps modernes*, Jean-Paul Sartre published his report on genocide, in which, pressured by the Turkish judge and his Pakistani colleague, he had stricken the history of the Armenian genocide from the pages of history. Such is the serenity of "justice."

It has always seemed difficult to me to situate colonial war crimes in relation to those of the Nazis. Responding to General Massu, I wrote, in 1972, that he was "less guilty than Eichmann and more guilty than Klaus Barbie."[121] As far as the number of victims went, I was certainly right. It is even correct to say that many of those victims were innocent according to the French law of the time. There remained, however, the case of the children of Izieu and their fate, which I was unaware of at the time, the only crime of which Klaus Barbie personally claimed to be innocent.

In the interim, the image of Israel had undergone a profound change, not in the Arab countries, for which the country constituted a foreign colony implanted in the Arab world, consisting of former "protégés" (*dhimmi*) who had banded together to form a state, but in Africa, in a large part of the Third World, and for all that was designated in vague terms as the new European left. That representation corresponded to facts that were by no means mythical. Israel prior to 1967 was, to be sure, a society built through a colonial process,[122] but it was not or was only very incompletely (as a result of the expulsion of the majority of the Palestinians) a colonial society. The conquest of the rest of Palestine created two societies locked in a mortal embrace and resulted in their rapid evolution toward a situation of apartheid. Even today the process has not been completed, but how is one to deny the evidence? Now the Israelis were Jews, which was not a favorable sign in the Arab world, which was a matter of indifference for a large part of the Third World, and which, from having been a positive sign in Europe, after the great massacre, was tending, according to a classical process, to reverse itself: once again the victims were becoming executioners. Already in 1967, a German newspaper of the extreme right, *Deutsche National und Soldatenzeitung*, ran the headline: "The Israeli Auschwitz in the Desert." Israel appeared as the enemy of the Third World. The reasoning underlying that schema involved, to be sure, some enormous simplifications. The idea of a Third World that would be pure suffering opposed to a purely exploitative West masks a number of essential conflicts. Should Saudi Arabia, for example, be taken as a Third World country? It was forgotten that black slaves had been sold and delivered by their black masters and that the Arabs had played a crucial role in that trade. Bloody events in Rwanda, Indonesia, and Cambodia revealed that the Third World had attained, dare I say, the dignity of genocide. And what is one to say of the current war between Iraq (which was the agressor) and Iran, which has been going on since 1980?

The Israeli invasion of Lebanon on June 7, 1982, the massacres of Sabra and Shatila in September, under the protection of the Israeli army, aggravated matters for Israel and, as a result, for the Jews. Not that the invasion had been, as was said at the time, a "genocide of the Lebanese-Palestinian people," and not that the siege of Beirut could be compared with the destruction of the Warsaw ghetto. But we were all the same able to see Annie Kriegel at the time attempting to play Faurisson, walking, as it were, both sides of the street: trying to explain, on the one hand, that the number of victims at Sabra and Shatila was in fact infinitesimal and, on the other, suggesting that the real killers might well have been not the Phalangists allied with Israel, but quite simply the Russians.[123] And to be sure, following the massacres, there was the enormous demonstration in Tel Aviv, the only true protest against the war in Lebanon, as well as a commission of inquiry—which was infinitely more responsible and more serious than the "Commission de sauvegarde" established by Guy Mollet in 1957—but the innocence of Israel was dead.

None is this is retrospective. The worst crimes that might be committed by Israel would not be justified by Treblinka, but conversely they do not change a single bit the totally criminal nature of Auschwitz and Treblinka. The present may transform the *image* of what the past was; it has no possibility of transforming the past itself in its reality. But it is true that men no more live on truth alone than on bread.

The Klaus Barbie trial (May 11–July 4, 1987) was going to put that change of values to the test. Before surrounding himself (as if to symbolize the unity of the Third World) with a Congolese lawyer, Maître M'Bemba, and an Algerian lawyer, Maître Bouaïta, between Bolivia's delivery (or sale) of Barbie on February 6, 1983 and the opening of the trial in May of 1987, Maître Vergès had carefully prepared the terrain.

It was to be a trial between the France that had emerged (quite distantly) from the Resistance and the Nazi police chief, the expediter of Jewish adults and children, a torturer and murderer of members of the Resistance. It was a trial with multiple parties, since it introduced the France of Vichy and that of the Algerian war, the state of Israel posited as a symbol of evil, on an equal footing with the Nazi state, the Jewish "collaboration" and a West guilty in its entirety of colonialism, not to mention a Resistance movement whose tensions and even betrayals it distorted with a number of perfectly monstrous accusations.[124] The Algerian war served as a launching pad. After recalling that he was bringing suit on behalf of Algerian clients for "crimes against humanity," Vergès declared to an Algerian weekly in Paris, which was devoting an issue to the twenty-fifth anniversary of the pogrom of October 17, 1961, that the high court of appeal should state "whether a crime against humanity is only a crime committed by some Nazis against some Jews, or whether it involves a crime that is far more serious, far more current, and far more frightening for the future: the crime committed by imperialists against peoples struggling for their liberation."[125] *Some* Nazis, *some* Jews: the words were not chosen accidentally; they were part of a rewriting of history. Vergès was to pursue that campaign in Algeria in April 1987,[126] which resulted in the publication, between April and June, of some violently anti-Semitic attacks (directed in particular against Jean Daniel) in the Algerian weeklies *Algérie-Actualité* and *Révolution africaine*.

But beyond the "Vergès case,"[127] it is true that the Klaus Barbie trial ran up against some unbearable contradictions from which no one quite managed to extricate himself.[128]

There were contradictions in the accusation. Barbie was indicted and judged for "crimes against humanity" (it was the first such trial in France). But what is a *crime against humanity*? According to the statute of the international military tribunal at Nuremberg (Article 6c) it was a matter of "atrocities or crimes including, but not restricted to, murder, extermination, enslavement, deportation, imprisonment, torture, rape or other inhuman acts committed against any civilian population, or persecution for political, racial, or religious reasons, with or without violation of the internal laws of the country in which such acts were perpetrated." But there is a kind of crime against humanity that is, dare I say, of a higher order, and that is genocide. Defined by the International Convention on Genocide, unanimously ratified by the United Nations on December 9, 1951, genocide is defined as the extermination of national, ethnic, racial, or religious—but *not* economic or social—groups. The convention, for example, does not concern the massacre of the kulaks. A fine convention that has never been applied, governments being hesitant to prosecute themselves.

The prosecution at Lyon had intended to restrict its accusation to complicity in genocide, that is, to Barbie's role in the deportation and death of Jews (thus excluding the torture, murder, and deportation of members of the Resistance, which were considered war crimes, and thus covered by the ten-year statute of limitations). But the criminal chamber of the Supreme Court, in a decision of December 20, 1985, had retained a less restrictive definition of crimes against humanity: "Inhuman acts and persecution which, *in the name of a State practicing a policy of ideological hegemony* [my emphasis], have been committed systematically not only against individuals for reason of their belonging to a racial or religious group, but also against adversaries of that policy, whatever the form of their opposition." This allowed for the deportation of members of the Resistance to be judged as a crime against humanity (without statute of limitations, unlike war crimes). Maître Vergès was openly jubilant at this decision: in his view, it opened up the possibility of arguing that France also—in Indochina, in Madagascar, and in Algeria—had committed crimes identical to those condemned in the text instituting the international military tribunal at Nuremberg.

And that being the case, one had to be logical: if one were to try Barbie, one would have to try those French citizens responsible for colonial crimes, which were as imprescriptible as those

of the Nazi torturer. But if one refused to admit that the crimes
of the French army were crimes—without statute of limitation—
against humanity, then one would also have to forgo trying Barbie . . . at least for equivalent crimes.

That logical contradiction cannot be swept away with a wave
of the hand. But it is perhaps not as clear-cut as Vergès claims.
First of all because his own logic is interrupted at midpoint: if he
equates the crimes of the French army with those of Nazism,
then he ought to extend that equation to other crimes, such as
that of Melouza, the village exterminated by the FLN at the end
of May 1957—something he is careful not to do.

But it is the very principle of the identification of the crimes
we committed with Hitler's genocide, as argued by Vergès, that
is debatable. Those French crimes were amnestied by our government on March 22 and April 14, 1962, without any distinction between "war crimes" and "crimes against humanity." The
imprescribility of those latter crimes, moreover, was instated
in French law only *after* the amnesty decrees, on December 26,
1964; it was not, in fact, until that date that the international
legislation adopted at Nuremberg was integrated into our national law. And no one at the time was thinking of France: only
the Nazi crimes were at issue. It is true that the latter had been
committed in the name of an inherently criminal ideology,
whereas the ideology of French Algeria proclaimed, in theory,
the equality of Algerians and Frenchmen within the French Republic, not the superiority of the latter over the former. Guy
Mollet's French government discreetly authorized torture; he did
not proclaim, *urbi et orbi*, the right to torture. In 1961, at the
time of the putsch attempt by the four generals, I heard the following argument being formulated: in what way is a Gaullist
bullet any less murderous than a "putschist" bullet? And there
was some truth to the argument. It is nonetheless the case that
democratic institutions and the existence of public opinion *also*
allowed for negotiations to progress.

The crimes of Massu, Bigeard, and Robert Lacoste were

against the laws of the republic, whereas those of Himmler and Eichmann were in *conformity* with Hitler's principles, and that establishes an essential difference between the two, contrary to the claims of J. Vergès. Is that a reason to whitewash the former? I still do not believe that to be the case.

Let us, however, temporarily accept the argument: the contradiction implicit in the Barbie trial remains, since a number of individuals guilty of participating in the genocide of the Jews, such as Messieurs Leguay or Papon, have still not been tried. With the passage of time, states do not like to judge those who have embodied their will.

Conversely, the defense itself was caught in the trap. It could not allow itself to "faurissonize," and the word was used, as designating a contemptible act, by Maître Bouaïta during his arguments on July 2, 1987.[129] But it also had to attempt to get Barbie acquitted, to present him as innocent, to explain that the torture inflicted was imaginary, and above all that a document (the telegram recounting the Izieu operation and signed by Barbie) could only be a forgery since it came from the Centre de Documentation Juive Contemporaine, which Maître Vergès regards (as did Paul Rassinier) as a factory of forgeries.[130]

Does an attempt to gain the acquittal of a torturer and a killer amount to a defense of the Algerians? Maître Vergès, in his way, revived what had been one of the temptations of the Arab world colonized by England and France: an alliance with Hitler's Germany. But it was the democracies, as Maître Rappaport has recalled, which, after much bloodshed, ended up emancipating the colonies. The very idea of a struggle against the Algerian war would have been inconceivable under a totalitarian regime. Two former Algerian leaders, Hocine Aït Ahmed and Mohammed Harbi, have said as much: "One does not defend a torturer by exhibiting other torturers, even if they were our enemies in the recent past. . . . Our struggle during the colonization can and should be identified with the struggle of the French Resistance during the German Occupation." It is preferable then to defend today human rights in newly independent countries rather than to defend someone who could have been their executioner.[131]

Insurmountable contradictions, no doubt, for anyone dreaming of a coherent system of justice, but not without an educational upshot: the screening of the film *Shoah* before an immense audience is reinstating the rights of a memory that has once again come close to being murdered.

7. *The Confusion of Feelings*

The months of the trial were also, in France, the time of an unprecedented "revisionist" offensive, with (among other treats) the publication of the first two issues of the *Annales d'histoire révisionniste*. But the important issue is not that, but rather a certain banalization of the phenomenon. Already, in April, the satirical periodical *Zéro* had initiated an investigation and published parallel interviews with P. Guillaume, the leader of the sect disseminating the gospel according to Faurisson, with Faurisson himself, and with the author of these pages, who had not been informed of that format, and whose "text" had not been shown to him. In May a political tract[132] arrived at the Lycée Voltaire with the suggestion that it be distributed to student delegates, several of whom are minors. The principal, who is neither a Nazi nor an anti-Semite, calmly followed the suggestion, and distributed the tract under the official stamp of the lycée, without even an explanatory note.[133] On May 28 the "Letters to the Editor" section of *Libération* published two revisionist letters, which provoked a rather devastating response the following day from Serge July—who has not always been so meticulous in such matters—and the dismissal of the person in charge of the letters section.

Other tracts continue to circulate, including one by a man who claims he spent forty-seven months at Mauthausen, and I see no reason not to take him at his word. Let us examine those various documents a bit. Nine years after the campaign began, the arguments have not budged at all. We are confronted with the discourse of a sect, which is totally incapable of evolving, of responding to arguments, or even of broaching the debate that it so vociferously demands. It is indeed a religious sect—or perhaps several sects—characterized by a taurine incapacity to communicate with anyone who does not immediately enter into their frame of thought, the signal feature of sects.

Let us look at the two letters to *Libération*. One is at the level of technical argumentation, so dear to Faurisson: how much fuel would have been necessary to transport, gas, and burn four million human beings at Auschwitz? The figure is false, of course, but is described as "commonly accepted." The second is not specifically about gas chambers, but claims that massacres, all massacres, from that of the Jews to that of the Palestinians, by way of Dresden and Hiroshima, are the pure application of the logic of capitalism. Maintaining that there was one camp in the war that was infinitely worse than the other is tantamount to "according a meaning to that unequaled killing, which created tens of millions of victims, for can it be admitted that such a hecatomb was needed to reabsorb the economic crisis of 1929 and allow capitalism to start off afresh on the right foot?"

The tract distributed at the Lycée Voltaire and elsewhere adds this note: "Hitler did not want any more Jews in Europe. As of 1933, the Jews wanted a general war against him. And the crusade of the democracies is what they got. England and France declared war on Hitler. . . . Germany at war treated Jews as the enemies they were, pursued and interned them. NEVER EXTERMINATED THEM. The German people paid the bill in firebombing and deportations, with massacres added on." The Germans are simultaneously the victims of the Jews and, by way of capitalism, their beneficiaries. "The Jews will never allow the Deutschmark to be endangered. It is the currency of their 'reparations.'"

Let us cut short these quotations. Which are enough to make one throw up. But what is to be done? Every society has its sects and its madmen. Punishing them would serve only to work toward their proliferation. It is with such individuals as with secret police agents or spies. Once they have been identified it is best to keep an eye on them and not let them out of sight. If they are arrested or expelled, others will show up to replace them and will be harder to locate. Judicial punishment is a dangerous weapon and can be turned against those using it. The lawsuit brought against Faurisson in 1978 by several antiracist associations ended with a decision by the Paris Court of Appeals on April 26, 1983, which recognized the seriousness of Faurisson's work—which is quite outrageous—and finally found him guilty only of having acted malevolently by summarizing his theses as slogans. Germany has experimented with legislation specifically aimed at deniers of the genocide.[134] Judging from the quantity of openly or discreetly revisionist publications in that country, one is hard put to view the effort as very successful. Perhaps contempt is a more effective weapon.

I am not, however, saying that the judicial weapon should never be used. There is a law against defamation and a law aimed at racist activities. In California, the institute financing revisionist activities had proposed a sum of $50,000 to whoever could prove the existence of a gas chamber. A citizen, Mr. Mermelstein, who had seen part of his family disappear at Auschwitz, accepted the challenge. Naturally, the conditions under which evidence was to be presented were such that only a dead person would have been an acceptable witness. The money was thus not awarded for reason of insufficient evidence. The candidate filed a suit, his case was heard, a settlement was reached under the supervision of the Los Angeles Superior Court, and the Institute for Historical Review apologized to the plaintiff and paid the promised amount.[135] Which is all to the good provided that one does not ask the courts to establish a point of history, but only a point of law. For to endorse such a request would be tantamount to accrediting the idea of two historical schools, one of which may crush the other. For there are not two historical schools, or rather, there are many more, and along with them there are those who say no and who will always say no. "It is not for the historian to attempt to convince Faurisson if the latter 'is playing' in a different mode of discourse, in which conviction, the obtaining of a consensus concerning a definite reality, is not at stake. If the historian persists in that path, he will find himself in the position of a victim." Such, according to Jean-François Lyotard, is the *differend*.[136] Any man has the ability to say: no, to all comers, and even to win disciples in the process. There are heroic forms of negation, and perverse ones as well.

Does this mean that one should capitulate in the face of such denial, sliding bit by bit toward a world in which all things are equivalent, the historian and the forger, fantasy and reality, massacres and car accidents?

> Twentieth century, old junkshop
> Feverish and problem-ridden.[137]

Plainly, we will have to come to terms with the fact that the world has its Faurissons, as it has its pimps and its pornographic film clubs. But there can be no question of yielding any ground to him.

It is not enough, in this matter, to be, on the whole, on the right side of the issue. What is needed is ceaseless work, the establishment of facts, not for those who know them and who are about to disappear, but for those who are legitimately demanding as to the quality of the evidence. Such archeological labor was useless in 1945, because the ruins were still steaming and the witnesses crying out; today it has become indispensable.[138]

One should also stop laying oneself open to the criticism not of the revisionists, whose opinion is of little import, but of the well-motivated. There is currently no historian, to be sure, who is prepared to retain the figure of four million human beings disappearing in Auschwitz. A million deaths is a reasonable—however enormous—hypothesis.[139] But it is true that the figure of four million is officially indicated all over Auschwitz through the auspices of the Poles, and Claude Lanzmann was wrong to write that "the most serious estimates hover around three and a half million."[140] I follow him more willingly when he writes, "One has to observe and ascertain, ascertain and observe. It is a wrenching task."[141] Ascertaining and observing also means extricating from those who maintain it the quasi-monopolistic hold on memory that they have arrogated to themselves and that they present to the public of the mass media. No need to name them, the reference will be understood. As for the rest . . .

8. *In the Guise of a Conclusion*

As I was preparing this melancholic essay, my friend François Gèze acquainted me with a tango by the Argentine poet Enrique Santos Discépolo. It seemed to him—and to myself as well— that it described rather well this world of ours, in which, all the same, there sprout every now and then a few flowers of truth that instill hope and whose gardener, along with many others, I do my best to be, without for all that knowing how to set things aright. Here it is, then:

Cambalache

That the world was and always will be a sty
I know quite well.
In fifteen hundred six
And in the year two thousand too.
That there have always been crooks,
Swindlers and dupes,
The contented and the embittered,
morality and lies.
But that the twentieth century is a torrent
of insolent nastiness
No one any longer denies.
We live in a flood of scum
and in the same mud,
All of us manipulated.

Today it's all the same
whether one's loyal or betrays,

Ignorant, erudite, robber,
generous or a con man.
Everything's the same!
Nothing's better than anything else!
A jackass the same as
A great professor!
There is neither punishment nor reward,
Immorality has leveled us.
Whether your life's a fake
Or you pursue your ambition,
Who cares if you're a priest,
a mattress-maker, king of spades,
mule-headed or a son of a bitch?

What a lack of respect,
What an insult to reason!
Anyone can be a lord!
Anyone a thief!
Mixed up with Stavisky
you'll find Don Bosco and the whore,
Don Chicho and Napoleon,
Carnera and San Martín . . .
As in the contemptuous storefronts
of the old junkshops,
Everything in life gets mixed together,
and wounded by an unsheathed sword,
you can watch the Bible weep against a water-heater.

Twentieth century, old junkshop
Feverish and problem-ridden.
Ask for nothing and you'll get nothing,
and if you don't steal you're a fool.
Go ahead then, don't worry.
We'll all meet up in hell's oven!
Don't think about it any more, stay in your corner,
No one cares if you were born honest.
It's all the same: the guy who slaves
Night and day like an ox,
The one who lives off of his girls,

The one who kills, the one who cures
Or the one who has become an outlaw.

Will truth have the last word? How one would like to be sure of it . . .

Notes

Foreword

1. For an evocation of Vidal-Naquet's contributions as a historian of ancient Greece, see Bernard Knox, "Greece à la française" in *Essays Ancient and Modern* (Baltimore: Johns Hopkins University Press, 1989), pp. 77–91, and Knox's preface to Vidal-Naquet, *The Black Hunter* (Baltimore: Johns Hopkins University Press, 1986). Among Vidal-Naquet's overtly political works, see *L'Affaire Audin* (Paris: Minuit, 1958); *La Torture dans la République* (Paris: Minuit, 1972); *Les Crimes de l'armée française* (Paris: Maspero, 1977).

2. Concerning the emergence of the term *intellectual* at the time of the Affair, see Jean Denis Bredin, *The Affair: The Case of Alfred Dreyfus*, translated by J. Mehlman (New York: George Braziller, 1985), part III, chapter 3, "Logicians of the Absolute."

3. P. Vidal-Naquet, "Les Juifs de France et l'assimilation" in *Les Juifs, la mémoire, et le présent*, volume I (Paris: Maspero, 1981), p. 78.

4. Ibid., p. 81.

5. See Hannah Arendt, *The Origins of Totalitarianism* (New York: Harcourt, Brace, Jovanovich, 1951). The most eloquent case for affirming a connection between the two sequences was probably made by Charles Maurras, the old royalist and anti-Dreyfusard leader, who upon being sentenced to life imprisonment in 1945 for collaborating with the enemy, exclaimed: "This is Dreyfus's revenge." See G. London, *Le Procès Maurras* (Lyon: Roger Bonnefon, 1945), p. 212.

6. Vidal-Naquet, *Les Juifs*, I:88.

7. Ibid., pp. 81, 110.

8. For a discussion of the Darquier interview and its aftermath, see Henry Weinberg, *The Myth of the Jew in France, 1967–1982* (New York: Mosaic Press, 1987), pp. 59–64.

9. Quoted in ibid., p. 62.

10. The article is reproduced in Faurisson's *Mémoire en défense: contre ceux qui m'accusent de falsifier l'histoire* (Paris: La Vieille Taupe, 1980), pp. 73–75.

11. Olga Wormser-Migot, *Le système concentrationnaire nazi* (Paris: P.U.F., 1968).

12. The letter appeared on January 16, 1979, in *Le Monde*, p. 13, and is reproduced in Faurisson, *Mémoire en défense*, pp. 84–88.

13. C. Colombani, "Des universitaires s'affrontent sur le cas Faurisson," in *Le Monde*, June 30, 1981.

14. Faurisson has discussed the verdict in "My Life as a Revisionist (September 1983 to September 1987)," *Journal of Historical Review* (Spring 1989):5–6.

15. C. Colombani, "Des universitaires."

16. Guy Hocquenghem, preface to Heinz Heger, *Les Hommes au triangle rose* (Paris: Persona, 1981), p. 9. The passage is discussed in Alain Finkielkraut, *L'Avenir d'une négation: Réflexion sur la question du génocide* (Paris: Seuil, 1983), pp. 159–161.

17. Reference to the gas chamber issue as a touchstone of French culture is to be found in ads for a Faurisson videotape in the *Journal of Historical Review*. See also Lyotard, *Le Différend* (Paris: Minuit, 1983), p. 16: "The plaintiff objects that he has been deceived concerning the existence of the gas chambers, that is, concerning what has been called the Final Solution. His argument is: to identify a site as a gas chamber, I shall accept as a valid witness only a victim of such a gas chamber; now according to my adversary, such victims can only be dead; otherwise the gas chamber would not be what it is claimed to be; thus there are no gas chambers."

18. See Finkielkraut, *L'Avenir d'une négation*, pp. 74–78.

19. "Narration et pouvoir" in *Change 38, La Machine à conter* (October 1979):110.

20. Faurisson has attached much weight to Martin Broszat's letter to *Die Zeit*, published in the August 19, 1960 edition of that newspaper under the title "Keine Vergasung in Dachau" ["No Gassing in Dachau"]. Broszat became director of the Institute of Contemporary History in Munich. See Faurisson, *Mémoire en défense*, pp. 179–221, "Une Révision déchirante de la thèse officielle (1960)."

21. In "The Faurisson Affair: His Right to Say It," in *The Nation* (Feb-

ruary 28, 1981, p. 231), Chomsky writes that his text was originally written not as a preface but as a statement about the civil libertarian aspects of the affair, which he sent off to a Faurisson associate, "telling him to use it as he wished."

22. N. Chomsky, preface to Faurisson, *Mémoire en défense*, p. xii.

23. P. Vidal-Naquet, "Flavius Josèphe et Masada" in *Les Juifs*, I:43–72.

24. Arno J. Mayer, *Why Did the Heavens Not Darken?: The "Final Solution" in History* (New York: Pantheon, 1988).

25. The innovation of their inclusion in Mayer's bibliography may be gauged by considering their absence from as representative a work as Michael Marrus, *The Holocaust in History* (New York: Meridian, 1987).

26. Mayer, *Why Did the Heavens Not Darken?*, p. 451.

27. Butz's review appeared in the *Journal of Historical Review* 9(3) (Fall 1989).

28. Faurisson's review appeared in the *Journal of Historical Review* 9(3) (Fall 1989):375–380. Passage cited is from Mayer, *Why Did the Heavens Not Darken?*, pp. 362–363.

29. "Pierre Vidal-Naquet's Friend" is a subtitle of Faurisson's review, p. 375.

30. Mayer, *Why Did the Heavens Not Darken?*, p. 349.

31. Vidal-Naquet has published a strikingly ambivalent preface to the French edition of Mayer's book, *La "Solution finale" dans l'histoire* (Paris: La Découverte, 1990), reprinted in *Les Juifs, la mémoire, et le présent*, volume II (Paris: La Découverte, 1991), pp. 235–266. In it he denounces Lucy Dawidowicz's attack (*Commentary*, October 1989) on the book for "revisionist" tendencies, but ends up rejecting Mayer's assertion that sources for the study of the gas chambers are "rare and unreliable" on the basis of a volume published after Mayer's own work: J.-C. Pressac, *Auschwitz: Technique and Operation of the Gas Chambers* (New York: Beate Klarsfeld Foundation, 1989).

32. Faurisson, *Mémoire en défense*, p. 3.

33. This point is also made by Finkielkraut, *L'Avenir d'une négation*, p. 18.

34. For a critique of this legislation, see Tzvetan Todorov, "Racism," *Salmagundi* 88–89 (Fall 1990–Winter 1991):47–53.

35. Ibid., p. 49.
36. The two texts are *L'Antisémitisme* and *Contre l'antisémitisme* (Paris: Editions de la Différence, 1982 and 1983). Vidal-Naquet has written a brief essay on the circumstances of Guillaume's republication of Lazare's work as well as on the use French anti-Semites have traditionally made of the first of these texts. See "Sur une réédition," in *Les Juifs*, II:85–87.
37. R. Faurisson, *A-t-on lu Lautréamont?* (Paris: Gallimard, 1972), p. 19.
38. See Finkielkraut, *L'Avenir d'une négation*, chapter 1, "L'ouvrier, martyr et sauveur," pp. 15–58.
39. *Notre royaume est une prison*, supplement to *La Guerre sociale* 3, October 1980.

Preface

1. "A Paper Eichmann" and its appendix, "Zyklon B," which I owe to Pitch Bloch, appeared in *Esprit* (September 1980):8–56; "On Faurisson and Chomsky" in the same journal in January 1981, pp. 205–208; these texts were subsequently reprinted in my anthology *Les Juifs*, I:195–289. "Theses on Revisionism" is my contribution to the colloquium at the École des Hautes Etudes en Sciences Sociales, *L'Allemagne nazie et le génocide juif* (Paris: Gallimard/Le Seuil, 1985), pp. 496–516, and is reprinted with the agreement of its first publishers. (An English version of the French volume has appeared as *Unanswered Questions: Nazi Germany and the Genocide of the Jews*, edited by F. Furet [New York: Schocken, 1989].) I have taken the occasion of this republication to either make minor corrections or complete my documentation. "On the Side of the Persecuted" is an article published in *Le Monde* on April 15, 1981.
2. I have borrowed the term, with his permission, from Yosef Yerushalmi, the author of *Zakhor: Jewish History and Jewish Memory* (New York: Schocken, 1982). Yerushalmi used it with reference to the "revisionists" on June 3, 1987, during a colloquium on forgetting—*L'Oubli*—organized by Editions du Seuil at Royaumont.
3. Ibid.
4. I regretted at the time that "A Paper Eichmann" had been presented on the cover of *Esprit* as a "Response to Faurisson and Several Others"; I protested against the presentation by the journal *Zéro* (April 1987) of

interviews conducted by Michel Folco under the banner "Exclusive: Faurisson vs. Vidal-Naquet."

5. For the same reason I do not reply, when addressed personally, to the lies accumulated by these "scholars," certain of which approach the grotesque (see, for example, P. Guillaume's preface to R. Faurisson, *Réponse à Pierre Vidal-Naquet*, or *Annales d'histoire révisionniste* 1 (Spring 1987):175.

1. A Paper Eichmann

1. "La politique hitlérienne d'extermination. Une déclaration d'historiens."

2. The texts published by *Esprit* in September 1980 dealt with Cambodia as well as with Auschwitz. At stake was the possibility of linking a totalitarian system and a practice of murder. I refer the reader to the issue, specifically to the responses of P. Thibaud and S. Thion.

3. Translation by Jeffrey Mehlman.

4. Marvin Harris, *Cannibals and Kings: The Origins of Culture* (New York: Random House, 1978); the phrase in quotation marks is taken from Marshal Sahlins's admirable review of the book in the *New York Review of Books*, November 23, 1978. Note that Harris would account not only for masculine supremacy but for the Oedipus complex (pp. 57–66).

5. W. Arens, *The Man-Eating Myth* (Oxford: Oxford University Press, 1979). A review by Rodney Needham, "Chewing on the Cannibals," may be found in the *Times Literary Supplement* of January 25, 1980; the February, March, and April issues returned on numerous occasions to the alleged debate. Marshall Sahlins had already said what he had to say in the *New York Review of Books* of March 22, 1979.

6. *New York Review of Books*, March 22, 1979, p. 47.

7. *Auschwitz ou le grand alibi*, p. 5. The italicized passages are underlined by the authors. This document was republished by its authors at the beginning of 1979, after the scandal provoked by Darquier de Pellepoix's statement to the effect that the only victims gassed at Auschwitz were lice (*Express*, October 28, 1978). A new preface clarified the position held at the time by the "Bordiguistes." I quote from the Vieille Taupe edition, and it is insofar as it expresses the Vieille Taupe position that the brochure interests me in this context.

8. Ibid., pp. 6–7.

9. Ibid., p. 9.

10. For the history of Joël Brand's mission, see the (quite personal) testimony of André Biss, *Un million de Juifs à sauver* (Paris: Grasset, 1966) and the analysis by Y. Bauer, *The Holocaust in Historical Perspective* (Seattle: University of Washington Press, 1978), pp. 94–155.

11. *Auschwitz ou le grand alibi*, p. 11.

12. Serge Thion, ed., *Vérité historique ou vérité politique?* (Paris: La Vieille Taupe, 1980), p. 139. Future references to this work will be under the title *Vérité*.

13. *Le Mensonge d'Ulysse* (sixth edition, 1979); *Ulysse trahi par les siens, Compléments au Mensonge d'Ulysse*, a new and considerably enlarged edition.

14. One has to be unable to read in order to write, as has J.-G. Cohn-Bendit (*Libération*, March 5, 1979, and *Vérité*, p. 133): "The mass murder occurred, something which neither Rassinier nor Faurisson call into question."

15. On this virtual *polycracy* of totalitarian systems, we at last have in French the crucial work of F. Neumann, *Béhémoth: Structure et pratique du national-socialisme* (Paris: Payot, 1987). It has taken forty-four years, and sixteen to translate Martin Broszat's *L'Etat hitlérien* (Paris: Fayard, 1986), which insists—perhaps excessively—on such polycracy.

16. Speech delivered at Posen before the Reichsleiter and Gauleiter on October 6, 1943; Himmler, *Geheimreden 1933 bis 1945 und andere Ansprachen* (Frankfurt, Berlin, and Vienna: Propyläen Verlag, 1974), p. 169. The edition is introduced by J. C. Fest and edited by B. F. Smith and A. F. Peterson.

17. Ibid., p. 201.

18. Materials on the Korherr report may be found in G. Wellers's excellent booklet, *La Solution finale et la Mythomanie néo-nazie*, edited by B. Klarsfeld and S. Klarsfeld (Paris, 1978), pp. 41–84.

19. One is embarrassed to have to recall this fact in the face of Rassinier's (and then Thion's, p. 164) denials. For published details, see the document signed personally by Himmler on January 6, 1942 (instructions for executions) in *Eichmann par Eichmann*, edited by P. Joffroy and K. Königseder (Paris: Grasset, 1970), pp. 257–258. As a matter of course, documents from Auschwitz combine two categories of death, "natural death" and S.B. (*Sonderbehandlung*): cf. *Dokumenty i Mater-*

ialy z czasów okupacji niemeckiej w Polsce, I, Obozy (Lodz: N. Blumental, 1946), p. 118. *Sonderbehandlung* could also have a perfectly benign sense.

20. J.-P. Faye, *Théorie du récit: Introduction aux "Langages totalitaires"*, (Paris: Hermann, 1972); *Langages totalitaires*, (Paris: Hermann, 1972).

21. "Mauthausen," *Revue d'histoire de la Deuxième Guerre mondiale* 15–16 (July-September 1954):41–80.

22. This was a principal point of the declaration by historians published in *Le Monde* (February 21, 1979), which I initiated and composed along with Léon Poliakov. A similar objective motivated the articles by O. Wormser-Migot (*Le Monde*, December 29, 1979) and F. Delpech (*Le Monde*, March 8, 1979, and "La persécution nazie et l'attitude de Vichy," *Historiens et Géographes* 273 [May-June 1979]:591–635).

23. There were gas chambers which were not put into service, whatever certain deportees and investigators may claim: such was the case for Dachau. I see no reason to doubt the existence of those of Ravensbrück, Struthof, and Mauthausen. Concerning the last named camp, P. S. Choumoff's demonstration, *Les Chambres à gaz de Mauthausen* (Paris: Amicale des déportés de Mauthausen, 1978), convincingly refutes the few pages on the subject by O. Wormser-Migot (*Le système concentrationnaire nazi*, pp. 541–544) and has effectively convinced historians such as P. Renouvin and J.-B. Duroselle. (This study has subsequently been continued by the same author in two articles in *Le Monde juif* 122/123 [April–June and July–September 1986]; the retractions of Michel de Boüard—an author who, in the study mentioned in n. 21, had spoken of a gas chamber at Mauthausen—which appeared in *Ouest-France*, August 2–3, 1986, have not yet taken the form of a demonstration.) Concerning Ravensbrück, see G. Tillion, *Ravensbrück* (Paris: Seuil, 1973).

24. Everyone can fill in what I have sketched here. The names of Christian Bernadec, Silvain Reiner, and Jean-François Steiner come immediately to mind. See Cynthia Haft's beautiful article, "Ecrire la déportation: Le sensationnel, avilissement du tragique" in *Le Monde*, February 25, 1972, and the conclusion of her book, *The Theme of Nazi Concentration Camps in French Literature* (The Hague and Paris: Mouton, 1973), pp. 190–191. See also R. Errerra, "La déportation comme best-

seller" in *Esprit* (December 1969):918–921. I myself have denounced
one of the most infamous of such falsifications, Sylvain Reiner's *Et la
terre sera pure* (Paris: Fayard, 1969; see *Le nouvel observateur*, December 8, 1969), and contributed, along with Roger Errera, to the banning
of that book for its pirating of *Medecin à Auschwitz* by M. Nyiszli. On
the other hand I fell into the trap laid by J.-F. Steiner's *Treblinka* (Paris:
Fayard, 1966); cf. my article in *Le Monde*, May 2, 1966, whose substance I do not retract.

25. C. Hauter, "Réflexion d'un rescapé" in *De l'Université aux camps
de concentration: Témoignages strasbourgeois* (Paris: Belles-Lettres,
1954), pp. 525–526.

26. V. Grossmann, *L'Enfer de Treblinka* (Grenoble and Paris: Arthaud, 1945, repr. 1966); for a serious study, cf. A. Ruckert, *NS Vernichtungslager in Spiegel deutscher Strafprozesse* (Munich: DTV, 1979)
or A. Donat, *The Death Camp Treblinka* (New York: The Holocaust
Library, 1979); I know only through the public praise it has received
from R. Hilberg Y. Arad's book, *Belzec, Sobibor, Treblinka: The Operation Reinhard Death Camps* (Bloomington: Indiana University
Press, 1987).

27. R. Hilberg arrives at a figure of 5,100,000 victims; see the concluding charts in *The Destruction of the European Jews* (New York:
Holmes and Meier, 1985), p. 767.

28. S. Klarsfeld, *Le Mémorial de la déportation des Juifs de France*
(Paris: Ed. Klarsfeld, 1978). A supplement has been published subsequently. This work is based for the most part on German police records;
it calls for a number of rectifications, and will certainly call for others
in the future, but it constitutes a good starting point. For a more recent
treatment, cf. G. Wellers, *Le Monde juif* (July-September 1980):75–
101.

29. Faurisson (*Vérité*) presents the numerical results of the investigations of the Comité d'histoire de la Seconde Guerre mondiale concerning the total number of racial or nonracial deportees as inaccessible.
Concerning the latter category, their total number may be found in J.-P.
Azéma, *De Munich à la Libération* (Paris: Seuil, 1979), p. 189: 63,000
deportees, of which 41,000 were members of the Resistance. Returning
full steam in a brochure written to answer me (cf. *infra*, n. 81), Faurisson (p. 31) gave the estimated figure of the Comité pour les Juifs:
28,162. Having consulted the *Bulletin du Comité d'histoire de la Deux-*

ieme Guerre mondiale 205 (May-June 1973), 206 (July-August 1973), 208 (November-December 1973) and 212 (August-September 1974), the committee realized that it had arrived at an absurd figure. One more hoax, then.

30. There are not only ideologues. Nazi persecution is occasionally exploited by run of the mill con men; cf., for example, C. Lipsky, *L'Affaire* (Paris: Presses de la Cité, 1977), pp. 53 and 76. This administrator of "Le Patrimoine foncier," a crooked firm, compares himself to Tristan Bernard saying after his arrest: "Until now we have lived in fear; now we shall live in hope."

31. Thion (*Vérité*, p. 341) has given only a very incomplete list of this literature. For a listing of such publications, see *infra* my "Theses on Revisionism." I still consider N. Fresco's devastating article, "Les redresseurs de mort" (*Les Temps modernes*, June 1980, pp. 2150–2211), a study that I had read in manuscript before writing my own, to offer an excellent ironic perspective on the phenomenon of revisionism.

32. For the case of *The Diary of Anne Frank*, cf. *infra*, "Theses on Revisionism," n. 94.

33. G. T. Rittersporn, "Staline en 1938: apogée du verbe et défaite politique," *Libre* 6 (1979):99–164, in which references to other works of the author, who was a sponsor of the publication of Thion's book, may be found.

34. G. Kolko, *The Politics of War* (New York: Random House, 1969); J. Kolko and G. Kolko, *The Limits of Power* (New York: Harper and Row, 1978).

35. It is bitterly grotesque to read the commentaries the line has received from Faurisson in person (*Vérité*, p. 91), S. Thion: "a sentence which is at the least maladroit, since it is ambiguous" (p. 72), or P. Guillaume, the man who was to cure Faurisson of his paranoid symptoms: "a sentence which is strictly true, even if Hitler did not in practice give a damn about what happened to the Jews" (p. 139).

36. In *Le Mensonge d'Ulysse* (pp. 170–171), Rassinier nevertheless admitted the plausible existence of a few gas chambers, perhaps due to "one or two madmen in the SS" and to "one or two concentration camp bureaucracies eager to please them," or vice versa.

37. Preface to T. Christophersen, *Le Mensonge d'Auschwitz* (Paris: FANE, 1973), p. 8.

38. Concerning these works, cf. *infra*.

39. A. R. Butz, *The Hoax of the Twentieth Century*, 4th ed. (Torrance, Calif.: Noontide Press, 1979), pp. 245–248. It goes without saying that if the Talmud contains imaginary statistics, such is the case for all ancient literatures.

40. See *Spotlight*, September 24, 1979, and concerning the congress, the previously mentioned article by N. Fresco. At present such congresses take place annually and their proceedings may be read in successive issues of the *Journal of Historical Review*; cf. also *infra*, p. 138.

41. *Journal of Historical Review* 1:57. I have slightly abridged the text.

42. Faurisson writes (*Vérité*, p. 111) and Thion confirms (p. 38, n. 31) that no expert evaluation of a gas chamber has been performed. This is false: I have before me an expert analysis performed at Cracow in June 1945 concerning the ventilation openings of the gas chamber at Birkenau (Crematorium No. 2), twenty-five kilograms of female hair, and metallic objects found in that hair. The analysis—which makes use, I am told by G. Wellers, of classical methods—revealed compounds of hydrogenated cyanide in that material. To which response will be made by invoking the trial of Marie Besnard, a famous case of alleged poisoning, and the Stalinist cast of Poland in 1945.

43. These key documents are four in number and were collected and published in a German translation (the originals are in Yiddish and, in one case, French) in *Hefte von Auschwitz* (Editions of the Museum at Oswiecim, *Sonderheft*, 1, 1973). There are several other cases of testimony by survivors of the Auschwitz *Sonderkommando*, such as that of D. Paisikovic, reprinted in L. Poliakov, *Auschwitz* (Paris: Julliard, 1964), pp. 159–171. The most detailed case of such testimony is that of Filip Müller, *Sonderbehandlung* (Munich, 1979), which has been incompletely and imprecisely translated into French (I am told by Claude Lanzmann) as *Trois ans dans une chambre à gaz à Auschwitz* (Pygmalion, 1980), with a preface by Lanzmann that makes the necessary comparisons. Lanzmann's film *Shoah* (1985) allowed the survivors to speak. In his *Mémoire en défense* (cf. *infra*, n. 103), Faurisson, for his part, has attempted to disqualify these texts (pp. 232–236).

44. See J. Kermisch's meticulous study, "Mutilated Version of Ringelblum's Notes," *YIVO Annual of Jewish Social Science* 8 (1953):289–301.

45. *Geheimreden*, p. 201.

46. *Goebbels Diary*, edited by L. P. Lochner (Garden City, N.Y.: Doubleday, 1948), p. 377.

47. Concerning this case, see L. Poliakov, *Bréviaire de la haine* (Paris: Calmann-Lévy, 1979), pp. 209–218. Concerning Stangl and several others, see, for example, Choumoff, *Mauthausen*, pp. 36–37, and G. Sereny's detailed account, *Into That Darkness: From Mercy Killing to Mass Murder* (New York: McGraw-Hill, 1974).

48. Gypsy members of the Wehrmacht arrived at Auschwitz wearing their decorations; cf. for example H. Langbein, *Hommes et Femmes à Auschwitz*, translated by D. Meunier (Paris: Fayard, 1975), p. 27; in general, see D. Kenrick and G. Puxon, *The Destiny of Europe's Gypsies* (London: Sussex University Press, 1972), pp. 59–184.

49. "I have analyzed thousands of documents. . . . I have tirelessly pursued specialists and historians with my questions. I have searched—but in vain—for a single former deportee capable of proving to me that he had seen a gas chamber with his own eyes" (*Le Monde*, January 16, 1979, and *Vérité*, p. 61).

50. Cf. Wellers, *Mythomanie*, pp. 14–15.

51. Thion offers (p. 345) a bibliography of the polemic; add the clarification by L. Poliakov and P. Vidal-Naquet (*Le Monde*, March 8, 1979) and a final series of documents presented by G. Wellers, "Encore sur le 'témoignage Gerstein,'" *Le Monde juif*, January—March 1980, pp. 23–35 (minutes of the interrogation of Gerstein before a French military court). Rassinier recounts the visit he received from a Nazi witness of the extermination at Belzec in *Le Drame des Juifs européens* (Paris: Sept Couleurs, 1964), pp. 79–91. The absolutely certain identification of that visitor as Pfannenstiel is established by Wellers (*Mythomanie*, pp. 32–35); see as well, concerning his deposition, S. Friedlander, *Kurt Gerstein* (Castermann, 1964), p. 112. A "diplomatic" edition of the report composed by Gerstein in French is found at the end of P. Joffroy, *L'Espion de Dieu: La passion de Kurt Gerstein* (Paris: Grasset, 1969). Since these lines were written, the polemic around Kurt Gerstein has resurfaced. In Nantes on June 15, 1985, an old student of Faurisson's, Henri Roques, defended a doctoral thesis on the value of the Gerstein file. The text of this thesis, along with a particularly dishonest introduction, may be found in A. Chelain's volume, *Faut-il fusiller Henri Roques?* (Paris: Ogmios Diffusion, 1986). The jury was composed of members of dubious competence: J.-C. Rivière, J.-P. Allard (a medievalist), and a historian of Hitlerian leaning, P. Zind. Following a scandal, the thesis defense was annulled on July 3, 1986. The press accorded the affair copious coverage in May and June 1986. For

a good critical account, see G. Wellers, *Le Monde juif*, January-March 1986, pp. 1–18. The most remarkable feature of the thesis was its failure to study the testimony of Professor Pfannenstiel.

52. I have discovered Rassinier's publications dutifully listed in a Polish bibliography devoted to the German camps.

53. *L'Insurrection du ghetto de Varsovie*, coll. "Archives" (Paris: Julliard, 1966).

54. The comparison was unfortunate since Bukharin recognized practically nothing except his political defeat; those who were actually judged publicly, moreover, were only a minority. Certain others among them, such as Krestinsky or Kostov, retracted their confessions.

55. D. Sperber, *Le Symbolisme en général* (Paris: Hermann, 1974).

56. It may be found, translated into French, in the anthology *Auschwitz vu par les SS* (Oswiecim Museum, 1974), pp. 141–209.

57. Rudolf Hoess, "Autobiography of Rudolf Hoess," in *K.L. Auschwitz Seen by the S.S.* (Oswiecim Museum, 1974), pp. 33–137.

58. L. Poliakov, ed., *Le Procès de Jérusalem* (Paris: Calmann-Lévy, 1963), p. 118.

59. I have not seen Hoess's manuscript, but H. Langbein maintains (*Le Monde juif*, 78, April-June 1975, p. 10) that there are photocopies of it in Vienna and Munich and that, contrary to what the "revisionists" have written, the text "is in a regular handwriting and is perfectly legible." Rassinier makes one of his habitual blunders concerning this text: "Its authentification can only be attempted by experienced specialists, such as those working on Egyptian palimpsests" (*Drame*, p. 44). (A palimpsest is a medieval manuscript written over an earlier obliterated manuscript.) I should say that the few pages by Hoess I have seen in photocopy entirely confirm Langbein's judgment: the perfectly legible handwriting of Hoess is that of an honest functionary; see the reproduction of Hoess's text on the final solution in *Bieuletyn Glownej Komisji badania zbrodni Hitlerowskich w. Polsce* 13 (1960):86–120. I owe this document, as well as a number of other Polish documents, to my friend B. Bravo. I have also received several photographs of the same manuscript from the Oswiecim Museum.

60. Testimony and interrogations of Hoess in *Procès de Nuremberg*, vol. 11, pp. 408–433.

61. The Polish edition of the crucial fragment of the Hoess memoirs (*Auschwitz vu par les SS*, pp. 35–142) contains numerous critical remarks.

62. This is but an example of the numerous errors and absurdities to be found in Rassinier. I will not burden these pages with them (except, below, concerning demography), but I have composed a small anthology of them for my personal use.

63. The technical rules in question are those of Anglo-Saxon procedure and are far more rigorous than those in use on the European continent. To write that the article "cynically authorized the use of forgeries" (Faurisson, *Vérité*, p. 71) is ridiculous.

64. Beyond the forty-two volumes of the official record, which I do not claim to have read, the bibliography is huge; for the juridical aspects, M. Merle, *Le procès de Nuremberg et le Châtiment des criminels de guerre*, preface by H. Donnedieu de Vabres (Paris, 1949); H. Donnedieu de Vabres, "Le Procès de Nuremberg," *Revue de science criminelle et de droit comparé*, 1947, pp. 171–183; for a German retrospecive view, G. E. Gründler and A. von Manikowsky, *Nuremberg ou la justice des vainqueurs*, translated by H. Lugert (Laffont, 1969); a Soviet account is given by A. Poltorak, *Le Procès de Nuremberg*, translated by H. Lusternik (Moscow: Editions du Progrès, 1969); a convenient synthesis by L. Poliakov, *Le Procès de Nuremberg* (Julliard, 1971); see as well, since then, R. Errera, "Nuremberg: le droit et l'histoire (1945–1985)," in *L'Allemagne nazie et le génocide juif* (Paris: Gallimard and Seuil, 1985), pp. 447–463. The offensive against the trials, from a Nazi perspective was launched by M. Bardèche, *Nuremberg ou la Terre promise* (Sept Couleurs, 1948).

65. Cf. Merle, *Procès*, pp. 123–124.

66. The most lucid overall evaluation remains that of Hannah Arendt, *Eichmann in Jerusalem* (New York: Viking, 1963). The most extreme "revisionist" point of view is given by Rassinier, *Le Véritable Procès Eichmann ou les Vainqueurs incorrigibles* (Sept Couleurs, 1962), a book it is impossible to take seriously.

67. *Eichmann par Eichmann*, p. 110, a text which I have verified by consulting the German original; it corresponds quite precisely to what Hoess says, but his interlocutor is Himmler (*Commandant d'Auschwitz*, p. 261); see also Hoess's declaration at Nuremberg, vol. 11, p. 410.

68. *Combats pour l'histoire* (Paris: Armand Colin, 1953), pp. 107–113.

69. My only personal contact with Rassinier was limited, in 1959, if I recall correctly, to a courteous exchange of letters on the subject of ac-

tivities of the Maurice-Audin Committee (against torture) during the Algerian war. I knew nothing at the time of his work; I note this fact to observe that Rassinier, throughout his shifts, remained an anticolonialist.

70. H. Coston, *Dictionnaire de la politique française* (Paris, 1972), II:560 (information supplied by E. Escobar, whom I thank).

71. Introductory note to *Le Mensonge d'Ulysse* (1979).

72. *Les Responsables de la Seconde Guerre mondiale* (Nouvelles Editions latines, 1967), p. 191; the book contains some remarkable considerations on the Jewish influences that perverted Roosevelt and on the good reasons Hitler had to persecute men who themselves admitted that "they were foreigners in Germany" (p. 114).

73. An amusing detail: Léon Poliakov has told me that the translation of his book was used in 1954 by *L'Unità* in its campaign against the rearmament of Germany.

74. Lenifying interpretations of the Korherr report have been advanced (Butz, *The Hoax*, p. 113). The most serious objection is that the figure for the inhabitants of the Theresienstadt ghetto is combined with that for Jews subjected to "special treatment." But do not all such military statistics deal with the dead and the wounded? It should nonetheless not be forgotten that the Korherr report concludes that the Jewish population in Europe, between 1937 and the end of March 1943, diminished by four and a half million individuals, a figure that included emigration.

75. His method has been well analyzed by Wellers, *Mythomanie*, pp. 38–39, whose argument I develop and specify here.

76. The "revisionists" all use the same sources. The same article by D. Bergelson is quoted by R. Harwood, "Did Six Million Really Die?" translated from the English, *Historical Review Press* (1977?):7; he adds a declaration by an American Jew in 1946.

77. At least that is how I understand the cryptic indications of *Drame*, p. 218. Perhaps one is to understand between 1947 and 1963.

78. *Le Véritable Procès Eichmann*, pp. 111–112.

79. *Etre un peuple en diaspora* (Paris: Maspero, 1975), pp. 10–11.

80. Preface to R. Marienstras, *Etre un peuple en diaspora*, pp. ii, iii; *Les Juifs, la mémoire et le présent*, I:111–112.

81. I have made an effort to verify it: the declaration of war is more than novelistic. In the *Jewish Chronicle* of September 8, 1939, one finds: 1) a letter from Chaim Weizmann, dated August 29, and thus

prior to the war, *in his function as president of the Jewish Agency*, which assures the British Prime Minister of the Jewish Agency's support for the cause of democracy: "The Jews stand by Great Britain and will fight on the side of the democracies"; 2) a declaration made at Jerusalem by the Jewish Agency assuring the British that—despite the White Book of 1939—the Yishuv in Palestine would remain loyal and would fight for the victory of the British Empire. It is quite clear that Faurisson has not read the text he refers to. He has acknowledged as much since then (*Réponse à Pierre Vidal-Naquet*, 2d ed. [Paris: La Vieille Taupe, 1982], p. 49), but has then gone on to repeat without significant change his argument or to base it on other equally representative "declarations of war," such as this headline of the *Daily Express* of March 24, 1933: "Judea Declares War on Germany" (from a tract given to me by Gilbert Brunet).

82. All this is clearly quite mythical; on the real process of the relations between the Zionist movement and Hitler's Germany, see E. Ben Elissar, *La Diplomatie du IIIe Reich et les Juifs, 1933–1939* (Paris: Julliard, 1969).

83. It is unfortunate that Faurisson did not list all the military measures that preceded and followed the yellow star, such as the decree published in Germany on May 15, 1942, which forbade Jews from owning domestic pets: dogs, cats, and birds (*Procès de Jerusalem*, p. 169). But it was no doubt a matter of preventing them from using carrier pigeons.

84. *Geheimreden*, p. 169.

85. See, for example (*Vérité*, p. 175), concerning Hoess's description of gassings: "One began to remove the corpses immediately"; note the word "immediately," in German: *sofort*.

86. *Dokumenty i Materialy I*, p. 110.

87. New testimony has just appeared, which entirely confirms all the rest: written in 1945 and confirmed in 1986, it comes from a non-Jewish prisoner at Auschwitz from April 15, 1944 to January 18, 1945, General André Rogerie, recently deceased. See *Le Monde juif*, no. 125, January-March 1987, pp. 3–14 (annotated by G. Wellers). I made the mistake, in the first edition of this text, of seeking support in aerial photos recently released by the CIA (*Le Monde juif*, no. 97, January-March 1980, p. 11); Georges Wellers is right to recall that on the days those photos were taken (June 26, August 25, September 13, 1944) no Jewish convoy arrived at Auschwitz; concerning the selection process,

see the testimony of P. Francès-Rousseau, *Intact aux yeux du monde* (Paris: Hachette, 1987), pp. 114–115.

88. Primo Levi, *Se questo è un uomo* (Turin: Einaudi, 1965), pp. 13–30; among much other testimony, see as well Marc Klein, in the anthology *De l'université aux camps de concentration: Témoignages strasbourgeois*, 2d ed. (Belles-Lettres, 1954), pp. 430–431.

89. Pierre Guillaume, whom I questioned on this matter, answered that these people were transferred at the station in Kielce, or rather, I was later told, in Kosel, 120 kilometers from Auschwitz. But why?

90. Hans Laternser, *Die andere Seite im Auschwitz-Prozess 1963–1965: Reden eines Verteidigers* (Stuttgart: Seewald, 1966), pp. 185–186.

91. The elements of the case, including the articles published in *Le Monde* on December 29, 1978, January 16, and February 21, 1979, are to be found in *Vérité*, pp. 63, 106, 109–110, 332–334; La Vieille Taupe announces (*Vérité*, p. 338, n. 3) the forthcoming publication of a Faurisson text (intended for his legal defense in a lawsuit brought by LICRA) under a sensational title: *Vous avez dit Kremer: un exemple de supercherie historique*; see this volume, chapter 2.

92. The German text was published in *Hefte von Auschwitz*, 13 (1971), pp. 5–117, with an introduction and notes by J. Rawicz; a French translation appears in the anthology *Auschwitz vu par les SS*, pp. 211–299.

93. My demonstration takes up and develops the one sketched by G. Wellers (*Vérité*, pp. 332–334) and, following him, N. Fresco, "Les redresseurs de morts."

94. R. Faurisson, *A-t-on lu Rimbaud?*, followed by *L'Affaire Rimbaud* (La Bibliotheque volante, July 1971), p. 4.

95. I have occasionally corrected the Polish translation in order to remain closer to the text.

96. *Frauenkonzentrationlager*: a concentration camp for women, in other words: Birkenau; the context shows that the "Muslims" referred to are women.

97. "Nothing allows one to say that the 'special actions' crudely recounted in the diary seized on the person of the Auschwitz surgeon . . . were gassings" (*Vérité*, p. 63).

98. The translation in the Polish edition quoted by Wellers said: "It is not for nothing that Auschwitz is called the *extermination camp*."

99. The translation by the Oswiecim Museum, from this point of view, is irreproachable.

100. *Vérité*, pp. 109–110. Faurisson refers in a note to *Auschwitz vu par les SS*, p. 238, n. 85.

101. This practice did not in any way exclude other forms of murder, specifically injections of phenol; on the (assuredly considerable) role of typhus as a cause of death at Auschwitz, see A. Fiederkiewicz, "Le Typhus exanthématique et les Epouillages au camp des hommes à Birkenau; Contribution à l'histoire du K. L. Auschwitz," in *Problèmes choisis de l'histoire du K.L. Auschwitz* (Auschwitz Museum, 1978), pp. 237–265.

102. Minutes of the interrogation of Kremer at Cracow, July 30, 1947, German text: *Hefte von Auschwitz*, 13 (1971), p. 113, n. 69.

103. The book, which has since been published by Faurisson, *Mémoire en defense*, contributes *nothing* requiring me to change my evaluation. Instead of a falsification of a few lines, we have a falsification of almost 280 pages.

104. Cf. Butz, *The Hoax*, pp. 113–144 and passim. Faurisson, in *Vérité*, p. 105; on the September 1944 visit by representatives of the CICR to the Auschwitz commandant, cf. *Documents sur l'activité du CICR en faveur des civils détenus dans les camps de concentration en Allemagne (1939–1945)*, 3d ed. (Geneva, 1947). A British agent in the Teschen camp tried, through intermediaries, to obtain information as to what was being said of gas chamber-shower rooms. He was unsuccessful: the representatives themselves appear not to have asked any direct questions: "We have the impression that the mystery is kept quite secret."

105. Concerning the outrage of lawyer Manfred Roeder at the fact that his "truth" had been received by swine, cf. *Mensonge d'Auschwitz*, pp. 30–36.

106. Hesiod, *Theogony*, pp. 27–29; cf. M. Detienne, *Les Maîtres de vérité dans la Grèce archaïque* (Paris: Maspero, 1967).

107. P. Gibert, *La Bible à la naissance de l'histoire* (Paris: Fayard, 1979).

108. Cf. Claude Lefort, "L'Ere de l'idéologie," *Encyclopaedia universalis*, "Organum," 17 (1973), pp. 75–93.

109. *Problèmes choisis de l'histoire du K.L. Auschwitz*, p. 53.

110. New York, 1946.

111. *Joseph Reinach Historien: Révision de l'histoire de l'affaire Dreyfus*, pref. Ch. Maurras (Paris: Editions A. Savaète, 1905).

112. H. Dutrait-Crozon, *Précis de l'affaire Dreyfus avec un répertoire analytique* (Nouvelle Librairie nationale, 1909); the third edition, published in Paris in 1938, contains an appendix concerning Schwartzkoppen, from which I have taken my quotation. It is regrettable that Philippe Ariès, in his beautiful autobiography, *Un historien du dimanche* (Paris: Seuil, 1980), did not tell us anything of the influence of this book on Action Française circles.

113. *Ulysse trahi*, pp. 82–120.

114. This quotation is from a letter by J. Bennett in the *Melbourne Herald* of October 26, 1979, p. 19; other texts by Bennett include one in *The Age* (March 15, 1979). On the issue of historical truth, a biting response from a specialist, John Foster, was published in *The Age*, March 23, 1979.

115. I quote a typewritten memorandum dated April 12, 1979 and bearing the same title as Butz's book. Thion refers to a first draft of this memorandum, which was published in the *National Times* of Melbourne, on February 10, 1979. From my Melbourne colleague Charles Sowerwine, whom I thank, I have received a whole file of letters and press clippings on the John Bennett case and the campaign that led to his exclusion from the Victorian Council for Civil Liberties and to his rapprochement with the extreme right.

116. The final sentence of "Sorcellerie, Sottise, ou Révolution mentale," *Annales ESC* 3 (1948):9–15; for an elaboration, cf. R. Mandrou, *Magistrats et Sorciers en France au XVIIe siècle* (Paris: Plon, 1968; reprt. Seuil, 1980).

117. I took a public position on the matter at the time: see "Le Navet et le spectacle," *Esprit*, April 1979, pp. 119–121.

118. Indeed it was.

119. The decision by the Conseil d'Etat of October 20, 1978, which I have before me, does not allow any decisive clarification of the matter.

120. *La Clé des Chimères et Autres Chimères de Nerval* (Paris: Pauvert, 1976).

121. Rassinier, *Ulysse trahi*, pp. 111, 155.

122. Robert Faurisson, "Le problème des chambres à gaz," *Défense de l'Occident*, June 1978; also in *Vérité*, p. 86.

123. Ibid., p. 88, as well as articles in *Le Monde* on December 29, 1978 (in *Vérité*, pp. 104–105), on January 16, 1979 (pp. 110–111), and on

March 29, 1979 (p. 112), and an interview with Faurisson in *Storia Illustrata* (August 1979; pp. 175–176, 203–204).

124. K. Winnacker and E. Weingaertner, *Chemische Technologie-Organische Technologie II* (Munich: Carl Hanser Verlag, 1954), pp. 1005–1006.

125. Institut National de Recherche et de Sécurité, "Acide cyanhydrique: Fiche Toxicologique No. 4" (revised ed., April 1969).

126. *Vérité*, pp. 88, 104–105, 110–111, 174–177, 203–204, 319–321.

127. *L'Extermination des Juifs en Pologne V-X*: depositions by eyewitnesses; Third Series: "Les Camps d'extermination" (Geneva: C.J.M., 1944), pp. 59–60.

128. They have subsequently been identified as R. Vrba and F. Wetzler; cf. G. Wellers, *Mythomanie*, pp. 14–15.

129. *Vérité*, pp. 87, 110, 175.

130. Ibid., p. 202, n. 1.

131. To my knowledge, this was indeed a myth [P. V.-N.].

132. Winnacker and Weingaertner, *Chemische Technologie*, p. 276.

133. *Vérité*, p. 312.

134. $CaC_2 + H_2 \rightarrow C_2H_2 + Ca(OH)_2$; see, for instance, G. Champetier, *La Grande Industrie chimique organique*, coll. "Que sais-je?," no. 436 (Paris: P.U.F., 1950), p. 65.

135. *Jüdische Rundschau Maccabi* 23 (June 5, 1980):5.

2. On Faurisson and Chomsky

1. *Mémoire en défense*; this is the book announced in n. 91 of my study "A Paper Eichmann"; the announced title has become a subtitle. A detailed refutation of this work has recently been published by M. Steinberg: *Les yeux du témoin et le regard du borgne* (Paris: Cerf, 1990).

2. That is what I wrote and believed in 1981, but further information has led me to realize I was wrong (note from 1987).

3. A falsification that has been modified without informing the reader remains, of course, a falsification. Where "special action" (the code name for gassing) was principally (*Vérité*, p. 109) the "sorting out of the sick from the healthy," it becomes additionally (*Mémoire en défense*, p. 34) the "cleaning of either third class or especially freight trains, in which the new detainees had just arrived." In the first hypothesis, why should "special action" concern those arriving from the outside and not yet afflicted by the epidemic? In the second, it could not

concern, for good reason, the "Muslims." And why, above all, should the same expression employed the same day have two different meanings?

4. Chomsky's preface, which is seven pages long, is entitled "Quelques commentaires élémentaires sur le droit à la liberté d'expression."

5. Ibid., p. ix.

6. This was already the case for the preceding book, by Serge Thion.

7. See this volume, pp. 39–40 and *Esprit*, p. 38.

8. *Esprit*, p. 52. I reprint these lines as they were published. For reasons of precision I rephrased them in the definitive version of my text, *supra*, p. 58.

9. Maurice Nadeau, *Histoire du surréalisme*, II, *Documents surréalistes* (Paris: Seuil, 1948), p. 154.

10. Concerning the refusal of the personnel of the Centre de Documentation Juive Contemporaine (a private foundation) to serve him, cf. *Esprit*, p. 52, and *supra*, p. 58.

11. These are words, American and English colleagues have told me, which might be said of a university thesis—and a good one!

12. For the sake of completeness, I will say that in his new book there is material on gas chambers that were either imaginary or did not function in the western camps, Buchenwald and Dachau. But it is all so poorly analyzed from a historical point of view that even such documentation is hard to utilize.

13. "Le Cambodge, les droits de l'homme et l'opinion internationale," pp. 112–113.

14. "Le Cambodge, la presse et ses bêtes noires," pp. 95–111.

15. When a regional director of LICRA protests against a performance of Shakespeare's *The Merchant of Venice* (cf. *Le Monde*, July 5, 1980), he is working for Faurisson, who is delighted to mention such venomous foolishness.

16. Cf. Stephen Lukes, "Chomsky's Betrayal of Truths," *Times* (London), Higher Education Supplement, November 7, 1980, p. 31.

17. See P. Guillaume, *Droit et Histoire* (Paris: La Vieille Taupe, 1986), pp. 158–159.

18. I possess a huge file of material; suffice it for me to refer to a small book published, alas, by Editions Spartacus (Paris, 1984), N. Chomsky, *Réponses inédites a mes détracteurs parisiens*.

19. P. Guillaume, *Droit et Histoire*, p. 54.

20. P. Guillaume signed a preface to Chomsky's book, *Réponses inédites*, with his initials.

21. My colleague and friend Professor Arno Mayer of Princeton spoke with Chomsky about his preface a few weeks before its publication.

22. See his letter in the *Village Voice* of March 18, 1986, p. 7, responding to an article by Paul Berman in the same newspaper (February 18, 1986).

23. I refer to the American edition of the *Biographical Companion to Contemporary Thought*, edited by A. Bullock (London: Fontana-Collins, 1983); details of this matter can be found in an article by G. Sampson (author of the note), "Censoring 20th-Century Culture: The Case of Noam Chomsky," *The New Criterion*, October 1984, pp. 7–16.

24. W. D. Rubinstein's article, "Chomsky and the Neo-Nazis," published in the Australian periodical *Quadrant*, October 1981, pp. 8–14, seems to me to miss the mark; it was followed by a published debate, in which Chomsky (setting forth his usual line) participated, as well as R. Manne (on the subject of Cambodia) (*Quadrant*, April 1982, pp. 6–22). In P. Guillaume's *Droit et Histoire*, pp. 152–172, one finds fragments of an unbelievable attack by one Chantal Beauchamp, characterized as a "professor and *agrégée* in history," against Chomsky, who is accused of being a closet exterminationist, and his accomplice P. Guillaume. One would like to know the elements of this delectable affair.

25. N. Chomsky, for example, appears not to have had any problem with La Vieille Taupe publishing the (genuinely Nazi) volume of W. Stäglich, *Le Mythe d'Auschwitz* (1986). To someone who asked him what he thought of it, he replied that he did not discuss things with fascists (testimony of Paul Berman, 1986). The most intelligent article written to defend Chomsky—C. Hitchens's "The Chorus and Cassandra: What Everyone Knows About Noam Chomsky," *Grand Street*, Autumn 1985, pp. 106–131—avoids confronting this type of question.

26. See his polemic against Nadine Fresco, for example, in *Dissent*, Spring 1982, pp. 218–220.

3. On the Side of the Persecuted

1. I refer to Jean-Marie Paupert and his article in *Le Monde* of January 4–5, 1981.

4. Theses on Revisionism

1. I thank all those who have helped me in the preparation and publication of this study, in particular P. Moreau, a connoisseur of the Ger-

man extreme right; J. Tarnero; P. A. Taguieff; D. Fourgous, J. Svenbro; S. Krakowski; A. J. Mayer; and R. Halevi. Since this text is part of a volume in the "Hautes Etudes" collection, *L'Allemagne nazie et le génocide des juifs* (Gallimard and Seuil, 1985), references to other studies in that volume are to its American edition, *Unanswered Questions.*

2. Cf. H. Dutrait-Crozon, *Joseph Reinach Historien: Révision de l'histoire de l'affaire Dreyfus*, preface by C. Maurras (Paris: A. Savaète, 1905).

3. See the space accorded to him in K. Stimley, *1981 Revisionist Bibliography: A Select Bibliography of Revisionist Books Dealing With the Two Wars and Their Aftermaths* (Torrance, Calif.: Institute for Historical Review, 1980). See also H. Barnes, *Revisionism: A Key to Peace and Other Essays*, preface by J. J. Martin (San Francisco: Cato Institute, 1980).

4. See, for example, his preface to L. Hamilton Jenks, *Our Cuban Colony* (New York: Vanguard Press, 1928).

5. See the classic work of Lord A. Ponsonby, *Falsehood in War-Time.* (New York: Dutton, 1928).

6. W. Roscoe Thayer, *Volleys from a Non-Combatant* (New York: Doubleday, 1919).

7. Letter reprinted in *Le Mouvement social*, January-March 1982, pp. 101–102; I thank Madeleine Rebérioux for having brought this text to my attention.

8. Text reprinted in *American Historical Review*, April 1951, pp. 711–712; cf. H. E. Barnes, *Revisionism*, p. 131.

9. *The Genesis of the World War* (New York: Knopf, 1929).

10. Ibid., p. 306.

11. *Un débat historique: 1914. Le problème des origines de la guerre* (Paris: Rieder, 1933), p. 224.

12. *Genesis of the World War*, pp. xi–xii, 103, 333–335.

13. One could proliferate references; see, for example, the republication by La Vieille Taupe, the principal organ of French revisionism, of Bernard Lazare's book, *L'Antisémitisme: son histoire et ses causes* (Paris: Editions de la Différence, 1982), or the pamphlet by the German Jewish revisionist J. G. Burg entitled, with all due calm, *J'accuse (Ich klage an)*, 2d ed. (Munich: Ederer, 1982), and, by the same author, *Zionnazi Zenzur in der B. R. D.* (Munich: Ederer, 1980), pp. 48–49.

14. See "Antisemitism" in *The Origins of Totalitarianism* (New York: Harcourt, Brace & World, 1968).

15. In America and in France; needless to say, German revisionists recruited for the most part among extreme right-wing neo-Nazis have no interest in "reviewing" or "revising" the German nationalist version of the First World War!

16. Such is the title of Butz's book, one of the bibles of "revisionism," *The Hoax of the Twentieth Century*.

17. Concerning Rassinier, see "A Paper Eichmann," *supra*, pp. 00–00. J.-G. Cohn-Bendit and several of his friends have expressed their views in *Intolérable intolérance* (Paris: Editions de la Différence, 1982).

18. A. Finkielkraut, *L'Avenir d'une négation: Réflexion sur la question du genocide* (Paris: Seuil, 1982), p. 121. In contemporary American revisionism, references to the war of 1914–1918 serve as a convenient mask donned by what is essentially an anti-Semitic propaganda effort; see, for example, in *Journal of Historical Review* I(2) (1980), the reproduction of a chapter of A. Ponsonby's book cited in note 5. I remind the reader that that review is the periodical of the American revisionist sect.

19. Cf. H. E. Barnes, *Revisionism*, p. 16, in which Rassinier is quoted along with A. J. P. Taylor, Maurice Bardèche, Alfred Fabre-Luce, and a few others. But he alone is deemed worthy of the epithet "courageous."

20. See "A Paper Eichmann," *supra*, pp. 00–00, and G. Wellers' volume, *Les Chambres à gaz ont existé* (Paris: Gallimard, 1981); the recent publication by R. Faurisson of a brochure entitled "Réponse à Pierre Vidal-Naquet" (Paris: Vieille Taupe, 1982) does not call for any further discussion on my part. I shall merely note that the text attributed to me in the preface by P. Guillaume is not mine. That error was rectified in a subsequent edition and replaced by other lies.

21. "The conclusion precedes the evidence"; I borrow the formula from an unpublished text by J. C. Milner. Moreover, it should be recalled that in speaking of a "total lie," I do not mean—through a totalitarian inversion—to affirm that all that the "revisionists" write, in its slightest details, is false. It is the whole which constitutes a mendacious system.

22. Arendt, *Totalitarianism*, p. 30.

23. *The Terrible Secret* (London: Weidenfeld and Nicolson, 1980); see as well Martin Gilbert, *Auschwitz and the Allies* (London and New York: Holt, Rinehart and Winston, 1981), which is more detailed and extends over a longer time span, but less acute. For a case of concrete testimony among many others, see E. Young-Bruehl, *Hannah Arendt: For Love of the World* (New Haven: Yale University Press, 1982).

Needless to say, Laqueur's book was immediately exploited in a revisionist sense: if the Allies themselves did not believe, it was because there was nothing to believe; see the articles by R. Faurisson and P. Guillaume in *Jeune Nation solidariste*, December 1981.

24. M. Gilbert, *Auschwitz*, p. 190, and above all R. Braham, *The Politics of Genocide: The Holocaust in Hungary*, 2 vols. (New York: Columbia University Press, 1981), II:708–724, 1109–1112.

25. Ibid., pp. 1095–1120.

26. Both expressions—at times simultaneously—are to be found in revisionist literature. Cf., for example, Butz, *The Hoax*, particularly, pp. 53–100; R. Faurisson, *Le Monde*, December 29, 1978 (reprinted in S. Thion, *Vérité*, pp. 104–105); W. Stäglich, *Der Auschwitz Mythos: Legende oder Wirklichkeit?* (Tübingen: Grabert, 1979), pp. 146–151; a French "adaptation" of this work exists under the title *Le Mythe d'Auschwitz* (Paris: La Vieille Taupe, 1986).

27. The case of the myths accompanying the great slaughter is similar to that of the religious phenomena which followed in its wake, and which by no means undermine its existence. This elementary truth has eluded the anthropologist J.-L. Tristani; see his "Supplique à MM. les magistrats de la cour d'appel de Paris," in *Intolérable intolérance*, pp. 161–172, a text, moreover, which is in no way anti-Semitic, but rather lacking in intellectual elaboration.

28. F. H. Hinsley, ed., *British Intelligence in the Second World War* (London: Her Majesty's Stationery Office, 1981), II:673.

29. N. Blumental, *Dokumenty Materialy z Czasów Okupacji Niemieckiej w Polsce, i Obozy* (Lodz, 1946), p. 118.

30. *The Terrible Secret*, pp. 97–98; it is discussed by revisionist authors, for example, Butz, *The Hoax*, pp. 60–62.

31. M. Broszat, "Hitler und die Genesis der Endlösung," *Vierteljahrshefte für Zeitgeschichte*, XXV, 1977, pp. 729–775 (English translation in *Yad Vashem Studies*, XIII, 1979, pp. 73–125); C. Browning, "Eine Antwort auf Martin Broszats Theses zur Genesis der Endlösung," ibid., XXIX, pp. 97–109; see, by the same author, "The Decision Concerning the Final Solution," in *Unanswered Questions*, pp. 96–118; this is, in my opinion, the most rigorous study of the subject.

32. D. Irving, *Hitler's War* (New York: Viking, 1977).

33. The references may be found *supra* (chapter 1, n. 67), to which should be added, insofar as Eichmann is concerned, a crucial document,

the manuscript he composed in Argentina and which was published by a neo-Nazi revisionist, Dr. R. Aschenauer, *Ich Adolf Eichmann: Ein Historischer Zeugenbericht* (Leoni am Starnbergersee: Druffel Verlag, 1980), p. 178. Despite his categorical affirmation, which was written prior to his capture, his publisher nonetheless is capable of writing without any loss of composure that Eichmann is alluding to a nonexistent order (ibid., p. 178, note). I note a slight discrepancy between Eichmann's manuscript and the version told at Jerusalem: the conversation with Heydrich takes place at the end of 1941 in the first case, at the end of the summer in the second (*Eichmann par Eichmann*, p. 110).

34. See, for example, H. Härtle, *Freispruch für Deutschland* (Gottingen: Schütz Verlag, 1968), pp. 201–204; Burg, *Zionnazi Zensur in der BRD*, pp. 173–176, uses the existence of monetary and postal institutions in the ghettos of Lodz and Theresienstadt to demonstrate that all was normal.

35. I had this opportunity at the beginning of April 1982, in the Yad Vashem library in Jerusalem.

36. The record seems to be held by R. E. Harwood (the pseudonym of the British neo-Nazi R. Verrall) in his famous booklet, *Did Six Million Really Die?* (Richmond, 1979), a minor monument of imaginary erudition. Several indications of the repercussions of that publication in England are to be found in Gill Seidel's book, *The Holocaust Denial* (Leeds: Beyond the Pale Collective, 1986).

37. The Institute for Historical Review, located in Torrance, California, which publishes, in addition to the journal bearing its name, a whole series of works.

38. One of the most precise studies of that International is by P. A. Taguieff, "L'héritage nazi," *Nouveaux Cahiers* 64 (Spring 1981):3–22.

39. I borrow this information as well as other items from the biography of the individual published in the *Journal of Historical Review* I(2) (1980):187; I have also made use of indications furnished by J. Jakubowski in *Expressen* (Stockholm) of July 17, 1981.

40. Its first issue was the object of a 1979 subscription campaign among members of the American Historical Association.

41. I have before me an issue published in 1981. Glued to the first page are a few strands of hair with the caption: "Please accept this hair of a gassed victim."

42. L. Marschalko, *The World Conquerors: The Real War Criminals*,

translated from the Hungarian by A. Suranyi (London: Joseph Sueli, 1958; reprt. New York: Christian Book Club, 1978). This remarkable book was revealed to me by J. C. Milner. A typical example of its scholarship: the Jewish nationalist newspaper *Shem*, published clandestinely in France, is said to have explained, on July 8, 1944, that conditions in the camps were on the whole good and that children between two and five years old went to kindergarten classes in Berlin (p. 115). One of the French sources mentioned is Maurice Bardèche.

43. In *Intolérable intolérance*, La Vieille Taupe thus published, along with texts that are inept but in no way anti-Semitic, a study by Vincent Monteil which, in its anti-Zionism, is fundamentally anti-Semitic.

44. Cf. *Le Monde*, June 2, 1982, quoting M. Bougenaa Amara from *L'Opinion* (Rabat), the periodical of Istiqlal: "Nazism is a creation of Zionism. The historical reality of the concentration camps remains to be authenticated. Doubts linger as to their very existence."

45. The most curious book on this theme that I know of is by Hussein Ahmad, *Palästina meine Heimat: Zionismus—Weltfeind der Völker* (Frankfurt: Bierbaum Verlag, 1975). It combines every form of anti-Semitism and revisionism.

46. See, for example, in *Revue d'études palestiniennes* 1 (Fall 1981), M. Rodinson, "Quelques idées simples sur l'antisémitisme," pp. 5–21, which denounces (p. 17) Arab use of the classics of anti-Semitism; these analyses strike me as far more pertinent than the maximalist ones undertaken by B. Lewis, *Semites and Anti-Semites* (New York: Norton, 1986).

47. The best known case is that of J. G. Burg (Ginzburg), who knew Europe under Hitler and Stalin, then Israel, before settling in Germany. His autobiography, *Schuld und Schicksal* (1962), 6th ed. (Oldendorf: K. W. Schütz ver. K. G. Preuss, 1979), moreover, is interesting and only marginally revisionist. Its subtitle may be translated as: "The Jews of Europe Between Executioners and Hypocrites." He has since slid toward revisionism and German nationalism. See, in addition to the books already mentioned, *Maidanek in alle Ewigkeit?* (Munich: Ederer, 1979 [banned]); *Sündenbocke, Grossangriffe des Zionismus auf Papst Pius XII und auf die deutschen Regierungen* 4th ed. (Munich: Ederer, 1980), books published by a specialty house. Burg has also published a collection of Jewish tales, *Jüdische Anekdotiade* (Munich: Ederer, 1970).

48. The most prolific author in this vein is Erich Kern, author of *Mei-*

neid gegen Deutschland (2d ed., 1971) and *Die Tragödie der Juden* (1979), both published by Schütz, a specialized subdivision of Preussisch Oldendorf. The French reader will note with interest the praise heaped on Robert Faurisson in the latter volume, pp. 289–299. One anthology has the interest of presenting ten authors (including the Englishman, D. Irving) with their biographies: *Verrat und Widerstand im Dritten Reich* (Coburg: Nation Europa, 1978). Note finally the works of U. Walendy, a specialist in photographs altered for propaganda purposes—there were some—as may be seen in the first issue of the *Journal of Historical Review* I(1) (1980):59–68. His books include *Wahrheit für Deutschland* 3d ed. (Vlotho-am-Weser: Verlag für Volkstum und Zeitgeschichtsforschung, 1976); and *Auschwitz im I. G. Farben Prozess* (Vlotho-am-Weser: Verlag für Volkstum und Zeitgeschichtsforschung, 1981).

49. See, for example, E. Kern, *Die Tragödie der Juden*, p. 83; W. Stäglich, *Der Auschwitz Mythos*, pp. 82–85, with references to *The American Hebrew* (New York) of May 24, 1934 and *The Youngstown Jewish Times* (Ohio) of April 16, 1936. They could also have mentioned *The Daily Express* of March 24, 1933.

50. See for example W. Stäglich, *Der Auschwitz Mythos*, p. 82, which makes reference, p. 395, n. 103, to all the revisionist authors (of whom the first was French, Rassinier) who have used the same document.

51. "Les redresseurs de morts" in *Les Temps modernes*, June 1980, pp. 2150–2211; S. Freud, *Jokes and Their Relation to the Unconscious* (New York: Norton, 1960).

52. For example, W. Stäglich, *Der Auschwitz Mythos*, pp. 28–65; E. Kern, *Die Tragödie der Juden*, pp. 122–133; Butz, *The Hoax*, pp. 211–214, retains only the second interpretation.

53. I have supplied the principal references in "A Paper Eichmann" *supra*, pp. 22, 41–42.

54. W. Stäglich, *Der Auschwitz Mythos*, p. 94, quoting and commenting on the Poznan speech of October 6, 1943. But the entirety of the author's "demonstration," pp. 89–103, could be adduced. One might also mention a page worth anthologizing about the "braggart" Himmler in a pamphlet of the Parisian extreme left, "De l'exploitation dans les camps à l'exploitation des camps," supplement to no. 3 of *La Guerre sociale*, Paris, May 1981, pp. 27–28; add as well R. Faurisson, *Réponse*, pp. 14–17.

55. One might refer at this point to a number of Rassinier's works, for

example, *Le Drame des Juifs européens*, pp. 79–91, and I have already mentioned L. Marschalko's astonishing book, but the masterpiece in the field is H. Härtle's work, *Freispruch für Deutschland*, see above all pp. 204–274.

56. *Hitler's War*, pp. 332 and 393. This alleged order is in fact the result of a minor intellectual hoax which has been denounced by both M. Broszat, "Hitler und die Genesis," p. 760, and G. Sereny and L. Chester, *Sunday Times*, July 10, 1977. It is a question of a telephone call from Himmler to Heydrich, emanating from the Führer's headquarters on November 30, 1941, on the subject of a specific convoy of Jews from Berlin, and the order was not to exterminate (*keine Liquidierung*) that specific convoy.

57. See the crucial testimony of H. J. Klein, *La Mort mercenaire*, preface by D. Cohn-Bendit (Paris: Editions du Seuil, 1980).

58. I was wrong to cite this text (*Frankfurter Allgemeine Zeitung*, December 15, 1972) following the interpretation it received from J. Tarnero (*Nouveaux Cahiers* 64 [Spring 1981]:28) and many others. My Italian friend and critic D. Lanza has drawn attention to the error; see my "clarification" in *Quaderni di Storia* 25 (January-June 1987):159–160.

59. Precise and verifiable information about this lobby, which publishes the weekly *Spotlight* (similar in format to the French *Minute*, but even more directly racist), may be found in *Facts* (an organ of B'nai B'rith) 26(5) (June 1980):1 and 2; see as well, concerning certain recent episodes in the life of the Institute for Historical Review, R. Chandler, in the *San Franciso Chronicle* of May 5, 1981. W. A. Carto chaired the 1981 revisionist conference; see his contribution, "On the Uses of History," *Journal of Historical Review* III(1) (1982):27–30.

60. There are debates in the United States about the more or less "libertarian" character of the revisionists and particularly of H. E. Barnes and his heirs; see the letters published in the *Village Voice* of July 1, 1981.

61. See, for example, A. Rabinbach, "Anti-Semitism Reconsidered," *New German Critique* 21 (Autumn 1980):129–141, particularly p. 141, n. 21.

62. A full-blown polemic appeared in the press in 1981: see, for example, the articles in *Svenska Dagbladet* on March 5, 1981, and *Expressen* on April 13, 1981, articles to which I myself responded (*Ex-*

pressen on July 16–17, 1981), which prompted additional articles by Myrdal (*Expressen* on July 18–19, 1981); one of Myrdal's texts, an attack against French intellectuals and their role in the Faurisson affair, was collected in his book *Dussinet fullt Skrifställining 12* (Stockholm: Norstedts, 1982), pp. 221–229; in this text, J. Myrdal, however, does not address the fundamental issue; there is material favorable to Faurisson in *Tidskrift for Folkets Rättigheter*, I, 1982.

63. Several indications in "A Paper Eichmann," *supra*, pp. 55–56, and above all Bennett's own comments on his action and the polemics it elicited, *Journal of Historical Review* I(2) (1980):115–120, "In the Matter of Robert Faurisson."

64. R. Faurisson had given an interview to *Storia Illustrata*, 261, August 1979, republished and corrected in S. Thion, *Vérité*, pp. 171–212; since then, Italian revisionism has developed around two individuals: a disciple of Rassinier, Cesare Saletta, a member or sympathizer of the Gruppo communista internazionalista autonoma, the author of a brochure entitled *Il Caso Rassinier* (1981) as well as of two others directed at the author of these pages, *L'onestà polemica del Signor Vidal-Naquet* and *In margine ad tua recensione* (1985 and 1986), both published by the author; and an avowed fascist, Carlo Mattogno, whose principal works have been published by Sentinella d'Italia. Both authors, moreover, develop the same themes, and it was the fascist author which La Vieille Taupe opted to publish in the first issue of *Annales d'histoire révisionniste* (Spring 1987), "Le mythe de l'extermination des Juifs: Introduction historico-bibliographique à l'historiographie révisionniste," pp. 15–107.

65. *Mémoire en défense.*

66. Lothar Baier, "Die Weisswäscher von Auschwitz: Robert Faurisson und seine Genossen," *Transatlantik*, July 1981, pp. 14–26; Paul L. Berman, "Gas Chamber Games: Crackpot History and the Right to Lie," *Village Voice*, July 10, 1981; L. Dawidowicz's article, "Lies About the Holocaust," *Commentary*, December 1980, pp. 31–37, is more international but also concludes with references to France.

67. "Never did Hitler order or accept that anyone be killed for reason of his race or his religion": that formula made Faurisson famous and was disseminated, it seems, in 1978. In 1974, the (neo-Nazi) revisionist W. D. Rothe ended his book *Die Endlösung der Judenfrage* (Frankfurt: E. Bierman) by affirming: "dass es nicht einen einzigen Juden gegeben

hat, der mit Wissen und Billigung der Regierung des Dritten Reiches, des damaligen Führers Adolf Hitler oder gar des Deutsches Volkes, umgebracht worden wäre, weil er Jude war."

68. Even though such trials do occur in the United States (without much publicity); see *infra*, p. 138.

69. In the previously mentioned volume, *Vérité*.

70. See, for example, in the *Journal of Historical Review* I(2) (1980):153–162, the exchange of letters between various revisionists and the editors of the *New Statesman* of London. I have it from G. Sereny that the highest moral and juridical authority of the English press debated the question and decided against a right to respond.

71. The Faurisson affair really began with the publication in *Le Monde* of December 29, 1978 of an article by Faurisson, followed by a response by G. Wellers. To be sure, *Le Monde* came out clearly against Faurisson, but one could read, for example, in the issue of June 30, 1981, concerning a trial, an article by C. Colombani entitled "Des universitaires s'affrontent sur le cas Faurisson [Academics confront each other over the Faurisson case]." The discussion was more intense in *Libération* (I participated in an interview with Didier Eribon, January 24–25, 1981); it appeared to come to a close in the July 11–12 issue with an article by F. Paul-Boncour entitled "Pour en finir avec l'affaire Faurisson," but resurfaced on several occasions, the last being the publication of two letters to the editor in which the two main themes of revisionism—the technical and the "Third World"—were combined. This led to a violent clarification by Serge July the following day and the disciplining of the editor responsible for their publication.

72. For example, aside from the books of Bardèche and Rassinier, in a volume by G. A. Amaudruz (a Swiss Nazi): *Un justicier au premier procès de Nuremberg* (Paris: Ch. de Jonquière, 1949).

73. See "A Paper Eichmann," *supra*, pp. 31–32.

74. I offer a few details concerning La Vieille Taupe in the second section of my study "A Paper Eichmann." It was specifically on the basis of what he knew or thought he knew of Rassinier that Noam Chomsky allied himself with the French group without, however, adhering personally to revisionist theses; see as well *infra*, pp. 116–120.

75. Those themes appear with perfect clarity in a tract distributed by these groups in October 1980 and entitled "Our Kingdom is a Prison." It was reprinted in the previously mentioned booklet (*supra*, n. 54), *De l'exploitation dans les camps*.

76. Concerning Drumont and the influence he exercised, see Z. Sternhell, *La Droite révolutionnaire, 1885–1914: Les origines françaises du fascisme* (Paris: Editions du Seuil, 1978), and M. Winock's collection, *Drumont et Cie* (Paris: Editions du Seuil, 1982).

77. E. Drumont, *La France juive* (Paris: Marpont-Flammarion, 1886), II:408–409.

78. See my texts "Des musées et des hommes," preface to R. Marienstras, *Etre un peuple en diaspora*, reprinted in *Les Juifs*, pp. 110–125.

79. A basic work on these historiographical practices and, in general, on the great massacre is L. S. Dawidowicz's book *The Holocaust and the Historians* (Cambridge, Mass.: Harvard University Press, 1981), a work which unfortunately yields too often to an excess opposite to the one it rightfully denounces (the banalization of the slaughter) and falls into Judeocentrism. Concerning the Soviet Union and Poland, this work nevertheless contributes crucial information and could be cited in each of the following notes; another work—by R. Braham—is announced as forthcoming.

80. Essentially C. Simonov, *Maïdanek, un camp d'extermination*, accompanied by a report by the Polish-Soviet Investigatory Commission (Paris: Editions Sociales, 1945), and V. Grossmann, *L'Enfer de Treblinka* (Paris: Arthaud, 1945, reprt. 1966), works without any real documentary value; aside from the indications of L. S. Dawidowicz, *The Holocaust*, pp. 69–79, see the brief study by E. Goldhagen, "Der Holocaust in der Sowjetischen Propaganda und Geschichtsschreibung," *Vierteljahrshefte für Zeitgeschichte* 28 (1980):502–507.

81. For the entire period prior to 1962, there is a good documentary guide in Polish, which does not deal with the camps devoted solely to extermination such as Treblinka, but which includes Auschwitz: Wanda Kiedrzynska, *Materialy do Bibliografi Hitlerowskich obosów koncentracyjnych* (Warsaw, 1964). Research was conducted in twenty-one languages, including Russian. It can easily be seen that the place occupied by works in that language is insignificant. The Russian translation of the classic work on Auschwitz by the Pole Jan Sehn bears the number 1382 and was published in Warsaw in 1961.

82. I quote the German translation introduced and annotated by A. Hillgruber and H. A. Jacobsen: B. S. Telpuchowski, *Die Sowjetische Geschichte des Grossen Vaterländischen Krieges (1941–1945)* (Frankfurt: Bernard et Graefe, 1961); on the Jews, cf. p. 272, on the camps, see pp. 422–424. The German publishers do not mention the author's

discretion concerning the genocide of the Jews even though their introduction and notes are quite critical. A few years later a narrative of the campaign of 1944–1945 was published: I. Konev et al., *La Grande Campagne libératrice de l'armée soviétique* (Moscow: Editions du progrès, 1975); on p. 71, there is discussion of "the gigantic extermination factory" of Auschwitz, with absurd statistics, but no mention of the Jews. For further details, see S. Friedländer, "De l'antisémitisme à l'extermination: Esquisse historiographique et essai d'interprétation," *L'Allemagne nazie*, pp. 13–38.

83. M. Broszat writes in "*Holocaust* und die Geschichtswissenschaft," *Vierteljahrshefte für Zeitgeschichte* 27 (1979):285–298 (see pp. 294–295), that the *Zeitschrift für Geschichtswissenschaft* in East Berlin, between 1953 and 1972, published a sum total of one article on the subject, in 1961, p. 1681, and that this was merely a review of works published in the West. This is not quite exact: see, for example, in 1962, pp. 954–957, the review of a Polish book; in 1963, pp. 794–796, the review of the series *Hefte von Auschwitz*; in 1964, pp. 5–27, L. Berthold's article on fascist terrorism in Germany and its victims, etc. But it is true that research articles are rare—incommensurate in quality and quantity with those published in Munich—and that a polemical accent against West Germany is characteristic; one study delves deeply into East German historiography on the subject and has the great merit of distinguishing among various chronological sequences; K. Kwist, "Historians of the German Democratic Republic on Anti-Semitism and Persecution," *Leo Baeck Institute Yearbook* XXI (1976):173–198; I owe this reference to Saul Friedländer.

84. See, for example, F. K. Kaul and J. Noack, *Angeklagter Nr. 6. Eine Auschwitz-Dokumentation* (Berlin: Akad. Verlag, 1966), which deals with complementary documentation concerning one of the defendants, Pery Broad, in the Auschwitz trial in Frankfurt.

85. I have given several examples of these qualities and deficiencies of Polish historiography in "A Paper Eichmann," *supra*, pp. 22, 26–27.

86. For incidental information concerning the Polish works (of the historians K. Iranek-Osmecki of London and C. Luczak of Poznan in particular), see the articles of S. Krakowski, "The Slaughter of Polish Jewry: A Polish Reassessment," *The Wiener Library Bulletin*, XXVI, 3–4, 1972–1973, pp. 13–20; "The Jewish Struggle Against the Nazis in Poland, According to Jewish and Polish Literature" (in Hebrew), VIIth

World Congress on the Sciences of Judaism, *Research on the History of the Holocaust* (Jerusalem, 1980), pp. 45–49; "The *Shoah* of the Polish Jews in the Book of the Polish Researcher C. Luczak," (in Hebrew) *Yalkout Morechet* (Jerusalem, 1980), pp. 183–198. It is hard for me to evaluate personally historiography in a language I do not know; a friend whose judgment I trust and to whom I transmitted S. Krakowski's articles tends to dismiss the two adversaries back to back, each one perceiving the chauvinism of the other; it is nonetheless the case that the symmetry, in this circumstance, can not be absolute.

87. See, for example, M. Teich, "New Editions and Old Mistakes" (concerning Reitlinger), *Yad Vashem Studies* VI (1967):375–384; N. Eck, "Historical Research or Slander?" (on Bettelheim, H. Arendt, R. Hilberg), ibid., pp. 385–430, and above all, concerning H. Arendt, the work of J. Robinson, *La Tragédie juive sous la croix gammée à la lumière du procès de Jérusalem (le récit de Hannah Arendt et la réalité des faits* (Paris: CDJC, 1969), translated by L. Steinberg. Israeli historiography has evolved in the interim, not in its entirety, to be sure, and not always at the same pace; but see in *Unanswered Questions* the contributions of A. Funkenstein and S. Volkov for example.

88. This was evident in the colloquium during which this paper was presented and particularly during the debate following the presentation of Arno Mayer, which has subsequently evolved into his book *Why Did the Heavens Not Darken?*

89. See the courageous article of the Israeli journalist Boaz Evron, "Interpretations of the Holocaust: A Danger for the Jewish People," French translation in *Revue des études palestiniennes* 2 (Winter 1982):36–52. The original appeared in Hebrew in *Yiton 77*, May-June 1980.

90. The Yad Vashem Institute is at once a scientific institute, a museum, and a place for meditation, each of them admirable, but one also finds in government tourist agencies in Jerusalem brochures inviting one to visit a "Holocaust cave" on Mount Zion, about which I prefer not to elaborate.

91. T. W. Adorno, *Dialectique négative* (Paris: Payot, 1978), pp. 283–286; I quote from pp. 283–284; for the intellectual context of Adorno's analysis, see J. P. Bier, *Auschwitz et les nouvelles littératures allemandes* (Brussels: Ed. de l'Université de Bruxelles, 1979).

92. An effort is needed to recall as much, but in the years following the

war, the symbol of the world of the concentration camps was not Auschwitz but Buchenwald. In consulting the Polish bibliography cited above (n. 81), one notes that in 1962 the number of works published on Buchenwald clearly exceeded the number devoted to the great Silesian slaughterhouse.

93. The notion of an absolute crime alas, functions in Israel and even elsewhere to justify relative crimes.

94. Concerning Dachau, cf. M. Broszat's letter to *Die Zeit*, August 19, 1960, which has since been reprinted numerous times and often deformed in the press and in revisionist literature. That being the case, one should not press the opposition between concentration camps and extermination camps too far. In the case of Dachau, precisely, personnel trained on the grounds were in many cases then used in Auschwitz and other murder sites. See the recent clarification by H. G. Richardi, *Schule der Gewalt. Die Anfänge des Konzentrationslager Dachau 1933–1934. Ein dokumentarischer Bericht* (Munich: Beck, 1983), pp. 241–248; on Krema I in Auschwitz, see W. Stäglich, *Der Auschwitz Mythos*, pp. 77 and 137. On this point, I have received photographic documentation from the Auschwitz Museum, which leaves no doubt as to tampering. It is on the subject of Anne Frank's *Diary* that the offensive has been conducted with greatest effectiveness; see, for example, R. Faurisson in S. Thion, *Vérité*, pp. 213–300, a study subsequently republished in English in the *Journal of Historical Review* III(2):147–209. Since then *The Diary of Anne Frank* has been published in a critical edition which appears to have resolved the problem of its authenticity; see H. Paape, G. van der Stroom, and D. Barnouw, *De Dagboeken van Anne Frank* (The Hague: Staatsuigeverij, and Amsterdam, Uigeverij Bert Bakker, 1986).

95. I borrow the phrase from J.-C. Milner, *Ordre et raisons de la langue* (Paris: Editions du Seuil, 1982), pp. 323–325.

96. See "A Paper Eichmann," section II.

97. This is a domain little studied in France. In Germany, recent revisionist literature has often been prompted by *Holocaust* (1979), as in the United States. See the articles of J. Herf, A. S. Markovits, R. S. Hayden, and S. Zielinski, *New German Critique* 19 (Winter 1980):30–96, which gives a quite complete overall view of the reception of the television series in Germany. An example of the revisionist reaction: H. Härtle, *Was Holocaust verschweigt: Deutsche Verteidigung gegen Kollektiv-Schuld-Lügen* (Leoni am Starnbergersee, 1979).

5. The Assassins of Memory

1. Thucydides, IV, 80, 1–4; the episode is told again, following Thucydides, by Plutarch in his *Life of Lycurgus*, 28, 6 but with a variant clearly due to an error: it was the Spartans who proceeded directly to sorting out the population and (by way of Diodorus of Sicily, XII, 67, 2) with a precision to which I shall return.

2. See A. Momigliano, "George Grote and the Study of Greek History," in *Studies in Historiography* (London: Weidenfeld and Nicolson, 1966), pp. 56–74.

3. I quote from the *History of Greece* (Paris, 1862), IX:103.

4. See P. Vidal-Naquet, *The Black Hunter*, translated by A. Szegedy-Maszak (Baltimore: Johns Hopkins University Press, 1986), pp. 168–188.

5. Xenophon, *Hellenics*, III, 3, 5.

6. Myron of Priena, quoted by Atheneus, *Banquet of the Sophists*, XIV, 657d (Jacoby, 106 F2); I am indebted for several ideas here to J. Ducat's excellent study, "Le mépris des Hilotes," *Annales ESC* 6 (1974):1451–1464, quotation on p. 1454. J. Ducat has just completed a manuscript on the Helots which he has authorized me to consult and from which I have profited.

7. See Grote, *History of Greece*, IX:103, who opts for a more recent date (425 B.C.) and who indicates, n. 2, the contrary position of his predecessor C. Thirlwall; Diodorus (see n. 1 *supra*) placed the episode in 424 B.C.

8. Cf. P. Oliva, *Sparta and her Social Problems* (Prague: Academia, 1971), p. 166; "There can be no doubt as to the authenticity of the episode"; G. Devereux, "Psychanalyse et Histoire: une application à l'histoire de Sparte," *Annales ESC* 1965 (1):18–44, has made rather singular use of Freudianism to account for the episode, but he does not treat it as a phantasm.

9. Nevertheless, Diodorus affirms, unlike Thucydides, that each man was killed in his own house.

10. Herodotus, IX, 29; this figure has obviously provoked much discussion.

11. See Max Weber, *Ancient Judaism* (Glencoe, Ill.: Free Press, 1952) and *General Economic History* (Glencoe, Ill.: Free Press, 1950); the concept has been taken up by Hannah Arendt, *The Jew as Pariah*, edited by R. H. Feldman (New York: Grove Press, 1979). For a discus-

sion, cf. A. Momigliano, "Le judaïsme comme 'religion-paria' chez Max Weber," in *Mélanges Léon Poliakov*, edited by M. Olender (Brussels: Complexe, 1981), pp. 201–207.

12. An expression borrowed from a manuscript on the genocide by Arno J. Mayer, which has since appeared as *Why Did the Heavens Not Darken?* I owe a good deal to Arno J. Mayer and extend to him my warm gratitude.

13. See M. R. Marrus and R. O. Paxton, *Vichy et les Juifs* (Paris: Calmann-Lévy, 1981), whose conclusions may be inflected by the documentation amassed by S. Klarsfeld, *Vichy-Auschwitz*, I and II (Paris: Fayard, 1983–1986).

14. I have already mentioned, p. 124, n. 82, S. Friedländer's study; we now possess M. R. Marrus's admirably informed article, "The History of the Holocaust: A Survey of Recent Literature," *Journal of Modern History* 59(1) (March 1987):114–160.

15. It is a historiography in which French researchers, whether from the University or the CNRS, cut a rather modest figure, despite the pioneering role of Léon Poliakov.

16. See, for example, in M. I. Finley's last book, *Ancient History: Evidence and Models* (London: Chatto and Windus, 1985) the chapter devoted to Ranke, the nineteenth-century founder of "positivist" history, pp. 47–66.

17. For a cumulative chronicle of Hitler's genocide, see Martin Gilbert, *The Holocaust: The Jewish Tragedy* (London: Collins, 1986), which is burdened by testimony and documents that are described but not criticized, and without explanatory investigation: see Marrus's judgment, "The History of the Holocaust," pp. 159–160.

18. I have already sketched an analysis of this debate in my "Theses on Revisionism," *supra*, p. 85; it is described with some precision in the article cited above by M. R. Marrus; see as well the luminous study, with its rich biography—which I was able to read, thanks to J.-P. Rioux, before its publication—by P. Burrin, "Maître ou serviteur: Hitler dans le Troisième Reich. Martin Broszat et l'interprétation fonctionnaliste du régime nazi," *XXe siècle: revue d'histoire*, October-December 1987.

19. This is the title of a major work by L. Dawidowicz.

20. I translate here the title of a famous article by Martin Broszat, mentioned *supra*, "Theses on Revisionism," n. 31. It has been republished

in English in a collection edited by H. W. Koch, *Aspects of the Third Reich* (London: MacMillan, 1986), pp. 390–429, and in German in M. Broszat's collection (edited by H. Graml and K. D. Henke), *Nach Hitler: Der schwierige Umgang mit unserer Geschichte* (Munich: R. Oldenberg Verlag, 1987), pp. 187–229.

21. F. Neumann, *Behemoth*, mentioned *supra*, "A Paper Eichmann," (n. 15), p. 513.

22. Arno Mayer does not fail to mention all these interventions in his unpublished manuscript (which has since appeared as *Why Did the Heavens Not Darken?*; see as well E. Ben Elissar, *La Diplomatie du IIIe Reich et les Juifs* (Paris: Julliard, 1939), p. 473; concerning Hitler's confusion, on four occasions, between this speech and that of September 1, 1939, the day on which the invasion of Poland began, and in which he had not spoken of the Jews, cf. L. Dawidowicz, *The Holocaust*, pp. 183–184.

23. *The Twisted Road to Auschwitz: Nazi Policy Toward German Jews, 1933–1939* (Urbana: University of Illinois Press, 1970); a summary of this work may be found in *Unanswered Questions*, pp. 54–70.

24. *The Twisted Road to Auschwitz*, pp. 214–254: "1938: A Road is Open."

25. I have already objected to this tragic conception of history in my introduction to the French translation of M. R. Marrus's book, *Les Juifs de France à l'époque de l'affaire Dreyfus* (1972); see *Les Juifs, la mémoire, et le présent*, p. 88. In this last case, the tragedy would have begun at the end of the nineteenth century.

26. My admiration for this film history, which is immense, need not conceal disagreements on details, on certain silences, for example, concerning the Gypsies, the attitude of American Jews, and above all, over the cruel manner in which the director questions Polish peasants, who inhabit a space of inherently impoverished discourse.

27. See E. Kogon, H. Langbein, and A. Rückerl, *Les Chambres à gaz, secret d'Etat*, 2d ed. (Paris: Seuil, 1987), pp. 184–185, where the principal testimony, including that of Hoess, may be found.

28. Ibid., pp. 24–71; Hitler's letter is quoted on page 28.

29. Here too I owe it to Arno J. Mayer to have thought of this dimension of the problem.

30. The essential book on the subject is G. Sereny, *Into That Darkness: From Mercy Killing to Mass Murder* (New York: McGraw-Hill, 1974).

31. On this point as well Arno J. Mayer's analysis is decisive.

32. L. Trotsky's article, "Le procès de Dantzig contre les 'troskystes'" was published in *Lutte ouvrière* on August 27, 1937; it is reprinted as an appendix to F. Jakubowsky's book, *Les Superstructures idéologiques dans la conception matérialiste de l'histoire*, translated by J. M. Brohm (Paris: EDI, 1976), pp. 207–212; this document was brought to my attention by Boris Fraenkel.

33. Cf. *supra*, "A Paper Eichmann," p. 30; one of the best syntheses on the subject known to me is C. Browning's "The Decision Concerning the Final Solution," in *Unanswered Questions*, pp. 96–118; Arno J. Mayer argues vigorously in terms of a response to failure: unable to take Moscow and Leningrad, Hitler at least had to destroy the demonized enemy.

34. *Why Did the Heavens Not Darken?*, chapter X.

35. Wirtschafts Verwaltung Hauptamt; for a rather detailed sketch of its evolution, see Wormser-Migot, *Le Système concentrationnaire nazi*, pp. 294–402.

36. Cf. "A Paper Eichmann," *supra*, p. 41.

37. See François Hartog, *The Mirror of Herodotus: The Representation of the Other in the Writing of History*, translated by J. Lloyd (Berkeley: University of California Press, 1988).

38. Michel de Certeau, *L'Ecriture de l'histoire* (Paris: Gallimard, 1975).

39. Hayden White, *Metahistory: The Historicial Imagination in Nineteenth Century Europe* (Baltimore: Johns Hopkins University Press, 1973); see also, concerning genocide, his lecture-article "The Politics of Historical Interpretation: Discipline and De-sublimation," *Critical Inquiry* 9 (September 1982).

40. In support of this affirmation, I would have to cite the complete intellectual output of Pierre Sorlin or, in a different genre, the films of Marc Ferro.

41. "Claude Lanzmann thus works like an anthropologist recording the 'living memory of a people.' In this respect his film is a great ethnological film about Jewish storytellers," writes P. Guillaume (*Droit et Histoire* [Paris: La Vieille Taupe, 1986], p. 57). And no doubt also about Nazi and Polish "storytellers." R. Faurisson's reaction to the film was two years in coming: "Ouvrez vos yeux, cassez la télé," Supplement no. 2 to *Annales d'histoire révisionniste*, a tract distributed in June 1987. It is extremely "vague," to use one of the author's preferred terms.

42. I have written a review of this lamentable work of fiction, whose effect was immense, in "Le navet et le spectacle," *Esprit*, April 1979, pp. 119–121.

43. An experience I had in May 1987 via television.

44. Concerning the existence of small gas chambers in the western camps, see E. Kogon, H. Langbein, and A. Rückerl, *Les Chambres à gaz, secret d'Etat*, pp. 222–255; the affirmation, to be found in all revisionists writings, according to which the German historian M. Broszat would have written in *Die Zeit* of August 19, 1980 that there were no gas chambers in the camps of the former Reich is a lie which has been effectively dismantled by G. Wellers, *Les Chambres à gaz ont existé* (Paris: Gallimard, 1981), pp. 141–143. M. Broszat spoke only of installations specialized in the annihilation of the Jews. The lie is nonetheless repeated in all the sect's tracts. That much being established, there *were* imaginary gas chambers and G. Wellers was wrong to glide over the subject a bit hastily (pp. 161–162).

45. See H. I. Marrou, *De la connaissance historique*, 7th ed. (Paris: Seuil, 1975), pp. 132–133.

46. "Comment s'en débarrasser?," *Le Monde*, June 18, 1987.

47. The expressions in quotation marks are borrowed from W. Stäglich, *Le Mythe d'Auschwitz*, p. 28.

48. I have given above, in "A Paper Eichmann," section VIII, the references to this document and the polemics it elicited.

49. This grotesque affirmation figures on the back cover of R. Faurisson, *Mémoire en défense*.

50. Robert Bonnaud drew my attention to this sentence.

51. A drolly sinister detail: Faurisson glosses this entry of September 3, 1942—"colic, diarrhea" (*Mémoire en défense*, p. 131).

52. In his article in *Le Monde*, January 16, 1978, and reprinted in S. Thion, *Vérité*, and in his book *Mémoire en défense*.

53. Above, p. 50.

54. *Réponse à Pierre Vidal-Naquet*, p. 55.

55. His detailed argument is to be found in a text printed at his own expense: *Mon analyse du 'Journal de Kremer,' médecin SS à Auschwitz* (Saint-Nazaire, 1981), and in *L'Antimythe*, no. 25, Draveil, 1981; a fragment of this last text was reprinted in the collection *Intolérable intolérance*, pp. 11–29.

56. *Mémoire en défense*, p. 35; I have replaced "my tenth" by "the tenth," which is more literal.

57. Concerning this interpretation, see above, p. 65.

58. Reference to this work is supplied above, chapter 1, n. 51. The thesis itself was annulled by Alain Devaquet on July 2, 1986, for administrative irregularities, after a press campaign. The measure, which shared the mediocrity of all administrative decisions, ignored the responsibility of the academics who were underwriting this hoax. An excellent clarification of the affair is to be found in the article by Michèle Cointet and Rainer Riemschneider, "Histoire, déontologie, médias: A propos de l'affaire Roques," *Revue d'histoire moderne et contemporaine*, January-March 1987, pp. 174–184.

59. I cite here an unpublished document, a tape recording of the Nantes defense. Concerning the friendship of Céline and Albert Paraz, an extreme right-wing writer who was the prefacer and friend of Paul Rassinier, cf. F. Gibault, *Céline, III, 1944–1961: Cavalier de l'Apocalypse* (Paris: Mercure de France, 1986), passim.

60. See the material assembled by G. Wellers, *Le Monde juif* 121 (January-March 1986):1–18; discussion of this affair continued in subsequent issues of the periodical, with an intervention by Henri Roques, who attempted in vain to explain his omission of this testimony.

61. J.-P. Allard, a professor at Lyon-III, has explained his position in this affair in various declarations, particularly in a letter of December 4, 1986, to his fellow Germanists which I have before me and which testifies above all to his cowardice.

62. Two volumes have been published through the efforts of Jean-Paul Dumont and Paul-Ursin Dumont, *Le Cercle amoureux d'Henry Legrand* (Paris: Gallimard, 1979); H. Legrand, *Adèle, Adèle, Adèle* (Paris: Christian Bourgois, 1979).

63. One should read the few literally insane pages P. Guillaume published in the first issue of *Annales d'histoire révisionniste* (Spring 1987), particularly pp. 178–180, an issue which was regrettably banned from public sale: in informing a Swedish diplomat of what was happening at Belzec, Gerstein was acting, according to Guillaume, on behalf of the Nazis. It was a matter of obtaining various advantages from the Nazis "in exchange for the improvement of the fate of the Jews."

64. The typography of the word *Annales* in the review I have just mentioned is borrowed from *Annales: Economies-Sociétés-Civilisations*. The circumstance speaks volumes as to the revisionists' will to respectability and appearances.

65. See above "A Paper Eichmann," section VI.

66. Much of what I know of La Vieille Taupe is borrowed from a megalomaniacal but fascinating article published in *La Banquise* 2 (1983):3–60, "Le roman de nos Origines." *La Banquise* is a dissidence of this dissidence, which broke with La Vieille Taupe over a number of issues, including that of Faurissonianism. It nonetheless retains a discreetly revisionist attitude, as evidenced by the book of one of its members, S. Quadruppani's *Catalogue du prêt-à-penser français depuis 1968* (Paris: Balland, 1983). Others broke clearly and definitively with the group over the Faurisson affair, and most particularly Jacques Baynac.

67. To my knowledge, no *history* of Socialisme ou Barbarie exists, even if projects of this sort have been formulated (particularly by the Danish professor Jules Lund), but the principal writings of the leaders of the group have been published: nine volumes in the Collection 10/18, from 1974 to 1979, edited by C. Castoriadis under the general title *Socialisme ou Barbarie*, and, by Claude Lefort, *Eléments pour une critique de la bureaucratie* (Geneva: Droz, 1971; revised and republished, Paris: Gallimard, 1979); see as well the collection of articles from the journal *Arguments*, edited by E. Morin, *La Bureaucratie* (Paris: 10/18, 1976). Finally, detailed interviews with C. Castoriadis, H. Simon, and C. Lefort were published in 1975 in the series *L'Antimythe*. So that matters may be clear, I shall state here that I discovered the journal in 1958, and that without ever being a member, I subscribed to the journal and to the dissident organ *Pouvoir ouvrier* from 1958 until their disappearance. It was at my initiative that the first group publication outside the journal appeared: Daniel Mothé's *Journal d'un ouvrier* (Paris: Editions de Minuit, 1959). I also collaborated with La Vieille Taupe in 1973–1974 in the effort to save the Spanish anarchist Puig-Antich.

68. I am paraphrasing and quoting P. Bourdieu, "Genèse et structure du champ religieux," *Revue française de sociologie* 12 (1971):295–334 (quotation on p. 321).

69. A savory detail: P. Guillaume and his friends were accused of succumbing to antifascism and a desire for publicity at the time of their collaboration with me during the Puig-Antich affair; cf. *La Banquise* 2:32–33, and those same critics, after their break and before the publication of *La Banquise*, in turn came to see me.

70. I am thinking of Miguel Abensour and the admirable collection

"Critique de la politique" (Payot), which has translated works of the Frankfurt School.

71. I underscored this role in my introduction to A. Schnapp and P. Vidal-Naquet, *The French Student Uprising*, translated by Maria Jolas (Boston: Beacon Press, 1971). The founders of Socialisme ou Barbarie, and E. Morin with them, have expressed their views in *La Brèche* (Paris: Fayard, 1968).

72. See above, "A Paper Eichmann," p. 111.

73. Testimony of Miguel Abensour.

74. See in *Mémoire en défense*, p. 270, the incredible letter of a Belgian Catholic fundamentalist publishing house, refusing to distribute Thion's book, a copy of which had been sent to it, because of the book's atheism. An alliance with such circles had thus been attempted.

75. Such a policy is rather singularly conducted on the international level, either with German neo-Nazis (see above, "Theses on Revisionism," p. 90) or with W. Carto's Liberty Lobby in the United States. Carto finances the *Journal of Historical Review*, of which Faurisson is a member of the advisory committee, and he has links with the Ku Klux Klan. There is much documentation concerning this group: see the American review *Facts*, the organ of the Anti-Defamation League, 26(2) (1980) and Ludi Boekel's film *The Other Face of Terror*, broadcast on Antenne 2 in 1984. In France, one should indicate the journal *Le Militant*, directed by a historian, A. Delaporte, and which voices a sensibility at once Catholic-fundamentalist and Nazi. Concerning these various tendencies, one may read (but with a critical eye) the works of P. A. Taguieff and J. Tarnero, for example in the anthology prefaced by R. Badinter, *Vous avez dit Fascismes?* (Paris: Arthaud-Montalba, 1984).

76. See the previously mentioned contribution to the collection *Intolérable intolérance*. V. Monteil was the distributor of the video cassette produced by R. Faurisson.

77. For instance, the Paris Iraqi magazine *Kol Al Arab* published an interview with Faurisson in April 1983. Other Arab (and particularly Palestinian) organs have had a quite different attitude—for example, *La Revue des études palestiniennes*. The generalizations in which B. Lewis indulges in *Semites and Anti-Semites* strike me as excessive. Having said that, I should state that it is a matter of some notoriety that Arab money, particularly from Saudi Arabia, financially supports the dissemination of anti-Semitic and revisionist texts. It has just been as-

certained (*Le Canard enchaîné*, August 5, 1987) that the famous Monsieur Gordji of the Iranian embassy helped underwrite the publishing-distributing house Ogmios, which distributes Henri Roques's thesis and works published by La Vieille Taupe.

In the first issue of *Annales d'histoire révisionniste*, pp. 110–115, S. Thion has published a study entitled "Histoire européenne et monde arabe." It is a preface to an aborted Arab edition of his book on the Faurisson affair, and in my opinion it is the sole text in these *Annales* which does not totally disgrace its author. That being granted, it should be stated that not for an instant does S. Thion ponder what effect the thesis of the "hoax of Auschwitz" might have on an Arab world at war.

78. Both were published by Editions de la Différence with prefaces by P. Guillaume in 1982 and 1983. In *Esprit* (June 1982), I had drawn attention to the dishonesty of the first republication.

79. These quotations are excerpted from a Vieille Taupe circular signed by P. Guillaume in 1986 and preceding the publication of W. Stäglich's book. Myth is not the only thing to have "died"; P. Guillaume's adversaries, who manifestly know him rather well, published his obituary in *L'Exagéré*, May 1, 1987: "The corpse of this revisionist-sic has been brought home to Paris to be at last given over to the gnawing critique of the scourers." The obituary goes on to stipulate that P. Guillaume passed away "at the residence of an officer of the Swiss army, Mme Mariette Paschoud." An officer and a teacher in Lausanne, Mme. Paschoud represents the Vaudois branch of revisionism.

80. Which has not prevented him from speaking, for years, about lies and hoaxes.

81. *Mémoire en défense*, p. 271.

82. A tract entitled "Le mythe de l'extermination des Juifs," signed by Faurisson and communicated to me by my Besançon colleague M. M. Mactoux.

83. Tract entitled "Info-intox … Histoire-intox … ça suffit! Chambres-à-gaz Bidon" (May 1987). The tract is signed by a Lycée Collective which, if I am not mistaken, had surfaced at the time of the Roques affair. It is accompanied by a drawing by the artist Konk (formerly with *Le Monde* and *L'Evénement du jeudi*, subsequently with *Minute*), taken from his album, *Aux voleurs* (Paris: Albin Michel, 1986). It was also distributed in Lyon, on April 27, 1987, in the context of the Barbie trial.

84. For France, see, in the beautiful series "Les lieux de la mémoire,"

published since 1984 at Gallimard by P. Nora, vol. II(1) (1986), *La Nation*, pp. 189–429, which goes back to the thirteenth century the better to underscore, in the nineteenth century, "the great cycle of the nation affirming its sovereignty" (p. 186).

85. See P. Nora's two studies, "Lavisse instituteur national," "Les Lieux de mémoire," *La République* I:247–289, and "*L'Histoire de France* de Lavisse," ibid., II(1):317–375.

86. See J. Chesneaux, *Du passé faisons table rase?* (Paris: Maspero, 1976). There are, moreover, many correct observations in this book, but its general thesis strikes me as open to criticism. Concerning national practices, see Marc Ferro, *Comment on raconte l'histoire aux enfants* (Paris: Payot, 1981).

87. I return here to what I wrote at the beginning of the volume of the "Peoples' Permanent Tribunal," *Le Crime du silence: le génocide des Arméniens*, p. 15. Concerning official Turkish historiography, see in that same volume the chapter entitled "Les Thèses turques," pp. 203–256. It is regrettable that this volume is introduced and concluded by François Rigaux, one of those who have denied the "crimes against humanity" committed in Cambodia under the reign of Pol Pot. For a far more detailed presentation of the Turkish conception of Armenian history, see Kamuran Gurun, *Le Dossier arménien* (Triangle, 1983).

88. All of this did not take place in a single day, and I hope that S. Friedländer will soon publish the presentation I heard him deliver on the subject in Haifa in January 1987 and which was replete with interesting details.

89. Occasionally, but not always, there appear works in the Diaspora which are far more "orthodox" and less critical than what is being produced in Israel. M. Gilbert's book *Holocaust* is an example.

90. In another Jerusalem neighborhood, on Mount Zion in the Old City, the "Holocaust cave" is a site intended to provoke fear of the return of the Shoah and not a place for meditation.

91. *Le Monde*, February 3, 1983; the article had the effect of shocking S. Quadruppani, *Catalogue du pret-à-penser français depuis 1968*, n. 66, pp. 344–346.

92. K. Jaspers, *The Question of German Guilt*, translated by E. B. Ashton (New York: Dial Press, 1948).

93. See B. Cohen and L. Rosenzweig, *Le Mystère Waldheim* (Paris: Gallimard, 1986).

94. Cf. *supra*, "Theses on Revisionism," p. 94.

95. See J. P. Bier, *Auschwitz et les nouvelles littératures allemandes* (Brussels: Editions de l'université de Bruxelles, 1979); as an individual case and because of its honesty and sincerity, mention should be made of L. Baier, *Un Allemand né de la dernière guerre, essai à l'usage des Français* (Brussels: Complexe, 1985).

96. See M. H. Kater's essential work, *Das 'Ahnerbe' der SS, 1935–1945: Ein Beitrag zur Kulturpolitik der Dritten Reichs* (Stuttgart: DVA, 1974).

97. Phrase used by A. Besançon, *La Confusion des langues* (Paris: Calmann-Lévy, 1978), p. 94.

98. And not the New Right alone: all those who derive from the work of G. Dumézil the idea, or rather the retrospective utopia, that, in the last analysis, European humanity embarked on the wrong ship when it became Christian (that is, Jewish). A fine example: J. L. Tristani, "La théologie comme science du XXe siècle," *Critique*, 1977, pp. 1085–1097. The case of Tristani, who is one of the collaborators of *Intolérable intolérance* and of P. Guillaume's book *Droit et Histoire*, is, from an intellectual point of view, particularly appalling.

99. One can get an idea of what such propaganda was like, with all that was true and occasionally imprecise in it, in the Thomas Mann volume translated into French as *Appels aux Allemands, 1940–1945* (Paris: Balland & Martin Flinker, 1985).

100. W. Stäglich, *Le Mythe d'Auschwitz*, chapter 4, n. 26, pp. 11, 12, 16.

101. Cf. *supra*, "Theses on Revisionism," p. 90.

102. Cf. Erich Kern, *Von Versailles nach Nürnberg: Der Opfergang des Deutschen Volkes*, 3d ed. (Göttingen: Schütz, 1971).

103. In France it has been the subject of a massive amount of documentation, and I shall therefore be brief. See S. Friedländer, "Sur le nazisme," *Le Débat* 43 (January-March 1987):184–187, which gives the principal references; by the same author, "Quelques réflexions sur l'historisation du National-Socialisme," *XXe siècle, revue d'histoire* (October-December 1987); under the title "Interrogations allemandes," *Le Débat* also assembled material by H. Bruhns, C. Meier, H. Mommsen, H. G. Haupt, and R. von Thadden, no. 45 (May-September 1987), pp. 140–169—this is the most complete assemblage of material in French; see also J.-J. Guinchard, "Passé nazi, passé allemand?," *Le*

Monde diplomatique, July 1987; E. François, "Allemagne: la révision du nazisme," *L'Histoire* 98 (March 1987):79–83; a good analysis with translated texts is to be found in Katharina von Bülow, "L'Histoire, une idole en faveur du finalisme politique," *Cosmopolitiques* 3 (May 1987):87–106. Finally a collection has just appeared—*Historiker-"Streit": Die Dokumentation der Kontroverse und die Einzigartigkeit der national-sozialistischen Judenvernichtung* (Munich: Piper Verlag, 1987)—which regroups all the essential texts. My thanks to P. Nora, Denis Vidal-Naquet, H. Bruhns, Arno J. Mayer, and J.-P. Rioux for the assistance they have given me.

104. "Vergangenheit die nicht vergehen will": I shall refer for the most part to "Between Myth and Revisionism?: The Third Reich in the Perspective of the Eighties" in H. W. Koch, ed., *Apects of the Third Reich*, pp. 17–38. The Nolte article, in German, is not the first to have appeared in a newspaper, but it was the one which served as a point of reference and, often, of counter-reference in the "Quarrel."

105. A. Hillgruber, *Zweierlei Untergang: Die Zerschlagung der Deutschen Reiches und das Ende des europäischen Judentums* (Berlin: Corso bei Siedler, 1986).

106. Martin Broszat, "Plaidoyer für eine Historisierung des National-sozialismus," *Merkur*, May 1985, pp. 373–385.

107. "Eine Art Schaudensabwicklung: die apologetishen Tendenzen in der deutschen Zeitgeschichtsschreibung," *Die Zeit*, July 11, 1986; J. Habermas was to return to the subject and attempt, in vain, to conclude in a second article published in *Die Zeit*, November 7, 1986, "Vom Offentlichen Gebrauch der Historie [On the public use of history]"; among the participants in the debate, mention should be made above all of the historian E. Jäckel, "Die elende Praxis der Untersteller [The miserable practice of the insinuators]," *Die Zeit*, September 12, 1986, who took the side of Habermas, and of the historian J. Fest, editor of the *Frankfurter Allgemeine Zeitung*, who published in that newspaper (August 29, 1986) "Die geschuldete Erinnerung [Indebted memory]" and took that of Nolte. On April 25, 1986, the same daily had published an article of the same tendency by the historian M. Stürmer, "Geschichte in geschichtlosem Land [History in a land without history]."

108. Quoted by K. von Bülow, "L'Histoire, une idole en faveur du finalisme politique," p. 103.

109. Thucydides, I, 23, 6.

110. H. Mommsen gives a gripping example of it in his study of the behavior of the Nazi leaders after the Reichstag fire, "The Reichstag Fire and its Political Consequences" in H. W. Koch, ed., *Aspects of the Third Reich*, n. 104, pp. 62–95.

111. E. Nolte, "A Past That Will Not Pass Away," p. 27. For the literally industrial exploitation by revisionists of T. Kaufmann's booklet— which is from 1941, not 1940, and which calmly looked forward to the sterilization of the Germans—see, for example, P. Rassinier, *Le Véritable Procès Eichmann* (*supra*, chapter 1, n. 66), pp. 109 and 239–243, or H. Härtle, *Freispruch für Deutschland* (*supra*, chapter 4, n. 34), pp. 255–256, or E. Kern, *Von Versailles nach Nürnberg* (*supra*, n. 102), p. 456; concerning Weizmann and the use to which he is put by Faurisson and several others, see my clarification in "A Paper Eichmann," section VII.

112. H. Mommsen discusses in this context (*Le Débat* 45:145–146) the projected Museum of German History, presently being planned in Bonn and Berlin, which runs the risk of freezing that history into an insipid state-inspired version. More than history books, museums function as the expression of national ideologies. One need only travel in Israel and in Poland; cf. "Des musées et des hommes" in *Les Juifs, la mémoire, et le présent*, I:110–125.

113. Samuel I, 15:1–3.

114. An example among many others: G. E. M. de Ste-Croix, *The Class Struggle in the Ancient Greek World* (London: Duckworth, 1981), pp. 331–332, and see the entry "genocide" in the index.

115. From the translation by E. Renan, *Histoire du peuple d'Israël* in *Oeuvres complètes*, VI (Paris: Calmann-Lévy, 1953), p. 501.

116. See *La Torture dans la République* (Paris: Editions de Minuit, 1972; reed. Maspero, 1975); *Les Crimes de l'armée française* (Paris: Maspero, 1975).

117. *Bulletin municipal officiel de Paris*, Session of October 27, 1961. M. Moscovitch was to repeat on January 15: "I have indeed regretted that the enemies of France were not exterminated . . . and I still regret it." (*Le Monde*, January 17, 1962).

118. The title of a brochure he published in 1961 with Maspero.

119. J. Vergès, "Lettre au docteur Servatius sur la défense de Robert Lacoste," *Les Temps modernes*, November 1961, pp. 563–565.

120. An allusion to the repression which followed the demonstration

of May 1945, particularly in Sétif. The figure of 45,000 victims is an exaggeration, but the repression was atrocious. That article by Vergès should be read in conjunction with the one he wrote on "the crime of colonialism" in *Les Temps modernes*, March 1962, pp. 1283–1295. The 1945 date is an allusion to the Nuremberg trial at which Dr. Servatius had been a lawyer.

121. *Le Monde*, March 22, 1972.

122. A demonstration of this had been given by Maxime Rodinson in his classic article, "Israël, fait colonial?" in *Les Temps modernes*, special issue (1967) and reprinted in his collection, *Peuple juif ou problème juif* (Paris: Maspero, 1981).

123. Annie Kriegel, *Israël est-il coupable?* (Paris: Robert Laffont, 1982), pp. 149–180.

124. See H. Noguères, *La Vérité aura le dernier mot* (Paris: Seuil, 1985), whose demonstration strikes me as irrefutable.

125. *Actualité de l'émigration*, October 15, 1986; I myself had collaborated (along with Didier Daenincks and Jean-Luc Einaudi) in this issue and our protest was published on October 29 together with a discouraging commentary.

126. See *Le Monde* of May 24–25, 1987 (article by F. Fritscher).

127. More than reading the book of this title [*Le Cas Vergès*] by Jacques Givet (Paris: Lieu commun, 1986), in order to become acquainted with the individual, one would do well to consult the astonishing self-portrait he published, with the assistance of J.-P. Chabrol, in *VSD* (May 21–27, 1987); the partial disavowal in the following issue will not convince anyone.

128. I have attempted to delineate several of these contradictions in *Le Monde* of June 16, 1987 ("Les degrés dans le crime").

129. See *Libération*, July 3, 1987 (article by Véronique Brossard): "Cette jeune génération montante d'intellectuels qui faurissonnent sur le colonialisme."

130. Cf. J.-M. Tholleyre in *Le Monde* of July 5–6, 1987.

131. Excerpts from and summary of a manifesto signed May 8, 1987, and published in *Le Nouvel observateur*, July 10, 1987.

132. The one cited above, n. 83.

133. Concerning this affair the most precise treatment is the one published in *Le Matin* of June 1, 1987.

134. Concerning this legislation, see E. Stein, "History Against Free

Speech: The New German Law Against the 'Auschwitz'—and Other— 'Lies,'" *Michigan Law Review* 85(2) (November 1986):277–323.

135. Cf. ibid., p. 281 and *supra*, n. 40.

136. Cf. Lyotard, *Le Différend*, p. 16, quotation on p. 38.

137. Excerpt from a tango by the Argentine poet Enrique Santos Discépolo, which the reader will find below.

138. I am thinking of the work undertaken by J.-C. Pressac, a former revisionist who, at Auschwitz, was overwhelmed by the evidence he had denied. See his *Auschwitz: Technique and Operation of the Gas Chambers* (New York: Beate Klarsfeld Foundation, 1989). I am thinking as well, of course, of all that Georges Wellers has contributed.

139. I recall, following J. Baynac and N. Fresco (*Le Monde* of June 18, 1987), that this was the conclusion reached by R. Hilberg in *The Destruction of the European Jews*, published in French translation by Editions Fayard in 1988.

140. Preface to Filip Müller, *Trois ans dans une chambre à gaz d'Auschwitz* (*supra*, chapter 1, n. 43), p. 12.

141. Ibid., p. 17.

Index

Abensour, Miguel, 183n70
"Abundance of Evidence, An" (Wellers), xiii, xviii
Academic gamesmanship, 7–8
"Accusation Against the Nuclear Powers," 125
Acetylene, 64
Action Française (organization), 54
Admirals, 30
Adorno, Theodor, 97, 98
Ahmed, Hocine Aït, 135
Algerians, 18, 128, 134
Algerian war, 127–129, 132, 135
Algérie-Actualité (newspaper), 132
Allard, Jean-Paul, 115, 153n51, 182n61
Allied Powers: atrocities of, 15–16, 88, 125; propaganda of, 19, 55, 83; racism of, 22
Amalekites, 126–127
Amara, Bougenaa, 168n44
American Historical Society, 80–81
American historiography, 80–81
American Indians, 4–5, 127
American Jews, 39
American revisionism, 80–81, 90
American War Refugee Board, 25, 84
Ancient Greeks, 99–102
Ancient historiography, 52
Ancient Jews, 33–34, 126–127
Annales d'histoire révisionniste, 136
El Ansar, 122
Anthropophagy, 3–7, 11

Anti-Semitism: of App, 20; of Faurisson, 67; in Paris, 75, 128; of Rassinier, 33; revisionism and, 90, 92
L'Antisémitisme, son histoire et ses causes (Lazare), 119
App, Austin J., 20
Arab revisionism, 16, 88, 184–185n77
Arab slave trade, 130
Archives, 17, 24, 26, 44, 69
Arcimboldo, Giuseppe, 110
Arendt, Hannah, x, 81, 82–83, 95, 96
Arens, W., 7, 8
Aristotle, 8
Armenian massacre, 56, 120–121, 129
Aschenauer, R., 167n33
Assyrians, 126
Athens, 99
Atlantis, 52–53
A-t-on lu Lautréamont? (Faurisson), xx
August, Clemens, 107
Augustine of Hippo, St., 112
Auschwitz: Butz on, 51; Czech on, 53; death categories of, 148n19; death statistics of, 19; "departures" from, 84; deportee selection in, 43–50; early descriptions of, 83–84; forced labor in, 109; gassings in, 106–107; Gypsies in, 24, 153n48; Kremer on, 45–50,

Auschwitz (Continued)
112–113; managerial conflict in,
12; Polish State Council and, 38–
39; *Sonderkommando* records of,
21–22; Soviet Army and, 108; as
symbol, 97, 122, 176n92; testimony about, 26, 27–29; typhus
in, xii, 45, 46, 48, 49–50, 65,
113–114; *see also* Birkenau
Auschwitz Museum, 95
Auschwitz Mythos, Der (Stäglich),
98, 119, 163n25
Auschwitz ou le Grand Alibi, 9
Australian revisionism, 91
Austria, 122
Aztecs, 5–6

Babi Yar massacre, 23
Baer, Richard, 23
La Banquise (periodical), 183n66
Barbie, Klaus, 129, 130, 131–135
Bardèche, Maurice, 32–33, 92,
168n42
Barnes, H. E., 80–81, 82, 90,
170n60
La Bataille du rail (film), 111
Baudrillard, J., 6
Baynac, Jacques, 112, 183n66
Beauchamp, Chantal, 163n24
Bebel, August, 90
Beirut siege, 131
Belzec, 26, 115
Ben Abdallah, 129
Ben-Gurion, David, 39
Bennett, John, 55–56, 91, 160n115
Berenice, 34
Bergelson, David, 36
Bergerac, Savinien de Cyrano de,
see Cyrano de Bergerac, Savinien
de
Bernard, Tristan, 151n30
Bernstein, Eduard, 79
Besnard, Marie, 152n42
Bibliothèque des histoires, 110

Bibliothèque Nationale (France), 2
Bigeard, Colonel, 21, 134
Birkenau, 62–63, 84, 97, 152n42,
158n96
Bitburg cemetery, 124
Black slaves, 130
Bloch, Pitch, 64
Blum, Léon, 32, 34
Boekel, L., 124
Bordiga, Amadeo, 9
Borwicz, Michel, 27
Bouaïta, Maître, 131, 135
Boüard, Michel de, 13, 149n23
Brand, Joël, 10
Brandt, Dr., 107
Brandt, Willy, 38
Bravo, B., 154n59
Breton, André, 68
Bréviaire de la haine (Poliakov), 34
British secret services, 84
Broad, Pery, 28, 174n84
Broszat, Martin: Browning and, 85;
Faurisson and, 144n20; on gas
chambers, 181n44; on German
history, 125; "Plea for a Histori-
cization of National-Socialism,"
124; on *Vergasung,* 23
Browning, Christopher, 85
Brunet, Gilbert, 157n81
Buchenwald, 14, 176n92
Bukharin, Nikolay Ivanovich, 27,
154n54
Burckhardt, J., 110
Burg, J. G., 168n47
Butz, Arthur: Auschwitz and, 21,
49–50; Bennett and, 55; on Willy
Brandt, 38; Centre de Documen-
tation Juive Contemporaine and,
34; on deportee selection, 43; on
"exterminationists," 50; Faurisson and, 91; on Gypsies, 24; *The
Hoax of the Twentieth Century,*
51, 98; *Journal of Historical Review* and, 19; Kremer diary and,

Index

45; Mayer and, xvii; obscurity of, 2, 90

Calcium carbide, 64
Calvin, Jean, 112
"Cambalache" (Discépolo), xvi, 140–142
Cambodian massacre, xv, 186*n*87
Cambodian totalitarianism, 70
Camos, 127
Cannibalism, 3–7, 11
Capitalism, 10, 137
Capitant, René, 128
Carto, W. A., 90, 184*n*75
Cartox, 61
Castillo, Bernal Diaz del, *see* Diaz del Castillo, Bernal
Castoriadis, Cornelius, 6, 116
Catholic Church, 105, 107
Céline, Louis-Ferdinand, 32, 115
Censorship, 55, 95
Centre de Documentation Juive Contemporaine, 2, 34, 58–59, 135, 162*n*10
Chateaubriand, François-Auguste-René, vicomte de, 57–58
Children, 40, 67
Chomsky, Noam: Cohn-Bendit and, 114; Faurisson petition and, 58; "Some Elementary Comments on the Rights of Freedom of Expression," xv–xvi, xx, 65–73, 91, 144–145*n*21; Stäglich and, 163*n*25; La Vieille Taupe and, 172*n*74
Christian clergy, 107
Christophersen, Th., 21, 43, 47, 51
Chronicles, 104
Cleisthenes of Athens, 8
Cohen, Kadmi, 33
Cohn-Bendit, Jean-Gabriel, 18, 66, 82, 113, 114, 148*n*14
Cold War, 17
Colonial war crimes, 129, 133–134

Comité d'histoire de la Seconde Guerre mondiale, 150*n*29
Comité pour les Juifs, 150–151*n*29
"Commission de sauvegarde," 131
Communist censorship, 95
Concentration camps: Belzec, 26, 115; Buchenwald, 14, 176*n*92; Dachau, 97, 176*n*94; deportee selection in, 42–50; Dora, 44; economic aspects of, 118; Maidanek, 109; *Sonderkommando*, 21–22, 25, 63; Teschen, 159*n*104; Treblinka, 15; *see also* Auschwitz; Birkenau; "Special treatment" (*Sonderbehandlung*)
Contre l'antisémitisme (Lazare), 119
Cortés, Hernán, 5
Costes (firm), 116
Coston, H., 33
Crimes against humanity, 30, 132–133, 134
Criminal revisionism, xx
Criminal trials, *see* Trials
Cyrano de Bergerac, Savinien de, 56
Czech, Danuta, 44, 53

Dachau, 97, 176*n*94
Dali, Salvador, 76
Daniel, Jean, 132
Darquier de Pellepoix, Louis, xi, xii, 147*n*7
Dawidowicz, Lucy, 104, 145*n*31
Day of the Shoah, 121
Death camps, *see* Concentration camps
Death statistics, 18–19, 21, 50, 139–140
Debray, Régis, xv
Défense de l'Occident (periodical), 92
Degesch (firm), 61
Deir Yassin massacre, 16
Delebecque, F., 54
Delousing metaphor, 12–13

Index

Delpech, F., 2
Demanjuk, J., 122
Deportees: Dutch, 47, 114; French, 33; Hungarian, 84; memoirs of, 13; "Muslim," 47, 114, 158n96, 162n3; selection among, 42–50; *see also* "Special treatment" (*Sonderbehandlung*)
Deutsche National und Soldatenzeitung, 130
Devaquet, Alain, 182n58
Diarrhea, 49
Diary of Anne Frank, The, xix, 17, 69–70, 97
Diatomit, 61
Diaz del Castillo, Bernal, 4–5
Différend, Le (Lyotard), xiv, 144n17
Dimitrov trial, 108
Diodorus of Sicily, 177nn1, 9
Discépolo, Enrique Santos, xvi, 140–142
Donabedian, Monique, 122
Dora camp, 44
Double Disappearance, A (Hillgruber), 124
Drame des Juifs européens, Le (Rassinier), 29, 34–38
Dreyfus Affair, ix-x; Algerian war and, 127; Faurisson conviction and, xiii; leftism and, xxi; revisionism and, xviii, xix, 54, 79, 81
Drumont, Edouard, 92–93
Ducasse, Isidore-Lucien, *see* Lautréamont, Comte de (I.-L. Ducasse)
Dumézil, G., 187n98
Dutch deportees, 47, 114
Dutrait-Crozon, Henri, 54

East European Jews, 36, 103
East German historiography, 94, 174n83
Education, 98
Eichmann, Adolf: Arendt on, 96; Browning on, 85; execution of, 57; Faurisson and, 24; Hitler and, 135; *Ich Adolf Eichmann,* 166–167n33; trial of, 30–31, 122; Vergès on, 128–129
Eichmann par Eichmann (Less), 30–31
Einsatzgruppen, 23, 35, 40, 104, 106
Encyclopaedia Universalis, 60
English revisionism, 91
Epaminondas, 101
Eribon, Didier, 172n71
Ether, 61
Euthanasia, 23–24, 107
Evidence, 29
Executions, 46, 49
Experimentation, human, 46
Extermination camps, *see* Concentration camps

Faure, Paul, 32
Faurisson, Robert, 111, 116, 125, 126; archives and, 15, 24; *A-t-on lu Lautréamont?* xx; Borwicz and, 27; Broszat and, 144n20; on conspiracy, 119; conviction of, xiii; on death statistics, 19; debate with, 2; defenders of, 58; on documents, 21–22; on exegesis, 45; on gassing, 23, 61–62; gay liberation and, xiv; Guillaume and, 118; Harwood and, 39; on Hitler, 18; Hoess and, 28; in imaginary scenario, 121; international interest in, 91; Jewish "war declaration" and, 157n81; *Journal of Historical Review* and, 19, 184n75; on Kremer, 48–49, 113–114; Kriegel and, 131; *Mémoire en défense,* xv, xix, 65–73, 113; personal misfortunes of, xiv-xv; "The Problem of the Gas Chambers, or Rumor of Ausch-

witz," xi-xii; on Rassinier, 31; Roques and, 114, 115; on *Shoah*, 180*n*41; sued, 138; Thion on, 38; on Veil, 44; on *Why Did the Heavens Not Darken?*, xvii-xviii; *Zéro* and, 136; on Zyklon B, 60

Faye, Jean-Pierre, 13, 72

Febvre, Lucien, 31, 56

Fejtö, F., 27

Felderer, Dietlieb, 86–87

Ferro, Marc, 180*n*40

"Findings", 68–69

Finkielkraut, Alain, xv, xxi

Folco, Michel, 147*n*4

Forced labor, 108–109

Forgeries, 22, 27, 82–83, 112, 135

Foucault, Michel, 110

France juive, La (Drumont), 92–93

Frank, Anne, xix, 17, 69–70, 97

Frank, Erwin, 7

Free speech, xv-xvi, 71, 72

French Army, 134

French Conseil d'Etat, 160*n*119

French deportees, 33

French historians, 2

French historiography, 54, 93

French Jews, 15

French Resistance, 31, 133, 135

French revisionism, 54, 91–93, 116–120

French Revolution, 6, 98, 103, 104

French Socialist party, xxi

French Supreme Court, 133

Fresco, Nadine, 89, 112

Fritzsche, H., 29, 30

Front National (France), 119

Gas chambers: of Birkenau, 62–63, 152*n*42; Broszat on, 181*n*44; Céline on, 115; Faurisson on, 162*n*12; Hauter on, 14; initial uses of, 104; Kremer on, 48–49, 112; Lyotard on, 144*n*17; pseudotechnical denial of, 23, 61–62; Rassinier on, 151*n*36; SS officers on, 22–23; of Teschen, 159*n*104; Thion on, 11; unutilized, 149*n*23

Gauchet, Marcel, 3

Geismar, Alain, 127

Genesis of the World War, The, 81

Genocide, 129, 133

German admirals, 30

German guilt, 122

German historiography, 94, 124–125, 174*n*83

German nationalism, 20, 88, 123

German National Socialism, *see* Nazi Germany

German revisionism, 165*n*15

German Revolution, 103

German Socialist party, 112

German-Soviet Nonaggression Pact, 30

Germany Must Perish (T. Kaufmann), 88, 126

Gerstein, Kurt, 26, 114–115, 116, 153*n*51, 182*n*63

Gestapo, 31; *see also Einsatzgruppen*

Gèze, François, 140

Giniewski, Paul, 16

Goebbels, Joseph, 22, 29

Gordji, 185*n*77

Great Britain, 157*n*81

Great Conspiracy Against Russia, The (Sayers and Kahn), 54

Greek literature, 112

Greek philosophy, 51–52

Greeks, ancient, 99–102

Greens (party), 125

Grossmann, V., 15

Grote, George, 100

Gruppo communista internationalista autonoma, 171*n*64

Guerre Sociale, La (organization), 116

Index

Guesde, Jules, xxi

Guillaume, Pierre: Chomsky and, 72; on deportee transfers, 158n89; Faurisson and, 24, 118; on Gerstein, 182n63; on Hitler, 151n35; Lazare and, xx; obituary of, 185n79; La Vieille Taupe and, 11, 116; *Zéro* and, 136

Gypsies, 24, 108, 123, 153n48

Habermas, J., 124, 126

Hadrian, 33

Hair, 152n42

Harbi, Mohammed, 135

Hardouin, Jean, 112

Harris, Marvin, 5, 6, 8, 11

Harwood, Richard, 39, 167n36

Hauter, Charles, 14

Hecataeus of Milet, 52

Hefte von Auschwitz, 44

Helots, 99–102, 103

Herodotus, 8, 103, 110

Hesiod, 4, 51

Heydrich, Reinhard, 30–31, 85, 170n56

Hilberg, R., 35, 95, 150n27

Hillgruber, A., 124

Himmler, Heinrich: Brand and, 10; Heydrich and, 170n56; Hitler and, 135; Hoess and, 155n67; Irving on, 85; on Jewish extermination, 14, 42; language of, 12–13, 22, 89; Laternser on, 44; on Warsaw ghetto, 41, 109

Histoire de France (Lavisse), 120

Historiography: American, 80–81; French, 54, 93; German, 94, 124–125, 174n83; Israeli, 53, 95–96, 121–122, 175n87; nationalism and, 120; Polish, 26–27, 53, 95; role of, 58, 83, 110–111; schools of thought in, 17–18, 138–139; socialist, 93–95;

Soviet, 53–54, 94; Turkish, 120–121; *see also* Revisionism

History of the Communist (Bolshevik) Party, 53–54

History of the Great Patriotic War (1941–1945) (Tepulchowski), 94

Hitler, Adolf: Davidowicz on, 104–105; Dreyfusard values and, 81; Eichmann and, 135; Faurisson on, 18; Guillaume on, 151n35; Himmler and, 135; Irving on, 85, 89; Israelite/Amalekite wars and, 127; on Jewish annihilation, 106; Laternser on, 44; Mayer on, 180n33; Operation T4 and, 107; Rassinier on, 156n72; Sade and, 126; Trotsky and, 54

Hoax of the Twentieth Century, The (Butz), 51, 98

Hocquenghem, Guy, xiii–xiv

Hoess, Rudolf: Browning on, 85; confessions of, 27; Faurisson on, 28; on gassings, 106; Gerstein and, 26; Himmler and, 155n67; memoirs of, 28, 154n59; Rassinier on, 29

Holocaust (television series), xviii–xix, 57, 59, 111

Holocaust exploitation, 16, 96, 121–122, 175n90

Homosexuals, xiii–xiv

Human experimentation, 46

Human sacrifice, 5–6

Hungarian Jews, 10, 84

Hydrocyanic acid, 60–61, 62, 64, 85, 152n42

Ich Adolf Eichmann (Eichmann), 166–167n33

Ideological discourse, 53

Indians, American, 4–5, 127

Industrial rationality, 11

"Inexistentialism," 3

Inmates, *see* Deportees

Insecticides, 61, 63
Institute for Contemporary History (Munich), 122, 144n20
Institute for Historical Review, 138, 167n37
International Committee of the Red Cross, 50
International Convention on Genocide, 133
Internationalist Communist party, 116
International League against Racism and Anti-Semitism, 16
Iraq-Iran war, 131
Irgun Zvai Leumi, 16
Irving, David, 85, 89, 124
Isaac, Jules, 80, 81
Israel, 55–56, 130–131
Israeli historiography, 53, 95–96, 121–122, 175n87
Israelites, 33–34, 126–127
Italian revisionism, 91, 171n64

Jabotinsky, Vladimir, 79
Japanese Americans, 16
Jaspers, Karl, 122
Jaurès, Jean, xxi, 81
Jeune Taupe, La (organization), 116
Jewish Agency, 39, 157n81
Jewish children, 40, 67
Jewish Historical Institute (Warsaw), 95
Jewish Information (periodical), 86
Jewish weddings, 86
Jews, 10, 103, 104, 105–106; American, 39; ancient, 33–34, 126–27; East European, 36, 103; French, 15; Hungarian, 10, 84; Russian, 37; Slovakian, 63–64
Jew Süss, The, 87
Josephus, Flavius, xvii
Journal of Historical Review, 19, 86, 152n40, 184n75
Journalism, 7–8

"Judeo-Bolshevism," 108
Juifs, la mémoire et le présent, Les, xvii
July, Serge, 136, 172n71
Jurisprudence, 29–30

Kahn, A. E., 54
Kaltenbrunner, Ernst, 28
Katyn massacre, 29
Kaufmann, Theodore, 88, 126
Kern, Erich, 124, 126, 168–169n48
Khrushchev, Nikita, 37
Klarsfeld, Serge, 15, 44
Kogon, Eugen, 13
Kolko, Joyce, 17
Kolko, Gabriel, 17
Konk (artist), 185n83
Korherr, Richard, 13, 35, 156n74
Kostov, 154n54
Kouchner, Bernard, 122
Kremer, Johann Paul, 45–50, 65, 112–113
Krestinsky, 154n54
Kriegel, Annie, 131
Ku Klux Klan, 184n75

Labor, forced, 108–109
Lacedemonia, 99, 100, 101, 103
Laconians, 100
Lacoste, Robert, 134
Langages totalitaires (Faye), 13
Langbein, H., 154n59
Lanza, D., 170n58
Lanzmann, Claude, 57, 106, 139–140, 152n43, 180n41
Laqueur, Walter, 83, 84
Larousse dictionary, 60
Larpent, G., 54
Laternser, Hans, 44
Latin literature, 112
Lautréamont, Comte de (I.-L. Ducasse), xx
Lavisse, Ernest, 120
Lazare, Bernard, xx, 82, 119

Lebanon, 131
Lefort, Claude, 116, 117
Leftism: Dreyfus Affair and, xxi; revisionism and, 90, 91, 92; terrorism of, 125; of La Vieille Taupe, 9; *see also* Marxists
Legrand, H. A. A., 115–116
Leguay, 135
Leibniz, Gottfried Wilhelm, 97
Lenin, Vladimir Ilich, 33
Less, A., 30–31
Levi, Primo, 42–43
Lewis, B., 184*n*77
Liberty Lobby, 90, 184*n*75
La Librairie Française, 33
Libraries, 2, 69
Lice metaphor, 12–13
LICRA, 16
Liebknecht, Karl, xxi
Lilienthal, Alfred, 58
Lipsky, C., 151*n*30
Literary exegesis, 45
Loriquet, 98
Los Angeles Colloquium (1979), 19
Los Angeles Superior Court, 138
Lund, Jules, 183*n*67
Luther, Martin, 112
Lycée Collective, 185*n*83
Lyotard, Jean-François, xiv, 116, 139, 144*n*17

Mactoux, M., 185*n*82
Maidanek, 109
Malamoud, Charles, 27
"Manifeste des Intellectuels" (Zola), ix
Maoists, 79
Mao Zedong, 37
Marienstras, Richard, 38
Marrus, Michael, ix
Marx, Karl, 110, 116
Marxists, 79, 97–98
Massu, 129, 134
Mattogno, Carlo, 171*n*64
Maurice-Audin Committee, 156*n*69

Maurras, Charles, 143*n*5
Mayer, Arno, xvii–xviii, 109, 145*n*31, 163*n*21, 175*n*88, 180*n*33
M'Bemba, Maître, 131
Meinhof, Ulrike, 90
Melouza massacre, 134
Mémoire en défense, see Faurisson, Robert
Mémorial (Klarsfeld), 15
Memorial foundations, 121
Mengele, Josef, 57
Mensonge d'Ulysse, Le (Rassinier), 13–14, 21, 32
Mentally ill Germans, 23–24, 107
Merchant of Venice, The (Shakespeare), 162*n*15
Mermelstein, 138
Messenians, 100, 101
Mexican natives, 5
Meyer, Dr., 46
Michelet, Jules, 110
Milner, J. C., 165*n*21
Mollet, Guy, 131, 134
Montaigne, Michel de, 56
Monteil, Vincent, 16, 119, 168*n*43
Mortality statistics, 18–19, 21, 50, 139–140
Moscovitch, Alex, 128, 189*n*117
Moscow show trials, 25, 27, 108
Munich Pact, 32
Muses, 51
Museum of German History (projected), 189*n*112
Museums, 189*n*112
"Muslims" (deportees), 47, 114, 158*n*96, 162*n*3
My Life (Trotsky), 54
Myrdal, Jan, 91
Myron of Priena, 101
Myth of Auschwitz, The (Stäglich), 98, 119, 163*n*25

National Center of Broadcasted Instruction, 71

Nationalism, German, 20, 88, 123
National Socialism, *see* Nazi Germany
National Vietnam Committee, 129
Nazi Germany: Arabs and, 135; Central Office of Economic Administration, 109; as chosen people, 123; documents of, 15, 21–22; Gestapo, 31; leadership of, 12; Neumann on, 105–106; Wehrmacht, 40; *see also Einsatzgruppen;* SS
Nerval, Gérard de, 59
Neumann, Franz, 105–106
New Right (France), 123
Nimitz, Chester, 30
Nolte, Ernst, 124, 125, 126
"Nuremberg laws," 104
Nuremberg ou la Terre promise (Bardèche), 32–33
Nuremberg trials, 28, 29–31, 132–133, 134

Ogmios (firm), 185n77
Old Mole (organization), *see* La Vieille Taupe (organization)
"Only Lice Were Gassed in Auschwitz" (Darquier de Pellepoix), xi
Ontological proof, 23
"Open Letter to My Jewish Friends" (Paupert), 75
Operation T4, 107
Orléans prostitution, xi–xii
Orwell, George, 56
Oswiecim Museum, 26
Oussedik, 129
Ovens, incinerating, 63

Palestinians, 16, 88, 122, 130
Papon, 135
Paraz, Albert, 32, 115
Pariahs, 103, 104
Paris Court of Appeal, xiii, 138
Parmenides, 52
Paschoud, Mariette, 185n79

Passage de la ligne (Rassinier), 32
"Past That Will Not Pass Away, A" (Nolte), 124
Pellepoix, Louis Darquier de, *see* Darquier de Pellepoix, Louis
Peloponnesian War, 99
Petit Larousse illustré, Le, 60
Petit Quillet-Flammarion, Le, 60
Pets, 157n83
Petty bourgeoisie, 10
Pfannenstiel, W., 26, 115, 153–154n51
Phalangists, 131
Phenol injections, 159n101
Philosophy, 51–52
Pivert, Marceau, 32
Platea, Battle of, 103
Plato, 52, 53
"Plea for a Historicization of National-Socialism" (Broszat), 124
Plutarch, 177n1
Poincaré, Raymond, 80
Poliakov, Léon, xiv, 31, 34, 149n22, 156n73
Polish Commission on War Crimes, 95
Polish historiography, 26–27, 53, 95
Polish "revisionist" tours, 87
Polish State Council, 38–39
Pol Pot massacre, xv, 186n87
Polycracy, 148
Pouvoir ouvrier (organization), 116, 117
Pressac, J.-C., 191n138
Prévert, Jacques, 68
Prisoners, *see* Deportees; War prisoners
"Problem of the Gas Chambers, or the Rumor of Auschwitz, The" (Faurisson), xi–xii
Programme communiste (periodical), 9
Propaganda, war, 80, 83
Prostitution, xi–xii

Protocols of the Elders of Zion, 82–83, 87
Prussic acid, *see* Hydrocyanic acid
Psychological warfare, 83
Puig-Antich affair, 183*nn*67, 69
Punishments, 46

Raeder, Erich, 29
Rajk, László, 27
Ranke, Leopold von, 17, 110
Rappaport, 135
Rassinier, Paul, 31–33, 82, 92, 116, 126; at Dora, 44; *Le Drame des Juifs européens*, 29, 34–38; on gas chambers, 151*n*36; German nationalism and, 20; Guillaume on, 11; influence of, 120; Italian revisionism and, 91; Maurice-Audin Committee and, 155–156*n*69; Arno Mayer and, xvii; *Le Mensonge d'Ulysse*, 13–14, 21, 32; *Passage de la ligne*, 32; Pfannenstiel and, 26, 153*n*51; self-perception of, 82; Thion and, 55; *Ulysse trahi*, 22–23; La Vieille Taupe and, 118; on Zyklon B, 60
Reagan, Ronald, 124
Red Army, 36–37, 108
Reinach, J., 54
Reitlinger, G., 95
Republic (Plato), 52
Resistance, French, 31, 133, 135
Resnais, Alain, 57
Revel, Jean-François, xi
Revisionism: Allied propaganda and, 55; American, 80–81, 90; Arab, 16, 88, 184–185*n*77; Australian, 91; "conscience" of, 81–82; criminal, xx; defined, x–xi, xxiii, 79; on deportee selection, 43; Dreyfusard, xviii, xix, 54; English, 91; French, 54, 91–93, 116–120; geographical distribu-
tion of, 90–93; German, 165*n*15; Italian, 91, 171*n*64; methods of, 18–24, 86–89; salutary, 14, 111; Soviet, 53–54; Swedish, 91
Révolution africaine (newspaper), 132
Revolutions, 103
Riegner, G., 84–85
Rigaux, François, 186*n*87
Ringelbaum, Emmanuel, 22
Rioux, J.-P., 178*n*18
Rivière, J.-C., 153*n*51
Roeder, Manfred, 19, 159*n*105
Rogerie, André, 157*n*87
Rolland, Romain, 82
Roosevelt, Franklin D., 156*n*72
Roosevelt administration, 16
Roques, Henri, 114–115, 118–119, 153*n*51, 182*n*60, 185*n*77
Rothe, W. D., 171–172*n*67
Rousset, David, 13
Russell Tribunal, 129
Russian Jews, 37
Russian Revolution, 103

Sabra massacre, 131
Sacrifice, human, 5–6
Sade, Marquis de, 6, 126
Sahlins, Marshall, 5–6, 7, 8, 147*nn*4, 5
Saletta, Cesare, 171*n*64
Sartre, Jean-Paul, 129
Saudi Arabia, 130, 184*n*77
Saul, King of Israel, 127
Sayers, M., 54
Schleunes, K. A., 106
Schuldfrage, 122, 123
Schutzstaffel, *see* SS
Schwartz, Laurent, 129
Schwartzkoppen, 54
Sehn, Jan, 173*n*81
Selection, deportee, 42–50
Semprun, Jorge, 57
Sept Couleurs, Les (firm), 33

Sereny, G., 172*n*70
Servatius, Dr., 28, 128–129, 190*n*120
Shakespeare, William, 162*n*15
Shamir, Y., 121
Shatila massacre, 131
Shoah (film), 106, 111, 136, 152*n*43, 180*n*41
Slansky, Rudolf, 27
Slaves, 130; *see also* Forced labor; White slave trade
Slavs, 107
Slovakian Jews, 63–64
Soap, 64
Socialisme ou Barbarie (organization), 116–117
Socialist historiography, 93–95
Socialist party: of France, xxi; of Germany, 112
Social science journalism, 7–8
"Some Elementary Comments on the Rights of Freedom of Expression," (Chomsky), xv–xvi, xx, 65–73, 91, 144–145*n*21
Sonderbehandlung, see "Special treatment"
Sonderkommando: Auschwitz, 21–22, 25; Birkenau, 63
Sophist, The (Plato), 52
Sorbonne, 2
Sorlin, Pierre, 180*n*40
Souyiri, P., 116
Soviet Army, 36–37, 108
Soviet-German Nonaggression Pact, 30
Soviet historiography, 53–54, 94
Soviet Investigatory Commission, 53
Soviet jurisprudence, 29–30
Soviet testimony, 26
Soviet Union, 107–108, 117, 131
Soviet war prisoners, 85, 106
Sowerwine, Charles, 160*n*115
Sparta, 99, 101, 102, 103, 177*n*1

"Special treatment" (*Sonderbehandlung*): Cohn-Bendit on, 113, 114; Faurisson on, 161–162*n*3; Himmler on, 13; Kremer on, 46–47, 50, 65, 113
Speech freedoms, xv–xvi, 71, 72
Sperber, Dan, 27
Spy Who Came in from the Far-Right, The (film), 124
SS (Schutzstaffel): deportee selection by, 42, 43; Faurisson on, 40; gas chambers and, 61–62, 63; ideology of, 123; Rassinier and, 82; testimony of, 22, 25
Stäglich, Wilhelm, 98, 119, 123, 124, 125, 163*n*25
Stalin, Joseph, 17
Stangl, F., 23
Statute on Jews (France), 104
Stern gang, 16, 121
Storm, Theodor, 51
Stürmer, M., 126
Swedish revisionism, 91
Système concentrationnaire nazi, Le (Wormser-Migot), xi

Talmud, 19, 152*n*39
Tamerlane, 127
Tarnero, J., 170*n*58
Temps modernes, Les (periodical), 128
Tepulchowski, Boris, 94
Teschen, 159*n*104
Theresienstadt ghetto, 156*n*74
Thibaud, Paul, 1, 70
Thion, Serge, 34, 71; Arab world and, 185*n*77; Chomsky and, 72; on documentary sources, 36; evidence and, 23; Faurisson and, 38, 91, 151*n*35; on Frank, 17; on gassing, 11; on "historical"/"political" truths, 55; intentions of, 16; on Rassinier, 31, 35; Thibaud and, 70; totalitarian language

Thion, Serge (Continued)
and, 13; *Vérité historique ou vér-*
ité politique? 15, 18, 19, 22, 24,
31, 44; on witnesses, 25
Third Reich, *see* Nazi Germany
Third World, 126–136
Thucydides, 99–100, 102, 109,
177*nn*1, 9
Tillion, Germaine, 13
Titus Flavius Vespasianus, 33, 34
Tocqueville, Alexis de, 110
Todorov, Tzvetan, xx
Torture, 134, 135
Totalitarianism, 11–12, 70, 84, 108,
148*n*15
Tourism, 87
Treblinka, 15
Trials: Eichman, 30–31, 122; Mos-
cow, 25, 27, 108; Nuremberg,
28, 29–31, 132–133, 134; war
crimes, 22–23, 25, 27, 44; witch-
craft, 25, 30, 56
Tristani, J.-L., 166*n*27
Trotsky, Leon, 54, 108
Trotskyism, 116, 117
True History of New-Spain (Diaz del
Castillo), 4–5
Truman, Harry S., 80–81
Tu quoque principle, 30
Turkish historiography, 120–121
Typhus: Faurisson on, xii, 45, 48,
65, 113; Kremer on, 46, 49–50,
113–114

L'Unità, 156*n*73
United Nations, 21, 29, 133

Veil, Simone, 44
Vergasung, 23
Vergès, Jacques, 128–129, 131, 132,
133, 134, 135
Vérité historique ou vérité poli-
tique?, see Thion, Serge
Verrall, R., 39, 167*n*36

Veyne, Paul, 17
Viannson-Ponte, P., 39
Vichy government, 104
Victorian Council for Civil Liberties,
160*n*115
Vieille Taupe, La (organization), 8–
11, 116, 117–118, 119; *La Ban-*
quise and, 183*n*66; Chomsky
and, 172*n*74; Faurisson and, 92;
Mémoire en défense and, xv;
Moscow show trials and, 27;
motto of, 69, 120; Ogmios and,
185*n*77; political allies of, 118–
119; Puig-Antich and, 183*n*67;
on Rassinier, 33; Stäglich and,
163*n*25
Vietnam War, 66, 129
Viollet-le-Duc, Eugène-Emmanuel,
93
Virgil, 112
Vishinsky, A. Y., 108
Voie de la Paix, La (organization),
32
Volleys from a Non-Combatant, 80
Voltaire, 97

Waldheim affair, 122
Walendy, U., 169*n*48
"Wannsee agreement," 89
War crimes trials, 22–23, 25, 27, 44;
see also Nuremberg trials
War prisoners, 85, 106
War propaganda, 80, 83
War Refugee Board (U.S.), 25, 84
Warsaw ghetto, 22, 40–41, 109
Weber, Max, 103
Weddings, 86
Wehrmacht, 40
Weizmann, Chaim, 39, 126, 156–
157*n*81
Wellers, Georges: "An Abundance of
Evidence," xiii, xviii; on Ausch-
witz convoys, 157*n*87; on chemi-
cal analysis, 152*n*42; Faurisson

and, 45, 48; on gas chambers, 23, 181*n*44

White slave trade, xi-xii

Why Did the Heavens Not Darken? (Mayer), xvii–xviii, 175*n*88

Wise, Stephen, 39

Witchcraft trials, 25, 30, 56

Witnesses, 25–26

Wolzek (imaginary camp), 28, 29

Works and Days (Hesiod), 4

World Conquerors, The, 87

World Jewish Congress, 25, 67

World War I, 80, 165*n*15

World War II, 15–16, 39–40, 107

Wormser-Migot, Olga, xi, 111

Wyclif, John, 112

Xenophon, 101

Yadin, Yigael, xvii

Yad Vashem Institute, 121, 175*n*90

Yad Vashem Studies, 95

Yerushalmi, Yosef, 146*n*2

Zéro (periodical), 136

Zind, P., 153*n*51

Zionism: Eastern European, 103; Holocaust exploitation by, 16, 121; Jabotinsky and, 79; in New York, 84; revisionist opposition to, 87; Thion and, 55

Zola, Emile, ix, xix, 51

Zyklon B, 59–64, 85, 106–107